VANISHING ACT

T0352536

VANISHING ACT

A TOM KNIGHT MYSTERY

Charlie Hodges

This edition published in 2020 by Farrago,
an imprint of Duckworth Books Ltd,
13 Carrington Road, Richmond, TW10 5AA, United Kingdom

www.farragobooks.com

First published in German, by Heyne Verlag in 2016

Copyright © Charlie Hodges 2020

The right of Charlie Hodges to be identified as the author of this
Work has been asserted by him in accordance with the Copyright,
Designs & Patents Act 1988.

All rights reserved. No part of this publication may be reproduced,
stored in a retrieval system, or transmitted, in any form or by any
means, without the prior permission in writing of the publisher.

This book is a work of fiction. Names, characters, businesses,
organisations, places and events other than those clearly in the public
domain, are either the product of the author's imagination or are used
fictitiously. Any resemblance to actual persons, living or dead, events or
locales is entirely coincidental.

Print ISBN: 9781788422635
Ebook ISBN: 9781788422628

Printed in UK by Clays Ltd.

Dedicated to Gervase Bradford,
the inspiration for Tom Knight.

He was a verray, parfit, gentil knight

Chapter One

By three o'clock he could barely concentrate. He walked, or rather marched along the seafront into the sun, filling his lungs with the warm air on every eighth stride. Around him Eastbourne basked in the contentment of high summer.

He had, of course, been mocked for moving here. It was true that the elderly flocked to the town, to visit, live or die. Dover for the continent, Eastbourne for the incontinent, his son had reminded him of the ancient maxim more than once. But if you stood on the beach by the pier and half-closed your eyes, the sweep of hotels along the seafront could pass for the south of France. Even when you opened them, there was a stateliness about the buildings, an understated aplomb, that soothed and reassured. There was a seamy underbelly too, hidden in the back streets where the tourists and trippers never went. If Brighton was a raucous teenager, Eastbourne was a benign, elderly aunt, outwardly respectable and prosperous, yet harbouring guilty secrets behind a graceful façade.

Such thoughts were far from Knight's mind on this particular afternoon. For days it had been as if a dormant bud hidden deep inside him had begun to flower, releasing fiery essences that had spread throughout his body and mind, gradually intoxicating him. It had been two years since Roz had died, two years of numbness and hibernation during which animal appetites had all but drained from his body. Yet here they were again, raucous old friends tumbling through the front door after a long absence, hell-bent on a good time.

An elderly lady in a mobility scooter drove past as he drew level with the Grand Hotel. She trailed a luxuriant crop of silver hair blown back by the offshore breeze, her aquiline features focused imperiously on the pavement ahead. She would have been beautiful once. Which dilapidation of old age had put her in the scooter at what, eighty, eighty-five? Stroke? Hips? And which would come for him? As if to stake a claim, his right knee ached and he leaned a little more heavily on his stick.

With desire had come doubt. Would he still be capable? As the day had drawn nearer excitement had become tinged with anxiety. So for the price of an excruciating lecture about safe sex he had extracted a prescription for Viagra from a twinkling lady doctor who had smiled encouragingly and wished him good luck. She had also called him Tom rather than Mr Knight, a familiarity that deepened his awkwardness given that she was not unattractive herself.

A car horn blared as he crossed the road, obliging him to redirect his thoughts to the task at hand.

Today's job was Colin Boyle, a recent guest of Her Majesty's Prison Service over the matter of an ear he had removed in a fight with a rival pimp. His claim in mitigation that the victim was deaf anyway had gone down badly, such that he had served eighteen months, his longest stretch yet. Boyle owed several thousand on a car that he had written off while drunk and the finance company wanted its money back. All Knight had to do was serve the writ, a seemingly straightforward job that had nevertheless defeated two investigators before him. He reasoned that Boyle would not be anxious to return to prison any time soon, but didn't exclude the chance of a cocaine-fuelled eruption that might result in serious injury. So he had chosen the Grand Hotel, trusting that its air of patrician assurance would undermine Boyle's confidence.

He left the pavement and walked up a driveway lined with gleaming Audis and BMWs that evoked the usual pang of envy. Inside, the lounge was populated by well-to-do weekenders and astute grandparents discussing inheritance planning with their financial advisers. He chose a table near the entrance and settled down to wait, his thoughts straying to the culinary arrangements for the evening ahead.

The first time Knight had cooked for Roz he had led with an aubergine soufflé. He had known even then to avoid the giveaway cliché of oysters and to woo her with light, uplifting food that would not leave them sluggish and yawning, which it hadn't. Roz was his second wife. After the divorce from the show jumper he had learned to cook, and then to cook well, marvelling at the transformation that this wrought upon his love life. Now he was cooking for Fran.

He had feared overstepping the mark by inviting her to his flat for supper on what would be only their third date. Yet she had accepted, with a smile and a raising of the eyebrows that reminded him of Roz, even though their lives could not have been more different. Fran worked in a retirement home, where she was paid a pittance to comfort, cajole and wipe its frail residents, which she did with a grace and humour that Knight found enchanting. That, and the way she looked even younger than her advertised fifty-three years. He was wondering if he had bought enough asparagus when Boyle entered.

He was an unhealthy yet menacingly feral specimen in his mid-twenties, his slight frame encased in a long leather coat. At the same age, Knight would have made short work of him, but now the odds would be heavily in the younger man's favour. With him was a pale blonde girl barely out of her teens. Eyes turned, detecting an alien presence. Knight's research had revealed that Boyle always accompanied his women on hotel visits, taking the money up front and waiting in the car while they serviced the clients. On the phone Knight had said he was a short man in his forties with medium length black hair, which was why there was no reaction from either the girl or Boyle when a balding, elderly gentleman of about six feet made a move in their direction.

He was within five yards of his prey. However much he willed himself to stay calm in these moments, a surge of adrenaline inevitably took over at the prospect of a kill. Quite unnecessarily, he accelerated. His left foot snagged a handbag by a chair and he went down, landing heavily on his right knee.

'Fuckin' hell!' Boyle looked down at the prostrate form beneath him. Unaccustomed as he was to helping his fellow man, he felt the eyes of the room upon him demanding action, so he assisted Knight to his feet while two waiters swooped in from either side.

'You alright, mate?'

'I think so. How clumsy of me, I'm so sorry.'

Still supported by the waiters, Knight reached into his inside pocket. 'By the way, this is for you. Witnessed by these two gentlemen.'

Boyle looked at the writ as a child might look at a tarantula placed unexpectedly in its hand by a party entertainer. He screamed an obscenity, drawing a gasp of horror from the onlookers, the more able-bodied of whom were now standing up to get a better view. Then he marched out of the hotel, dragging the girl with him.

Knight limped to the nearest table and ordered a vodka. Bloody Mulberrys, some of them were nearly the size of a kitbag. He would have given short shrift to any soldier who left one in such a stupid place.

***

Later the same afternoon, Fran changed Joan Baldwin's trousers and incontinence pad for the third time that day. The old lady was close to tears.

'I'm so sorry, dear. It just comes without warning, I don't know how to stop it.'

Fran smiled reassuringly.

'Don't worry, that's what these are for. It won't take me a moment.'

The urine smelt acrid. Another infection was brewing, which would make the dementia worse. Fran knew little of Joan, only that she had once been a dancer and was to all intents and purposes alone in the world. According to Mrs Grayling she had no children and no other relatives apart from a nephew who never visited. The one mercy of dementia was that she no longer knew this.

'There you go, ready to rock and roll.'

Joan laughed, despite herself. She liked it when Fran looked after her. Some of the other staff would have snapped, but Fran always made light of the humiliations that beset her. Taking care not to stress the bad hip, Fran helped her off the bed and onto the walking frame. It was hard to imagine she had danced a season at the Royal Ballet; perhaps that was what had done for the hip.

As they began the long haul back to the dining room, Fran's thoughts turned to the evening ahead. The ad had been her daughter's idea, repeated until it had become easier to say yes than to keep arguing about it. She had even written the description, to which Fran had eventually consented. 'Vivacious divorcee, 53, slim, optimistic with good s.o.h. seeks tender, amusing and reliable man 40-60 for friendship and maybe more.'

The only thing that wasn't true was the claim of optimism. Fran was not optimistic about men, a feeling entirely justified by her initial encounters with Eastbourne's finest. There had been a widowed traffic warden who had spent an hour explaining the extent of his prostate problem, followed by a married thirty-five-year-old body builder with a fetish for older women, who had assumed she was desperate to go to bed with him. She thought back down a dismal chain of unreliable men, all the way to the drummer.

Tom Knight was different, however. He was certainly tender and amusing, and thus far reliable. She had to admit he looked older than his fifty-nine years, but took it to indicate a life intensely lived. An ex-army officer, he had spent time in the Intelligence Corps and the SAS before taking himself to university as a mature student. He had then been a teacher for two years until the prospect of riches lured him into the world of commercial investigations, which he freely admitted amounted to industrial espionage. Now he was a private investigator. He was twice married, his second wife having died in a car crash, and he had three grown-up children. Fran's daughter said he was a catch. But did she want a catch? Did she even want to be fishing?

They reached the tea table and she settled Joan back into her chair. A patrician voice meanwhile boomed from the opposite side.

'His darkly tanned skin glistened in the midday sun as she worked the oil into his naked buttocks.'

A ripple of resigned disapproval arose from those of the dozen or so occupants of the table who had heard her. 'She's off again!' said someone.

'Whose buttocks were those then?' Fran asked.

'Her lover's of course! He was twenty, she fucked him on the beach and in the sea.'

'Language, Brenda!'

'Nothing wrong with fucked! Fine old English word!'

Brenda Newham had once been a television drama producer. Her credits comprised a handful of long-forgotten series that had drawn little in the way of critical acclaim, but had washed easily enough over their Sunday evening audiences. She had bravely transformed herself into a novelist, peaking in terms of sales if not creative fulfilment with a publisher who claimed to be second only to Mills and Boon in the romance market, but was probably fourth or fifth. Despite several bestsellers she had been poorly paid, leading to less genteel circumstances than she might have hoped for at this time of her life. Hence her presence at New Horizons Rest Home. Her dementia was as advanced as Joan's, but played out in a different way. Random fragments of her stories floated through her mind like the scattered pieces of a broken jigsaw, intensely experienced and quickly forgotten.

'What happened next?' asked Fran. Brenda frowned imperiously.

'What happened to whom?'

'To the man lying in the sun.'

Brenda looked blank. 'I've no idea what you're talking about!' she snapped, and fell silent.

Fran wiped a blob of cream from Joan's chin, wishing the kitchen wouldn't send up vanilla slices. Next to Joan sat Susan, an anxious, near-catatonic woman who wore gloves all day. She had been brought here by her son a fortnight ago for a 'trial'. He had stipulated that she be left to herself as much as she wished because enforced contact with strangers made her depression worse. It was not an approach with which Fran agreed, but Mrs Grayling who owned the home had issued instructions that these wishes were to be respected. So other than at mealtimes and on the days when her son took her out, Susan remained in her room, a captive in the prison of her mind. She walked slowly with a stick and was able to wash and dress herself, for which Fran was grateful.

Her mind drifted away as tea inched forward. She had no doubt that Tom was attracted to her; even to her blunted antennae this much was clear. Not that he had ever been pushy. In contrast to the vast majority of men she had met, he was a perfect gentleman. But was she attracted to him? Certainly not the way she had fancied the drummer. Even allowing for the fact that she had been a carefree teenager then, no one had ever come close. His parting gift after a year of carnal delirium had been her daughter. Goodbye art school. There had been two more children, both boys, with two more fathers, one of whom she had married and divorced. There followed a series of unsatisfactory entanglements until finally she had given up on men altogether. For ten years now she had been single and celibate, glad of the peace of mind it brought. Her one sorrow was that she didn't see the boys more, but she consoled herself that Australia was a better place for them than England.

The clock crept towards six and the end of her shift. She wondered if she was mad.

* * *

12

Knight surveyed the offering with a critical eye. In the end he had decided against sushi on the grounds that the rice might prove cloying, and had opted instead for couscous laden with roasted tomatoes, accompanied by smoked tuna drizzled with olive oil and capers. There was also manchego with figs and membrillo, while in the oven a brace of aubergines was cooking in a marinade of soy and mirin. Had he overdone it? It was too late to worry now.

He had nearly forgotten to put the aubergines in. After delivering the writ he had dropped in on Merv and smoked some white widow, with the predictable effect on his memory. A few years ago, shortly after moving to Eastbourne, he had witnessed a fight in a pub car park between Merv and another man. Knight had given evidence contradicting the man's assertion that Merv had started it, thanks to which the charges were dropped. His drunken opponent, one Detective Constable Bullock, had joined Knight's list of enemies, but Knight and Merv had become friends and occasional accomplices. An ex-infantryman in his forties who dabbled in money-making schemes on the fringes of legality, he was a resourceful man with his ear to the ground. Romance, however, was a foreign land to him.

'So, you reckon you're going to pork her tonight?' he had asked.

Knight had affected an air of disdain.

'How very charming. The voice of experience from the heart of the farmyard.'

'True, but at least I don't go round lying about my age.'

This latest twist in the Mad Major's life looked like a winner to Merv. As far as he could see it had lust, lies and comic delusion, everything he liked in a drama.

'So, when are you going to tell her, before or after?!'

'Piss off.'

Merv subsided into a laughing fit while Knight wondered again when he should tell her. Surely there was no particular need at this point? It wasn't as if they were going to start a family, and it hadn't really been a lie, more a survival tactic. Given that the ad said 40–60, she wouldn't have agreed to meet him if he had told the truth. He had got in under the wire, phase one completed. Naturally, he would tell her in due course, though he couldn't be sure if it would be tonight.

The wind was dropping. Knight decided it would be warm enough to eat outside and began taking the food to a table on the balcony. The knee was not nearly as painful as before, the smoke and the codeine had seen to that, but it was hard to feign normality. His stick had not been present on their first two dates and was banished on this occasion too, hidden in the back of a cupboard.

Next to the table were two business class airline seats with extending footrests and decent-sized trays that folded up out of the armrest. Many years ago a client had needed to get rid of them quickly for reasons he didn't care to explain, and Knight had bought them for a song. They had remained with him ever since, faithful companions through good times and bad. The doorbell rang.

She was wearing a black silk blouse with white culottes and a pair of light gold heels that matched her hair. Around her shoulders was a cream pashmina that intensified her deep blue eyes.

'You going to let me in?'

He stopped staring and led her into an airy sitting room dominated by a vast sofa opposite two ancient leather armchairs. The floor was carpeted in coir matting, frayed in places. The businesslike masculinity was in contrast to the brightly coloured array of prints on the walls. Fran dimly recognised some dancing women, Emil Nolde perhaps. Was she in a sophisticated haven of good taste or a classy bachelor shagpad? Not that they were mutually exclusive.

'The best bit's the view. Come and see.'

Fran stepped onto the balcony and found herself facing a wall of sea and sky split at the centre by the horizon. Over the pier, a cloud of starlings faded in and out of vision like a great, grey genie.

'It's beautiful!' She said it with unaffected, almost girlish, enthusiasm.

Knight agreed. He had inherited the flat from his aunt shortly after Roz died. He had thought of selling it, but had been seduced by the healing qualities of the sea view. On a spur of the moment decision, he had moved from London to make a new start.

'What are *they*?!' Fran had found the seats.

'The most comfortable way of taking in the view. Try one.'

Fran settled into a seat and was pleasantly surprised by its eagerness to cosset her. 'What's this for?' She pulled a lever and the seat tipped back, taking her with it. 'Oh my god!' The throaty laugh. She brought the seat up again and noticed the food for the first time. 'What's that?!' Wide-eyed with delight, she got up and inspected the plumage of Knight's culinary display. 'This is amazing, Tom!'

'Oh, it's all quick stuff, looks more trouble than it is.' He felt a surge of optimism as he poured two glasses of wine. He also felt a brief urge to get the truth about his age out of the way, but the oven pinged for the aubergines and the moment passed.

* * *

Replete but by no means drowsy, Fran put her feet up on the sofa. She had seldom experienced such delicacies. She had drunk four glasses of wine, the fifth sat on the coffee table beside her. Never had she been so thoughtfully wooed.

Over supper, in between the shrieks of the seagulls, he had told her tales of encounters with snakes in Borneo and gangsters in London. Also about his first wife, the show jumper. He had married her when she became pregnant, even though she miscarried before the wedding. A far cry from the drummer, Fran noted.

As the traffic below grew quieter they could hear the waves washing over the beach. She told him about riding the road with the band, about all-night parties in Amsterdam and Ibiza, a wild child in a Winnebago. They compared notes on the drugs they had taken. In his time at the University of Sussex, he had made a point of trying almost everything at least once, reasoning that, if he was there to broaden his horizons, he should do so thoroughly. She applauded his intellectual rigour, recognising a spirit of adventure that matched the one she had lost. Or thought she had.

Knight was in the kitchen making coffee. A rich Brazilian voice came from a loudspeaker somewhere, an alpha dove calling to its mate, punctuated every so often by the hiss of water over sand on the beach. A carved African woman held a flickering candle in one hand while the other supported a child feeding at her breast.

What would it be like to go to bed with him? He was certainly handsome. There was a determined set to his mouth that she liked, and he had inquisitive brown eyes that nevertheless seemed trustworthy. In the dim light the bags beneath them were almost invisible. As far as she could see he had good muscle tone, with a stomach that was on the modest side, certainly no worse than her own. She hadn't really inspected his teeth yet, and made a vague mental note to do so. Had she detected a limp?

On the other hand, this was only their third date. By the standards of her youth it was an eternity, though she had long felt that the standards of her youth left much to be desired. But as her daughter never tired of pointing out, life was short. Why wait if something felt right? Not having entertained such thoughts for over a decade, now that she did she found them intoxicating and took another sip of wine.

In the kitchen, Knight carefully arranged rose and violet creams on a silver dish as he waited for the water to boil. He felt a growing compulsion to step into her life so that he might protect her from further blows. He also knew that he was getting ahead of himself, but it was a feeling that refused to abate, that and his desire for her.

Should he sit next to her on the sofa? He didn't wish to invade her space, but recalled from distant memory that the choreography of these things was important. There was also the question of when to take the Viagra. Now was as good a moment as any. He took out the pill that he had positioned strategically in his shirt pocket and swallowed it. What would Roz think if she could see him now? Knight did not believe in an afterlife, but it seemed to him that she would have looked favourably on the proceedings. He filled the cafetiere and advanced into the sitting room.

Fran wondered what he would do next. He wasn't the pouncing type, she had seen enough of them to be fairly certain of that. Should she make room for him on the sofa? She raised herself just as he stooped to put the tray on the table beside her. For a moment their faces were level with each other, yet he seemed uncertain of himself. Perhaps it would not be wrong to help him.

'You're a lovely man, Tom. Thank you for doing this for me.'

She placed a hand on his face and kissed him softly.

For a moment they looked at each other in silence. Still stooping, Knight put his hand behind her head and drew her gently to him. The kiss was long and intense. When they parted he moved next to her on the sofa. He put his arm around her and kissed her again, pulling her gently down over him, massaging her shoulders. There was a clatter of falling coffee cups as his foot clipped the table. Knight's heart sank. But it was as if a guardian angel was looking over him.

'Why don't we go to the bedroom?' she whispered.

She had decided that if they were to go to bed, then bed it would be. However large the sofa, the thought of it as a venue for sex brought back memories she did not wish to relive. For his part, Knight could barely believe what he had heard.

'Yes,' he replied, his voice disintegrating into a croak.

She got up and put her arms around his neck as he rose from the sofa. A sudden skittishness overtook her, possibly born of a moment in a film she had seen, and on a whim she pulled herself up onto him, wrapping her legs around his waist. She did not mean for him to carry her, but Knight interpreted her action as a challenge, and duly set off on the long march to the bedroom.

The weight was bearable but his knee throbbed dangerously with every step, conjuring up the catastrophic vision of a fall. Pushing doubt and pain to the back of his mind, as he had been trained to do, he moved slowly across the sitting room to the corridor while she smothered his neck and face with her mouth. His heart was pounding, he guessed it was approaching one seventy, one eighty, dangerously high. Summoning his last reserves of willpower, he forced himself to breathe without gasping. His throat was dry, he needed water.

By way of a parting gift, the guardian angel had left the bedroom door open.

'Just a moment.' Knight set her down as gently as he could at the threshold and disappeared into the bathroom opposite.

He held the sink for support, frantically sucking air into his lungs and hoping she couldn't hear him. He turned the tap on and plunged his head towards the gushing water, misjudging the distance. His mouth collided with the tap handle, but he barely noticed. He put his mind to winning the battle for control over his breathing.

Fran meanwhile was admiring a wide, perfectly made bed. She decided to undress as far as her underclothes. No need to make Tom run the passion-killing gauntlet of clasps and hooks. As she stretched out on a sea of crisp, white linen, something on the bedside table caught her eye.

Knight was breathing more steadily now, though his heart rate was still uncomfortably high. No matter. He dried his face and returned to the bedroom.

The vision of heaven that greeted him was all too brief. Something was wrong. Why was Fran staring at him with such furious disgust?

'You filthy liar!' Knight froze. She was holding the passport he had forgotten to tidy away earlier when he had come back stoned from Merv's.

'You told me you were fifty-nine and I believed you! How could you do that to me?!' She was shouting now, her mascara streaked with tears.

'You're seventy-bloody-three!'

Knight opened his mouth to speak, but all that came out was the crown of his front tooth. It fell noiselessly to the floor, leaving him gaping like a vandalised gargoyle. Fran screamed. Gathering her clothes, she pushed past him and fled from the room.

Tom went after her. 'Fran, please!'

'Stay away from me!' she shrieked.

She turned and jabbed an accusing finger at him.

'You know what you are? You're a dirty old man!'

* * *

Chapter Two

The broken crown cost more than two months of Knight's state pension. He was not so poor that he had to live off it, but the expense was nonetheless a hammer blow to his finances. When Roz had died he had sold everything, paid off their considerable debts, and divided the little that was left between his children, the youngest of whom had left home the year before. That left him with a small army pension and an even smaller one from Corporate Intelligence Partnership. He regretted not having paid in more, but there had always been more pressing demands. The flat had been a godsend. Without it he would have been renting an overpriced bedsit somewhere in London. He usually had just enough each month to pay for the basics of life. To do more, which included the enrichment of his dentist, he had to work.

This was why he was sitting in a beachfront café a few tables from an amiable middle-aged accountant and a likewise cheerful woman in her late thirties. It was a referral job from a London agency to which he had given business in the past. Now the boot was on the other foot and he was glad of the work.

The accountant had told his wife he was going to see a client in Eastbourne. She suspected otherwise, with good reason. Knight had already established that the man had booked a room for the afternoon in a seafront hotel, where he photographed them checking in and going to the lift. There was no time to arrange a recording of subsequent events in the bedroom, so a good liar may yet have constructed a plausible narrative that would save the day. But now, obligingly, the couple kissed.

Knight felt a pang of loss. This time a week ago, he had been awaiting Fran's arrival like a nervous schoolboy. Forcing his mind to the task in hand, he flicked open a stamp-sized flap on the handle of his walking stick. The handle itself was made of solid steel, painted to look like oak. It made the stick a highly effective if not lethal weapon when wielded like a club. It was not strictly legal, but had gone thus far undetected by the authorities.

Beneath the flap was a tiny lens set in a touchpad, which he now pressed. Hidden in the stick's shaft, a camera no bigger than a sugar lump recorded the happy embrace and relayed the images to the phone in his pocket. The couple looked at peace in each other's company. Knight toyed with the idea of reporting that nothing had happened, but that would be a lie. He had told many lies in his life, most of all as a commercial spook. But he had seldom lied for personal gain, and never before to a woman with whom he felt himself falling in love. The knowledge that he had crossed that line filled him with shame.

He had, of course, tried to phone Fran, but she had ignored his calls. After many attempts, he had written a long letter of apology and received no reply.

The couple moved on, no doubt back to the hotel for round two. Knight didn't follow; there was more than enough to bring their pleasurable arrangement to an end. He slumped in his chair, with Merv opposite. Knight had hired him for the day to do the legwork, partly out of concern that his own might not be up to the task, and partly for company. It wasn't much money, but Merv was going through a dry patch and every little helped.

'When are you going to stop moping? This is getting daft!'

Knight had not revealed the full extent of his feelings, but Merv had never seen his friend in such a woeful state.

'Forget about her, mate. You'll pork the next one, bet you anything you like.'

Knight winced. 'I don't want to "pork" anyone!' he snapped, a little too loudly. An elderly lady with a pug looked up, possibly wishing someone might do as much for her.

'Only trying to help,' said Merv, quietly.

Knight sighed. 'Sorry. I just can't believe I was so stupid. I still don't know what got into me.'

He knew full well what had got into him. A raw obsession more appropriate to a teenager than a man of his years. Compounding his woe, the vision of Fran in her underclothes had taken up permanent residence in his mind. Did that make him a dirty old man? Perhaps it did.

'I just need to talk to her.'

'And tell her what? That you were a complete pillock and you want a second chance? Forget it!'

Knight lapsed into silence. What was he going to say, and where was he going to say it? He had a working knowledge of the area where Fran lived, in the quiet suburbia between the town centre and the retail park, but did not have her address. He could find it easily enough, but how would she react were he to appear uninvited on her doorstep? She might accuse him of stalking her. A dirty old man and a stalker, there was a thought.

The other option would be to wait outside New Horizons. She had told him where it was, so he could hardly be accused of using the dark arts of espionage. He also knew that she was on nights this week. But Merv was right. What could he say that wouldn't make things worse?

'Think about it – if she comes out and sees you waiting for her she's going to do her fucking nut! Leave it, mate, it's dead!'

* * *

Shortly after eleven, Fran began another round of checks. She hated night shifts. During the day, you could talk to the ladies and laugh with them at the unfolding farce of old age. At night, all you could do was wait for something to go wrong.

Leaving the office, she crossed the hallway to a dimly lit corridor leading to the two ground floor rooms. She looked in first on Susan Hillfield, who had seemed more withdrawn than ever today. Fran had noticed her staring at her once or twice, as if pleading for someone to throw open the cell door and free her from the darkness. But when Fran had tried to engage her in conversation, she had mumbled that she would like to go to her room, and shuffled away on her stick. At least she was sleeping peacefully now. Fran wondered what she dreamed about.

It was Brenda next. She had disgraced herself earlier by baring her breasts to the chiropodist. A devout and charitable Muslim who charged the old ladies a fraction of his normal rate, the experience had done little to raise his opinion of Western womanhood. There were no male residents. Until a year ago, there had been an ex-merchant seaman. He had died of a heart attack after a lethal encounter with a whisky bottle following a similar ambush by Brenda.

Fran returned along the corridor and made her way up the staircase. Her experience with Knight had left her in a state of profound dejection. She cursed her daughter for having the idea in the first place and cursed herself for being so naive. Had she learned nothing of men and their ways? Most of all she cursed Knight. He had lied, opening up old wounds she thought were healed. Equally distasteful was the thought that she had nearly slept with someone not far off the age of her charges. She felt uncomfortable admitting to something perilously close to ageism, but there was a grossness about it that made her shudder. He was just too old.

As she reached the top landing, she heard the floorboards creak downstairs. It was probably just the house murmuring to itself, or maybe Brenda had woken up and gone wandering. She made a mental note to check on her again when she came down.

Room three belonged to Lotty, an ex-headmistress. She was physically frail but mentally vigorous, still reading the classics in her nineties. Next was Joan. Her urinary infection had cleared but now she had a cough and rasped loudly as she breathed. Beyond Joan was Denise. Fran moved on past a succession of lives, some richly fulfilled and others not, but all at peace for the time being. She began to relax.

Having confirmed that Brenda and Susan were still in their rooms on the ground floor, she returned to the office and settled down again with a storage box as a footstool. The office was basically a large cubicle constructed from glass panels, affording a convenient view of the entrance hall on one side and the dining room on the other. As on countless previous occasions, this was to be her billet for a night that would be, at best, tedious. She picked up her magazine and took several swigs of water, the hot weather making her thirstier than usual.

There were meant to be two of them on night duty, but her colleague Jana had been called home to a sick child. It was a strict rule that Mrs Grayling should be informed in such circumstances, but Jana had twice left early in the past fortnight, obliging Mrs Grayling to step in at short notice. She feared for her job should it happen again, which was why Fran had colluded with her. The risk of detection was low. Mrs Grayling usually looked in at seven thirty in the morning to oversee the shift change, and Jana would be back well before then.

Fran was drawn to the young woman. She was from a small village in the east of Slovakia where apparently nothing happened. Barely more than a schoolgirl, she had come to England to seek her fortune and believed she had found it in the form of a wealthy bookmaker, recently separated from his wife. He had become infatuated with her, so much so that he proposed one night that they should have a child together. The fact that he was well into his fifties had not bothered her at all, so glad was she of the fast track to the good life that she longed for. With a little more experience of the world she might have detected something odd in the perfectionism with which he managed every experience they shared.

It was not until she became pregnant that he had revealed himself as a domineering fantasist to whom the notion of a baby was no more than an expression of sexual vanity. Once it was real, the prospect of another child appalled him. When Jana refused to have an abortion he had threatened to kill her, obliging her to flee to a women's refuge. Once the baby was born he refused to acknowledge its existence, while using his accountant to ensure she received the bare minimum of support, or preferably nothing at all. Despite all this, there was no question in Jana's mind of returning to the village where nothing happened. Two years on, she was doing nights at New Horizons while her toddler slept at the tiny flat they shared with her cousin.

Fran drank some more water, and opened her magazine. After a page or two she found herself yawning, which was unusual so early in the shift. She blamed Knight. The turmoil brought about by his deception had exhausted her.

* * *

Knight had abandoned any hope of sleep. As dawn broke, he sat in his office next door to the bedroom at a wide, leather-topped desk, bringing his accounts up to date.

Boarding school and Sandhurst had seen to it that he was a man of stoic self-discipline. When struck by misfortune, his standard procedure was to dust himself down and move on as quickly as possible. It annoyed him that he could not dislodge Fran from his mind, for Merv was obviously right. The chances of antagonising her by visiting unannounced were appallingly high.

On the other hand, not to do so felt like giving up and he was not a man to quit easily. It could be a weakness as much as a strength, he understood that perfectly well. It was the reason he had left the army under something of a cloud. He had witnessed a suspect being badly beaten in Northern Ireland and had refused to be quiet about it when told to do so by a senior officer. There had been a court case and the senior officer had been forced to resign. Afterwards, Knight had been left in no doubt that he could forget any chance of further promotion, and had resigned in disgust. But that had been a matter of principle. No principle was at stake here, only a desperate hunger to see her again.

As the arguments and counter-arguments attacked and retreated in his mind, a solution of sorts presented itself. He would write her a note saying that he would be in his car outside the home at eight o'clock this morning when she finished her shift. If she would consent to hear his apology in person he would be grateful, but if she refused he would understand fully and trouble her no further.

It was now approaching six. He had ample time to write the letter and drop it through the door before she left.

* * *

Fran was trapped in a dark place by an orc with bad teeth. It had her by the shoulders and was shaking them hard.

'Fran, wake up, what's wrong with you?!'

The gargoyle transformed into Jana, arriving in the nick of time to cover up her absence.

'It's twenty past seven, Mrs Grayling will come!'

Fran sat up quickly, with the guilty realisation that she had slept through the night and missed her late rounds.

'Jesus Christ, how did that happen?!'

She packed Jana off to get the early morning tea going and hurried away to check on the ladies. Brenda was awake, already narrating the particulars of a romantic tryst. Susan was still asleep, the duvet rising and falling gently with each breath. She went up the stairs to Lotty's room.

Lotty was lying on her back, staring peacefully up at the ceiling.

'Morning, darling, sorry tea's late.'

Lotty didn't reply. She continued to stare at the ceiling.

'What are you looking at up there?'

Still she didn't reply. She wore an absent yet oddly contented expression, her skin pale and cool. She wasn't breathing. Fran checked the pulse, knowing she wouldn't find one. Tears welled in her eyes, though part of her rejoiced that this fine old soul had been lucky enough to pass away here in her sleep and not in a hospital ward. Only then did it occur to her that, had she done her rounds, she could have called for help.

She heard the front door open and went out to the top of the stairs.

'Mrs Grayling, can you come up here a minute, please?'

She tried to sound calm, but Mrs Grayling instantly sensed trouble. It was not a welcome start to the day, given the problems that already beset her. The home was barely making a profit and she was behind with the improvements demanded after the last inspection. Nevertheless, a wave of sadness passed through her when she entered the room and saw the body; she too had been fond of Lotty.

'I'll call the doctor,' she said, quietly.

There was an established routine when someone died. After the doctor, the ambulance would come and everyone would be kept away while the body was taken out. Later there would be an announcement when they were all together at the table. Several residents had passed away in the years that Fran had worked at the home, but it never shocked her any the less. She was glad she didn't have to work in a hospital.

'Are you OK to carry on?'

Fran nodded and left the room. Mrs Grayling sighed, her thoughts turning to the problem of lost income.

Next door, Joan was facing away from the door, still fast asleep. She was usually the last to rise. Fran noted with approval that the wheezing had stopped. She crossed to the other side of the bed and opened the curtains, which usually had the effect of waking her. As she turned back to Joan, the first thing she noticed was a mark on the exposed arm that hung down by the side of the bed. Then she saw that her face had taken on the same bleached pallor as Lotty's. Fear gripped her as she felt for the non-existent pulse. Fran screamed for Mrs Grayling and ran next door to Denise.

She was dead too.

* * *

Knight felt more at ease now that there was to be a final throw of the dice. In his exhausted state he didn't see the flashing blue lights until the police car was close behind him, announcing with a blast of its siren that it wished him out of the way. He pulled over sharply into a row of empty parking bays, braked late and skidded to a stop inches away from an expensive coupe. Knight's own car was a Skoda, a utilitarian and suitably anonymous vehicle that bore the scars of several minor accidents for which he had been largely responsible.

He waited for the adrenaline to subside and set off again. On high alert now, he saw the next police car in good time as it hurtled out of a side street and disappeared with a squeal of tyres towards the station. As he drove up the hill away from the town centre, an ambulance passed him, suggesting a major accident on the highway further ahead. But then it turned right into a residential area, taking the route that Knight himself intended to follow.

Even in broad daylight, he found the strobing blue lights oppressive. Altogether there were five police cars and three ambulances blocking the street and pavements on either side of New Horizons. Knight parked in the next street and walked back to the home, the adrenaline surging again. He recognised the young WPC putting up tape across the gravelled driveway where two cars were parked, one of them Fran's.

'Hello Tom, you're out early!'

Bev was an ally. Once in a while she and Knight traded favours and information, very discreetly.

'Couldn't sleep. What's happened?'

'Three old ladies dead, I'm afraid. Looks like they were injected with something.'

In other circumstances, the surreal nature of the situation might have appealed to Knight. Instead he felt queasy.

'Looks like we got who did it, though. Even found a syringe and a couple of bags on her.'

'On who?' he asked, rather too anxiously.

Before Bev could reply, the front door opened. It was Bullock. He was a big man with close-cropped ginger hair, small eyes and a turned-up nose that was faintly porcine. He glared at Knight as if he had discovered something foul on the sole of an expensive new shoe.

'May I ask what brings you here, Mr Knight?'

Most people would have found his tone intimidating, but Knight enjoyed putting him in his place. In the army, he wouldn't have lasted more than a few months.

'Out for a stroll, Detective Constable. And may I say what a joy it is to see a public servant hard at work at such an early hour.'

'You trying to be funny?' Bullock took a step closer so that they were inches apart. It was a technique that usually worked but had no effect on Knight, even though the detective was appreciably larger. He was tempted to wind Bullock up further, but the door opened again and two uniformed officers came out.

Between them, being hustled along like an animal scenting the abattoir, was Fran.

* * *

27

Chapter Three

Knight sat on a bench facing the sea, watching the metallic sheen sparkle under another cloudless sky. Normally, the sight would have soothed him, but today it felt full of menace. What unspeakable acts were taking place down there as its inhabitants hunted and ate each other?

'You met her on a dating site?!'

'Yes. So what?'

Bev had not meant to sound incredulous. She took another bite of her sandwich and allowed the unlikely fact of Knight's love life to sink in. Knight remained silent, unsure how this cast him in her eyes. A foolish old man? A dirty old man?

After Fran was led off, he had returned to his car where he sat for a few minutes in mental disarray. It did not seem remotely possible that Fran had killed these women, but then how well did he know her after just three meetings? Had he narrowly missed being a victim himself? For want of a better idea, he had driven to the police station and asked to see her during a break in questioning, but was flatly refused. Eventually Bev had passed a message to Fran that Knight wished to see her. The offer was declined, which did not surprise him.

'And now, if I've understood this right, you want me to give you information that might help her get off?'

'I just need to know what happened, nothing you wouldn't tell the press.'

It fascinated her that Knight had responded to a dating ad. She had done it once when she was sixteen, as a dare. A man in his thirties had spiked her drinks and she was only saved by her inexperience of alcohol. After three pina coladas she was violently sick in the bar, much of it over her date as it happened, and passed out. An off-duty policewoman had stepped in and called an ambulance. When Rohypnol was found in her blood the man was arrested. That was when she decided on her future career.

Much though she sensed danger, she trusted Knight and did currently owe him a favour.

'I'll tell you what I know, but you didn't hear it from me, OK?'

'Of course not!'

'Alright. There were three dead ladies with needle marks. Bullock found a syringe in your friend's bag, and there were wraps under the front seat of her car that looked like heroin.'

Knight reeled.

'How do you know they were hers?'

'Because they've got her fingerprints all over them.'

He reeled again. At first, it seemed that the odds on him having dated a psychopath had shortened considerably, but then it struck him that there was something excessively overwhelming about the evidence that invited doubt.

'Who else was there?'

'Foreign girl, eastern European. She was in hospital with her kid all night; we checked.'

It didn't surprise Knight that Bullock was convinced he had found his killer. This would be a quick clear-up, good for the statistics and even better for the promotion he craved. The foreign girl must be Jana. Fran had told him a little about her.

'So, you're saying that she took a load of heroin to work, killed three people and waited for you to find her?'

It had not occurred to Bev to question the general interpretation of the morning's events. The evidence was conclusive, at least the way she had been trained.

'It's not what I say that matters, it's what he says. He's already charged her.'

'What about CCTV?'

'The home has a system, but it was switched off.'

That was too much for him.

'For god's sake, Bev, surely even Bullock can see how ridiculously convenient that is? What's her motive supposed to be?!'

29

'Calm down, Tom, I'm not in the witness box here!'

She had never seen him quite so heated. The more she thought about it, the more it did seem odd. But she was as yet untouched by cynicism and had faith in the system.

'I don't know, sometimes there isn't a motive, is there? Sometimes you get…' she was going to say nutters. 'Look, I'm sorry it's your friend, OK?'

They ate in silence for a while. Eventually Bev couldn't hold back the question.

'So what happened between you two?'

Knight bridled.

'What do you mean what happened?! Nothing happened!'

'I didn't mean *that*. I just mean… what went on between you? Like, you're asking *me* all these questions.'

She had a point. He gave her a brief outline of their three dates, concluding tersely that Fran had changed her mind about him. He did not say why.

'Well, maybe you're better off out of it.'

Knight would have sprung to Fran's defence again, but a way ahead of sorts was forming in his mind. He'd be pushing his luck, but Bev could help him take the first step.

'Do you think you can find out who the next of kin are?'

Now it was Bev who bridled.

'No, and if I did I wouldn't tell you. You think I want you poking around and getting me into trouble?'

'Come on, no one's going to find out.'

'Sorry.' She got up. 'Thank you for the sandwich. This has been a very interesting conversation, but it didn't happen, OK?'

She turned as she walked away.

'Be careful, Tom.'

* * *

Jana was making ready to leave at the end of the next night shift. The past twenty-four hours had only served to darken an already sombre mood.

She had seen bodies in open coffins at family funerals, so the sight of the three dead women had not unnerved her. Fran's arrest, however, had shaken her to the core and the experience of being questioned by Bullock had reduced her to tears. He had dismissed her shortly afterwards, as if some deep-seated instinct had been satisfied. Although she felt physically sick, it had not occurred to her to ask for time off, given the disgrace in which she now found herself.

For his part, Bullock had concluded swiftly that little was to be gained by questioning the surviving residents in any depth, a decision hastened by Brenda's insistence that she had recently massaged him under a palm tree. Once the police had left, an air of normality had descended. By lunchtime, several residents had already forgotten what had happened and were only vaguely aware that there was more space at the table than usual. By tea time, those who did remember had fallen into a state of silent despondency tempered by relief that they had been spared, apart from one or two who took the opposite view. Susan Hillfield had taken permanently to her room.

But all this lay in the past. What Jana was quietly dreading lay in the very near future.

She was deep in debt. For over a month now, Brian had sent her no money and she was resolved to confront him. He had long covered his tracks so well that she had no way of making contact, but she knew he would be at the dog track in Brighton that afternoon. She intended to confront him in public and threaten to keep coming back until he paid up, her calculation being that it would cost him less than what he would lose if he stopped going to the track.

When she stepped out of the front door Knight was waiting for her.

'Excuse me, are you Jana?'

She had lived in England long enough to detect a richness and civility in his voice, which compensated for being intercepted by an old man she had never seen before. He held a business card out for her to take. It just said, 'Tom Knight' and below that 'Investigations,' with a phone number and an email address.

His first thought was that she was beautiful. Dark eyes, high cheekbones and slightly pouting lips, long black hair. She reminded him of his daughter in her goth phase.

'I'm a friend of Fran's, I'm trying to help her.'

The word 'investigations' on the card disquieted her. She had been investigated enough of late, but the man seemed benign. His practised courtesy reminded her of her grandfather.

'I have to get home, someone is expecting me.'

'May I walk with you? If you don't mind going a little more slowly than usual?'

She assented and told him how she had found Fran asleep, then heard the commotion and witnessed the bodies. She was outside the office when Bullock asked to look inside Fran's handbag, to which Fran had not seemed to object. She had looked astonished when, from the depths of the bag, he had produced a syringe.

'Did anything in the office look different from when you left the night before?'

She tried hard to picture the scene when she took the call from her sister before hurrying home.

'I'm sorry, I can't think of anything. Why do you want to know?'

'Because I don't believe Fran did it. Do you?'

She had not given the question much thought. Like Bev, she assumed that someone with a syringe in their bag was likely to be guilty.

'She was the only one in the house, apart from the old ladies.'

'How can you be sure of that if you weren't there?'

She frowned. He was right, she couldn't be sure.

'Please, you're the only person who can help me, and Fran too if she's innocent.'

He took a memory stick from his pocket.

'If you download the hard drive of the office computer onto this, I'll pay you fifty pounds.'

She thought for a moment. Her job was hanging by a thread, but it would be an easy thing to do, and fifty pounds was a week's food shopping. The chances of being caught were low; all the staff used the computer regularly, and there was only one password.

Life had been rigorous in teaching her to drive a hard bargain wherever possible. She thought of trying to up the price, but had a better idea.

'Alright,' she replied. 'But if I help you with this, you must also help me with something.'

* * *

Knight returned to his car, apprehensive about the deal he had just struck. The girl had her head screwed on, he would give her that.

Some fool had parked too close to him. Forgetting about Jana, he applied himself to the tedious business of repeatedly inching backwards and forwards in order to get out. Inevitably, he lost patience and scraped the car in front of him. His conscience forbidding any further act of dishonesty for the time being, he wrote a note and left it on the windscreen.

As he passed New Horizons, a man and a woman were coming out. The man was middle-aged with a dark complexion and was carrying a suitcase. The woman was old and walked with a stoop. In the mirror he saw them turn up the road towards the scene of his mishap, the woman clinging to the man's arm for support. It would be worth driving round the block to get a better look at them.

What should have been a simple operation turned sour in the next street, where a refuse truck was blocking the way. Only a few yards further on was a gap between the parked cars that would easily accommodate it. Knight hooted and was ignored. A bin man glared at him. He hooted again and was about to get out when the driver grudgingly made a half-hearted attempt to move into the space.

With the sun in his eyes, Knight crept into the narrow gap, attracting more disapproval from the bin men. On one side the truck towered over him, on the other he faced an obstacle course of parked cars. He edged forwards with millimetres to spare, but was undone by a Range Rover. His mirror caught the rear corner and was pushed back as far as it would go. There were shouts from the bin men, the words 'old git' were used.

It was impossible to reverse. Even if he could twist his neck enough to look round, he had no confidence at all in his ability to thread his way back past the truck. He pushed forward, wincing as his mirror rasped along the behemoth's flank, where it left a highly visible line in the paintwork. Knight cursed the owner for wanting such a bloated, pointless thing. The bin men cheered when the housing of Knight's mirror cracked loudly and fell off. This time there would be no note. He doubted they would take his number, and was in any case past caring.

When he turned the final corner the couple was nowhere to be seen. At war with humanity, he was halfway home before it occurred to him that he had not looked to see if the small car he had scratched was still there.

* * *

33

The dog track was busy for a weekday afternoon. Knight sat at the front of the grandstand, opposite the betting pitches by the finishing line. He wondered again if he had been a soft touch, compelling though the girl's story had been.

They had driven in his car, with Milada in the seat he kept for his youngest grandson. She was quiet for a two-year-old, only mildly curious about her new surroundings. Now mother and child stood hand in hand at the back of the queue for one of the pitches amidst the commotion of punters seeking last-minute odds.

Facing them, fishing happily in the teeming waters of the credulous and the desperate, was Brian Denning. He was bigger than Knight had expected, a burly man of over six feet who looked as if he could take care of himself. When he saw the pair in the queue, his face filled with a panic that would have been comic in other circumstances. A heated conversation ensued while frustrated punters moved to the neighbouring pitches. Eventually he wiped the odds off his board to signal that he was closed, took his money satchel and walked away with Jana and Milada behind him. Jana looked briefly in Knight's direction and nodded.

Although seething with rage, Denning had lied well enough to convince Jana he had her money in an envelope in his car. He had been meaning to send it, he had been busy, there was no need to embarrass him like this. To his relief, she had taken the bait, and now he meant to punish her. That was his limit of rational thought; the possible consequences did not even occur to him.

Knight followed them, holding his stick as still as possible while the camera relayed the scene to his phone. He stayed close to the cars so that he could duck out of the way if Denning looked round.

With the races underway, the car park was deserted. Denning kept looking up, as if searching for something. He stopped by the side of a tall van. Knight realised he had chosen a spot where he could not be seen by the security cameras.

'So, you'd like what you're owed, is that right?'

Jana was at last beginning to sense danger, but it was too late. He grabbed her by the throat and slammed her head against the side of the van. Milada screamed.

'If you ever, ever do that again,' he shouted, banging her head each time he said 'ever', while Jana kicked out uselessly at him, 'if I ever see you anywhere near me ever again…'

'Denning!' With a roar that would have felled a squaddie at twenty paces, Knight strode towards them. 'Put her down at once!'

The impact of Knight's voice was such that Denning instinctively obeyed, but then he saw that it came from an old man with a walking stick.

'Who the fuck are you?'

'I believe you owe this young lady some money,' said Knight, calmly. He held up the phone for Denning to see. The images of the attack played on the screen.

'You've just committed a violent assault on the premises of the racetrack. What do you think the committee will do when they see it?'

Denning lunged clumsily for the phone. Stepping smartly sideways, Knight grabbed his wrist and pulled hard, stretching out his foot at the same time. Denning stumbled and fell, cracking his face on the wing mirror of a car as he went down. He got to his feet, his mouth dripping with blood. Knight moved closer to the van, keen to avoid the security camera should he need to use the stick.

It seemed he did. Denning lumbered towards him like a maddened bull, intent on savage retribution. Knight swung too soon, missing the kneecap and landing a painful but harmless blow on his opponent's thigh. They fell to the ground together and rolled apart. Now Jana was screaming too.

Denning was up first. He straddled Knight, grasping for his throat and gaining purchase. Yet, considering the circles in which he moved, he was an inexperienced fighter, perhaps because he delegated this kind of work to others. He allowed his face to get too close, allowing Knight to jab his thumb as far as it would go into the socket of his right eye.

Denning squealed and lurched backwards. As he did he felt a familiar and deeply unwelcome spasm in his lower spine, infinitely worse than what he was experiencing in his eye.

He bellowed with pain, then whimpered and gasped as he sought a posture to placate the rogue vertebra that had chosen this moment to dislodge itself again. Knight wriggled free, causing more jolts to the stricken back.

'Help me, please! I can't move!'

'We should call an ambulance, no?' Jana was holding the sobbing child in her arms, trying to calm her. Knight shook his head. He picked up the money satchel and gave it to her.

'No. Not until he's paid the money he owes you.'

Pointing his stick at Denning as if to indicate the position of litter on a parade ground, he added: 'If you ever touch her or miss another payment, my film will do the rounds of every racetrack in the country. Got that?' Denning nodded, his pain exacerbated by the sight of Jana counting out the money.

The next day, Jana had the memory stick.

* * *

Chapter Four

Outside Eastbourne Magistrates Court, a handful of photographers leapt like a troop of monkeys as the prison van emerged, pointing their cameras randomly through the tinted windows. It took a moment for Fran to understand the source of the flashes illuminating her cubicle like some strangely mute thunderstorm. The hard seat jolted her spine as the van bumped over the kerb.

'You're famous, darlin'.' The voice from the neighbouring cubicle was rasping and low. 'You'll be a star at Holloway, they love a murderer up there.'

Another jolt. She thought she might be sick, but the moment passed.

'I didn't do it,' she said, quietly.

'Course not, never said you did.' This came with a disparaging laugh, followed by a lengthy bout of coughing. After gasping for breath the voice continued.

'Pig told me they found a fair bit of smack on you. Where'd that come from?'

'I don't know!'

'It's just that most gear that gets sold in this town I tend to hear about. Sort of explains what I'm doing here, know what I mean?'

'I told you, I don't know!' In the past forty-eight hours the words had become a mantra.

'Well, let's just say, if you do happen to remember I'd like to know, alright?'

To Fran's relief, the voice lapsed into silence, but the question echoed on. How had the heroin got into her bag and her car?

When she had first seen the syringe it seemed prosaic. Syringes were a common item at the home and, in any case, she was still reeling from the discovery of the three dead women. Even when Bullock asked if it was hers it took a moment for the implication to sink in.

There had been a glimmer of hope when Mrs Grayling remembered the CCTV system, but the key to the cupboard in which it was housed was missing. Bullock forced the door, only to discover that the hard disc had been removed. When a further examination of her handbag revealed the key in an inside compartment, she began to feel as if she were observing herself in a dream.

At the police station there was a second interview, for which a duty solicitor was produced. World-weary and aching for a pension that was still years away, his assumption that Fran was guilty was palpable even before the fingerprints on the syringe had been identified as hers. Having advised her to make a full confession, his application for bail was at best half-hearted, and the magistrate had shown no hesitation in remanding her to prison.

One thing was clear. The net that entangled her had been designed and cast with immense skill. It was inconceivable that any of the residents could have the desire let alone the wit to carry out such a ruthlessly efficient plan, which left only one explanation. Someone had entered the house, injected the women and left the heroin to incriminate her, at the same time disabling the CCTV and planting the key in her bag. But who? And why? For several hours a jumble of unanswerable questions spun through her mind. The van slowed to a crawl as it reached the traffic-choked streets of London and inched its way north.

When at last she was led out into the prison yard she was surprised to see that her neighbour and fellow remand prisoner was a tiny, dark woman with sunken cheeks and close-cropped hair. Two of her top teeth were missing; most of the rest were nicotine-stained stumps.

'I'm Cindy,' she said, as they made their way to the reception office. 'Anything you want in here, I know how to get it.'

* * *

It was a grey Sunday afternoon as Knight made his way down a line of handsome Edwardian villas, the drizzle failing to dent his newly returned optimism. He had never taken great pleasure in physical violence, but there was no doubt that the despatch of a younger man in physical combat had raised his spirits. A lunchtime smoke with Merv had raised them further, so that the hunter within him was now rampant, scouring the terrain for a trail he was confident of finding.

The degree of planning involved in killing the women and framing Fran suggested competence and rational purpose. In the civilian world that purpose was nearly always money. Find the money and the rest would follow; it was an article of faith that had seldom failed him. The next of kin were the obvious starting point, if only to exclude them from the investigation. Even Bullock would have recognised this had he not been seduced by the prospect of a quick result.

Knight's strategy in such circumstances was straightforward and usually effective: put people under pressure and make them lie. If they lied they were hiding something, and once you knew what it was you could work on them. But, first, you had to find the pressure point. As his sergeant in Borneo used to say, you had to have their balls in your hand before you could squeeze them.

First on his list was the nephew of Joan Baldwin. An hour of desk research and a few phone calls had revealed that, until three years ago, Harry Baldwin had been a director of a profitable insurance brokerage in London. He had moved to Eastbourne in his late fifties to expand the business, but soon after this the company was taken over and its new owners were not sufficiently convinced of his talents to invite him to stay. According to the published accounts, he had cashed out with two million pounds. To Knight the money represented a retirement pot of inconceivable size, yet there was no evidence that he supported his aunt in any way or indeed had anything to do with her. The fees for New Horizons were paid by the council.

Antonia Baldwin was twenty years younger. Her Facebook account spoke of a leisurely round of lunches, gym and travel. There were mentions of two grown-up stepchildren but far more about her nut allergy, which on two occasions had nearly done for her. She wrote of these events in graphic terms, placing herself at the centre of what seemed a self-obsessed melodrama. Further research revealed an acting career that had peaked with a minor role in EastEnders before petering out into the pages of swimwear catalogues. There was no trace of the previous Mrs Baldwin, leading Knight to suppose that she had been quite literally replaced by a newer model.

The man who opened the door was bald with high colour and a well-developed double chin. He looked blankly at the elderly tweed-jacketed gentleman leaning heavily on a stick.

'I'm terribly sorry to bother you, but are you Mr Harry Baldwin?'

Baldwin noted, as intended, that the old man seemed nervous and unsure of himself. 'Yes. Who are you?'

'My name's Ronald Bowles.' Knight held out his hand, which Baldwin felt himself somehow commanded to shake. 'I'm Fran Haskell's uncle.' Baldwin withdrew his hand as quickly as decency allowed.

'What do you want?' There was a note of hostility now, though Knight hadn't expected him to be friendly. He hesitated for a moment, as if steeling himself.

'I know that this might sound upsetting to you, but I don't believe she did it. Could I come in and talk to you?'

Baldwin's face went an even deeper shade of red. Knight looked him straight in the eye with the most imploring expression he could muster.

'It'll only take a couple of minutes. Please, I've come a very long way.'

Knight disliked deploying the pathetic old man persona. He had an irrational fear that, each time he used it, he was taking a step nearer to the real thing, but it was one of his most effective ploys for getting a foot in the door. Though not today apparently.

Baldwin shook his head. 'I'm very sorry, but we've said everything we have to say to the police.'

'What is it darling? Is something wrong?'

Antonia Baldwin appeared, alerted by her husband's raised voice. Knight found it hard not to stare. She was about five foot six, in knee-length lycra training pants and a tight vest that stretched halfway down an impossibly flat stomach. A honeyed tan and gleaming teeth completed the vision of the perfect trophy wife. In one hand she still held a training weight and there was a faint sheen of perspiration on her skin. But what he noticed most were her green eyes. They made unwavering contact in a warm, welcoming caress, as if bidding him to hidden pleasures.

'This gentleman is the uncle of the woman who killed Aunt Joan. He thinks she didn't do it.'

'I'm so sorry to be a nuisance,' Knight wheezed. He upped the pace of his breathing and swayed momentarily on his stick, which had the desired effect.

'Please, come in.' Her voice was melodious and somehow cosseting, with a vestigial twang of south London.

To Baldwin's evident disapproval, Knight staggered past him and followed his wife down a corridor lined with prints of harbour scenes. He tried but failed to avert his eyes from the pert curves beneath the lycra, and wondered what she was doing with a deadbeat like Baldwin until he remembered the two million pound payout.

They entered a spacious living room where a pair of shiny leather sofas faced each other over an unfeasibly large coffee table. Gratefully accepting a glass of water, Knight produced what he claimed to be a heart pill and made a show of allowing his hand to tremble as he put it in his mouth. There was little question of being forcibly ejected; few people wanted a cardiac arrest on their hands.

'How do you think we can help you?' She sat next to her husband, facing Knight over the coffee table, the eyes working on him as they had doubtless worked on Baldwin. He sighed, raising his hands outspread in a gesture of futility.

'Well, I know it's an obvious question, but can you think of anyone else who might have wanted to harm your aunt or the other ladies?'

'Of course not!' snapped Baldwin. 'If we had, we'd have said so to the police!'

Antonia stroked her husband's arm. 'Harry, the gentleman's upset.' She turned back to Knight. 'The honest truth is, we were both very bad at visiting Auntie Joan, so we didn't really know what went on at the home.' In a more conciliatory tone Baldwin added, 'We're busy people, Mr Bowles. We knew she was being well looked after or we'd have moved her somewhere else.'

Knight nodded sympathetically, knowing full well they had never lifted a finger on her behalf.

'When was the last time you saw her?'

Antonia shifted uncomfortably. 'I can't quite remember, can you darling?'

Her husband glowered.

'We were never close, I just happened to be her last surviving relative.'

Knight was developing a deep dislike of the man and was tempted to make him squirm further. But he was walking a tightrope. If he pushed too hard they would become suspicious and ask the police about him. There was a fair chance of that happening anyway, but he didn't want the distraction of Bullock, just yet, if he could help it. On the other hand, if he didn't push hard enough he was wasting his time.

'So, you wouldn't know if any of the other victims were wealthy?'

Baldwin bristled. 'Well, obviously not. But if you must know, Joan had five hundred pounds that she left to a cats' home.'

An inheritance was easy enough to check, so it was unlikely to be a lie.

Antonia stroked her husband's arm again and said gently, 'I can see this is very difficult for you, Mr Bowles, but from what I've heard the evidence against your niece is pretty convincing.'

Knight frowned and looked bewildered. 'You're right. It's just… it's almost too convincing. It's as if someone had set her up.'

Baldwin gaped like an angry goldfish, but Antonia smiled at Knight as if consoling a severely disappointed child.

'I know. It must be dreadful.' She hesitated. 'Please don't take this the wrong way, but have you thought of talking to a counsellor?'

Now it was Knight's turn to feel affronted, albeit on behalf of the fictional Mr Bowles. Instead he replied, 'Perhaps I should. And I'm aware how distressing this must be for you.' He shook his head sadly, before adding as solicitously as he could, 'Where were you when it happened?'

He watched them keenly. Would either of them touch their faces or look away? Would their eyes flicker to the left, which some believed was the sign of a lie? It wasn't a proven science, but it added to the picture. Yet his powers of observation failed him, for he found himself drawn again into the garden of green delight.

She shrugged. 'I expect we were here. Watching television probably.'

Knight sensed the well running dry. Harry Baldwin seemed an unpleasant enough man, and Antonia was in every likelihood an accomplished gold-digger. But in the case of Joan Baldwin and her five hundred pounds there was no gold to dig.

* * *

Chapter Five

The temperature had topped thirty for the second day in a row. Knight shielded his eyes from the whitewashed glare of a Victorian terrace a few yards back from the seafront, where the houses contained warrens of small apartments inhabited by the single and the elderly. The high-pitched voice on the phone had directed him to number 57E, and now invited him down a flight of external stairs to a basement flat. For the past three decades this had been the lair of Carol O'Brien, the only daughter of Lotty Smith.

The voice combined with the heat had led Knight to imagine someone young and petite, but what greeted him at the door was eighteen stones of flesh in a plunging smock and leopard-spot leggings. A string of jagged beads cascaded down her chest like a minor rockfall down a mountainside, atop of which a small, smiling face was set within a cladding of jowls and chins. She looked in her late sixties.

'Mr Richards? How lovely to see you!' There was a sing-song quality he had not noticed on the phone.

He followed her down a dingy corridor. The false name was his only subterfuge. Jana's espionage had revealed not only Carol's address but also her occupation, so all he had needed to do was book an appointment. She entered a sparsely furnished room almost devoid of natural light and ushered him into an armchair. Beside it was a low table draped in black silk.

'So, have you had a reading before, or is this your first time?'

Knight confessed that it was. He claimed that a good friend had been greatly helped through difficult times by recourse to the Tarot and had urged him to give it a try. Her eyes lit up at the prospect of an easy client who would be unlikely to challenge her interpretations with his own.

'So, are *you* going through difficult times?' she cooed.

He sat back and looked away, as if reluctant to speak. After a moment's silence he turned back and looked straight at her.

'Well, you see, I've been having dreams about my late mother.'

Her eyes widened slightly.

'In the dreams she's calling me,' he faltered, 'and... I know this sounds stupid, but I keep wondering if it means I'm going to die soon.'

He had shrunk at first from adopting such a morbid approach, but if she was harbouring guilt he needed to get her emotionally off balance.

She breathed audibly but held his gaze. 'It's not stupid at all, lots of people worry about that. Why don't we see what the cards say?'

She asked him to shuffle the pack, then laid the cards out on the table, leaning forward to reveal the crevasse that was her cleavage. Knight wondered if he was being invited to stare. He had never shared the fascination that some men held for massive breasts, indeed large amounts of flesh made him queasy. He had once been challenged by a similarly proportioned woman, a fellow student on his gender studies module at Sussex, who had insisted that fat was a sexist construct. In the spirit of scientific enquiry, he had spent a drunken night with her, investigating whether his aversion could be overridden by rational thought. Mercifully for both of them, the amount of alcohol he had consumed rendered the experiment null.

She explained that the cards did not tell the future but would help him find his way through doubts and fears onto a path leading to peace and harmony. Doubtless with repeat sessions in mind, she emphasised how patience was required. A first reading could not always be expected to reveal everything he needed to understand.

She picked up a card showing a golden circle bearing runic inscriptions. It was carried through clouds by a crudely drawn naked man with the head of a horse.

'The Wheel of Fortune.' She spoke the words as if announcing the title of a story. 'When it appears in this position it can mean there's change ahead. But it can also be about expanding your consciousness and seeing life in a different way to what you see now.'

She picked up the next card, which showed two ragged men shivering in the snow at the foot of a stained-glass window. The window displayed five golden circles, each containing a five pointed star.

'And here we have the five of Pentacles.' The sing-song delivery was starting to irritate him. She hesitated uneasily, then continued, choosing her words carefully, 'Sometimes it's associated with ill health, but that doesn't automatically mean you're going to get ill. It's like I said, the cards don't tell the future, but they can tell us about things it might help us to be aware of.'

Knight's knee let out an unprovoked twinge at the mention of ill health.

'But here we have the nine of cups. The pleasure of the senses.' She said this with a certain amount of relief, which Knight shared. 'So, this could be asking if you're listening to your body and giving it what it needs.'

He strongly suspected he wasn't. Pushing aside the thought that there might be something in the cards after all, he took a ranging shot.

'You know,' he said excitedly, as if a great idea had suddenly sprung upon him, 'I've just thought what might have triggered those dreams. Did you see that awful story about the murders in the retirement home?'

He knew the ploy was clumsy but was confident he had established enough credibility not to arouse suspicion. If she had something to hide, it was more likely than not that she would glide over the topic and change the subject back to the reading. She might, of course, do this as a matter of professional practice, in which case he would continue to probe. He didn't expect her eyes to fill with tears.

'Excuse me.' She stood up and moved away, keeping her back to him. He heard a muffled cry, and saw that she was covering her face with her hands. Her body was shaking. Intrigued but disquieted, Knight raised himself from the chair and approached her.

'Are you alright?' he asked kindly.

She turned, her face smudged with mascara. 'My mother was one of those women!' she sobbed. Then she broke down and wept uncontrollably.

Knight felt skewered by guilt. 'I'm so sorry,' she wailed. 'It's not your burden to bear.'

'No, I'm the one who should be sorry, I had no idea.'

Feeling he should show a modicum of human solidarity, he attempted to put his arms around her, but they only reached as far as her shoulders. The gesture was accepted gratefully nonetheless. She flung her arms around his neck and squeezed her bulk against him, resting her head against his neck. She smelt of wine.

Gradually, the sobbing and heaving subsided. Knight waited for what seemed an age until she loosened her grip and took a step back.

'You're a very kind man,' she murmured, and then, abandoning any pretence of professional detachment, 'I don't suppose you fancy a drink?'

Over a bottle of Tesco Bulgarian white she treated him to her life story. There had once been a Mr O'Brien, who had prevaricated on the matter of children until it was too late and then walked out on her. After that had come the Tarot, guiding her through the dark days to a new life. But chiefly there had been her mother, Lotty, the one steadfast companion who had shielded her from a drunken father and stood by her through every subsequent setback, of which there were many.

As one episode followed another, interwoven with earnest praise for the power of the cards, Knight's sympathy gave way to a sense of claustrophobia. It was as clear as day that she was no more a murderer than Fran. When he managed to turn the conversation briefly to the murders in the hope of unearthing something new, it was only to open up a new seam of Tarot. Keen to bring things to a close, he waited until she paused to draw breath and suggested it must be of comfort that the guilty party had been apprehended.

A flicker of agitation crossed her face.

'I hope so,' she said quietly.

It seemed odd that she should entertain doubt. As far as the world was concerned, Fran's guilt couldn't be plainer.

'It's just that I did some readings not long ago for old Denise Brewer, you know, one of the other ladies who died.'

She looked for a moment as if she might break down again, but taking a deep breath she went on, 'Death came up in the same position twice. I thought it would upset her, but she said she wasn't worried about dying, because when the time came her daughter would do it for her.'

Knight showed no flicker of emotion.

'Did you mention it to the police?'

She shook her head. 'It was only afterwards I remembered. I thought about going, but… the cards didn't lead me there.'

Knight didn't ask why not, knowing the answer could take another hour. Invoking a doctor's appointment, he beat as hasty a retreat as decency allowed and emerged blinking in the sunlight. He was exultant. After two relatively simple forays he had an excellent lead, quite possibly the breakthrough that would enable him to secure Fran's release.

Carol's optimism was higher still. It had been a long time since a male of the species, presentable or otherwise, had paid any attention to her, let alone the amount lavished by Knight. Indeed, there had been no one since the days of Mr O'Brien, unless you counted the unfortunate webcam experience. But the cards had always insisted on the existence of a man who would sweep her away. Admittedly, she had sometimes mistaken this man for strangers she had met on buses or in pubs, though, when she looked back, she could always see where she had missed meanings.

She quickly re-dealt the cards, keen to see which would come last. It was The Lovers.

* * *

Chapter Six

Barbara Dawson was the youngest daughter of Denise Brewer. She had an elder brother who lived in Hong Kong. As far as Knight could see from her Facebook account, he had not set foot in England recently.

As with his previous outing, he needed little in the way of subterfuge. On her website she offered therapeutic massage from her home overlooking a leafy park some two miles from the seafront. A string of qualifications indicated that her services were of a strictly therapeutic nature. A photo showed a brown-eyed woman of medium build, in her fifties. Her husband was a surveyor. Knight found a picture of him at a Rotary dinner, a slight, pallid man with thinning hair.

The website image did little justice to the woman who answered the door. There was a lustre to her curly brown hair and deep tan that suggested holidays far away from England. Yet there was something about the line of her mouth, the way it turned down a little at the corners, that suggested dissatisfaction. He recalled that the voice on the phone had been businesslike, verging on the brusque, and so it was now.

'Mr Atkins? This way please.'

It was an impeccably restored Edwardian villa with high ceilings presiding over immaculate cornices. The walls were white, lit by discreetly positioned spotlights. Here and there was an etching of a classical ruin.

She led him to a sparsely-furnished ground floor room looking out onto a courtyard garden. While she interrogated him about his medical history, he assessed the terrain. They were sitting by a desk in a corner near the window. He noted with satisfaction that the desk drawers had no locks and that her mobile phone lay next to an open laptop. In the opposite corner was a filing cabinet, the top drawer of which was slightly open. He reckoned three minutes would be sufficient if Merv could keep her talking that long.

'And how long has the knee been troubling you?'

It seemed sensible to extract whatever additional value he could from the session, so he told her about the occasional collapses that had begun about two years ago.

'And it's only now that you've decided to do something about it?!'

He caught the tone of disapproval, akin to a dentist discovering a tooth left carelessly to rot.

'The chances are it's the bone that's damaged, and that's not something I can really help you with.'

He mumbled that he'd be grateful for anything she could do to ease his various aches and pains, whereupon she instructed him to strip to his underpants and lie face down on the massage table.

At first, the sensation was pleasant as she ran her lightly-oiled fingers up and down his back on either side of his spine. This, however, was merely an overture, a scandalously unrepresentative one at that. Soon her thumbs were quarrying painfully between his shoulder blades, enough to make him growl in protest.

'You're completely locked up, I'm surprised you can even turn your neck.'

He caught the disapproving tone again. It was true that he had neglected his body. Years of rugby injuries, skiing accidents and other misadventures had been allowed to accumulate unchecked, bringing not only his knee but also his ankles and hips to a state where total disintegration at some point in the future was a distinct possibility. In other circumstances, he might have lapsed into morbidity, but the topic of physical decline was helpful.

'Well,' he gasped, between waves of deep discomfort, 'I suppose it's the price one pays for living too long.'

'No, it's the price you pay for not looking after yourself. If you have good genes there's no reason your body shouldn't last a hundred years.' She had moved to his lower back now, tunnelling to either side of his coccyx and along the upper ridge of his pelvis.

'True, but would you really want to live that long? What's the point of the body holding out if the mind goes?'

'Because at least the body is not in pain. Or in as little pain as possible.' As if to emphasise the point, she used what must surely have been her elbow to plough a furrow down his thigh to the back of his knee. Stifling a yelp, he replied as casually as possible, 'I think the main thing is to go quickly, whatever state you're in. I mean take those women at the retirement home. Most people would say it's a terrible thing, but you could argue someone did them a favour.'

She remained silent. He regretted that he could not see her eyes. After a moment he added, 'What do you think?'

She stopped massaging.

'That's one way of looking at it.'

He heard irritation. He had crossed a line into private territory and it seemed to irk her. There was, of course, no reason to assume that an unwillingness to talk about the murders indicated guilt. In contrast to the Tarot reader she might simply hold strong views about privacy and self-control. On the other hand, if she had euthanised her mother and killed the other two women to cover her tracks, she would need to be as hard as nails. Superficially, she seemed to fit that bill equally well.

Meanwhile, she had redoubled her efforts, moving back to his shoulder blades and grinding the muscle over the bone. Knight prided himself on having a high pain threshold. Once his unit had lost their medical kit during a skirmish deep in the jungle. He had taken a bullet in the leg, lived with it for a day and a night before they reached camp. Perhaps time had dulled his memory, but even that seemed preferable to what he was going through now.

'Can you try to relax please?'

After what seemed an eternity, but was in fact two minutes, the doorbell rang. She tutted impatiently, excused herself and left the room. Dizzy from pain, Knight slid from the bed, steadied himself for a second and went to the desk. He attached a SIM reader to the phone and put the memory stick into the laptop to copy her documents.

There were raised voices from the door. Merv's attempt to conduct a council survey about the neighbourhood's recycling options was not going down well. By the sound of it, he was already past the affable phase and into the respectfully firm one. Next would come the foot in the door. Merv enjoyed these outings. He took pride in the thoroughness with which he prepared his personae and in the forged identity cards that were seldom challenged.

The desk drawers contained little of interest. Bills, business stationery, a cheque book and a speeding ticket which he photographed before moving to the filing cabinet. Barbara was now threatening to call the police unless Merv removed his foot, while Merv assured her in a weary voice that there was no point in taking that kind of tone with him.

The top drawer of the cabinet contained her client files. There was no time for these; he had to hope that most of this information would be on the laptop. There were also some dog-eared booklets about male impotence. Knight thought back to the scrawny surveyor in the photo and wondered if they had been acquired with him in mind. The lower drawer was concerned mostly with accounts and suppliers. But in the very last folder, tucked away at the back, was a framed certificate awarding one Barbara Keller an MD from University College London. It seemed odd that it did not occupy pride of place on the wall. And why was she reduced to offering massages when she was qualified to practise as a doctor?

At the door, she was shouting to a passer-by for help, which meant that there were seconds left before Merv would withdraw. Moments after Knight removed the SIM reader and the memory stick, she returned in a foul temper, apologising for keeping him waiting and complaining bitterly about the arrogance of officialdom. In her unsettled state there was now a chance to catch her off-balance. After reassuring her that he had been glad of a moment's respite, he turned the conversation back to the murders.

'I got to thinking about those women again while I was lying here. Can you imagine what it takes to inject three old ladies with heroin in cold blood? I mean, what kind of monster do you have to be to do that?'

He was facing up now so that she could work on the front of his thigh above his knee. She seemed somewhat taken aback, but other than that she gave nothing away.

'I've no idea. Why are you so interested in them?'

'I'm not interested in them particularly, just my mind wandering. It seems to do that more and more lately.' He made it sound casual, a wittering old fool with not enough to occupy him. It was time to push harder and see what happened.

'My memory's not what it was either. Do you know I can't even remember what I was doing that night?'

It was a crude non-sequitur but it served its purpose, for she was staring at him with a distinct aura of fear. He pressed on.

'I mean is that normal? Can you remember what you were doing that night?'

Her mouth dropped slightly open. There was a sharp intake of breath.

'I was with a friend at the cinema,' she replied rather quickly. She turned away and went to the filing cabinet where she made a show of looking at a brochure. Her hands were trembling.

'Oh yes, what did you see?'

'I really can't remember. Perhaps my memory's going too.' Her voice shook slightly. Convinced she had seen through him but determined to assert his cover to the last, Knight remained cheerily garrulous, enthusing about films he had seen and complaining about the price of tickets.

Still avoiding his gaze, she returned to the massage table and delivered a few desultory thrusts to the muscle around his kneecap before announcing tersely that there was indeed little she could do for him. Minutes later he was back on the pavement, itching to inspect his booty.

**

'So, case closed, eh?'

Knight lazed in business class while Merv cooked on the barbeque.

'Let's say I'm quietly optimistic.'

The visit to Barbara Dawson had yielded treasure beyond expectation. Keller was her name from her first marriage, made when she was still a medical student, and the name under which she qualified as a doctor. The career lasted scarcely longer than the marriage. In her late twenties, she was struck off for ending the life – deliberately it was asserted – of a terminally ill patient with an overdose of diamorphine. She only avoided a murder conviction because the jury had been unable to decide whether a lesser dose would have been sufficient to quell the patient's pain. The case had polarised opinion, the tabloids leading the way with headlines that pitted the Angel of Death against the Angel of Mercy.

But this was only the first gem to be plucked from the treasure chest. The speeding ticket had been acquired courtesy of a camera that Knight knew well, on the main road that led to New Horizons. At first, he had not believed his eyes when he saw that it was timed at 9.30 on the evening of the murder. All the town's cinemas lay in the opposite direction.

Eclipsing them both was the phone. He had started by ringing the numbers in the call log, claiming that he wished to buy a car he had seen advertised in Manchester. By feigning feebleness of mind, he had gained a degree of sympathy from the recipients, enabling him to extract a rough idea of their location and identity. One was a man with an Asian or Middle Eastern accent. In the background, Knight had heard a female voice asking if a prescription was ready. When the man broke off for a moment to deal with it he picked out another voice, male this time and less distinct, but clear enough for him to hear the mention of a car park.

He played back the recording several times, piecing together the fragments of a diatribe about hours spent in outpatients and the cost of parking. He recalled that the local hospital had been savaged for profiting from rising waiting times through rip-off parking charges. The dispensary, which was surely where the diatribe had taken place, would be a plentiful source of diamorphine.

Half an hour later, he was watching a queue of dejected people as they waited for their prescriptions. Behind the counter a harassed woman was attempting to convey dosage instructions to an uncomprehending Somali couple with a shrieking baby. She sounded similar to the woman in the recording. Behind her, searching for medicines among stacks of shelves, was a dark, well-built man in his forties. He had large, powerful hands squeezed into white gloves. Holding his phone behind his back, Knight pressed the redial button and watched him fumble in his pocket.

He felt the rush of blood that always came when a case cracked open. Barbara Dawson had killed a patient and offered to do as much for her mother, then lied about where she was on the night of the murders. And now he was looking at a contact who had daily access to heroin. It was that good.

'Excuse me?'

A middle-aged woman with a squint had materialised beside him. A badge identified her as a volunteer helper.

'You look a bit lost there – can I help you?'

In his haste to get to the hospital, he had neglected to prepare a cover story. 'I'm fine thanks, I'm just, er…' his mind went blank.

'Do you have an appointment, dear?'

The man in the dispensary glanced in their direction. Knight turned his back to him, anxious not to be remembered.

'I've just come to see someone. But thanks very much.'

He marched off in what he hoped was an appropriate direction, ignoring further offers of help. He wanted to stay longer and watch the man, perhaps follow him home, but now in a glass door he caught a reflection of the thwarted Samaritan talking to a security guard. Cursing all do-gooders, he found a side exit and left.

Over the pier, the starlings were performing their vanishing act again. He wondered if the solution he had so skilfully unearthed might itself disappear as easily. Stretching his limbs, free of pain since the massage, he dismissed the thought. The chain of logic was too strong. There was, of course, the question of hard evidence, but he was confident of its existence and even more so of his ability to find it.

'So, you reckon that, if you crack it, she'll come running back to you?' Merv seemed to find the thought amusing.

'And your point is?'

'My point is, you're risking a pile of shit just to get your leg over. Would you be doing this if it was some fat old slag?'

Knight was affronted by the reduction of his motives to base carnality, but the moment passed as Merv brought his steak.

'If she was a fat old slag, as you so gallantly put it, it's highly unlikely I'd have been seeing her. The point is that she's innocent.'

He bit into the tender meat, the hunter's reward. It had already occurred to him that there might be a grain of truth in Merv's assertion. He had more than enough circumstantial evidence to go to the police. Even Bullock would have to concede there was something here that demanded investigation. Was he trying to hog the glory, the better to appear the all-conquering hero? He decided not. Bullock would investigate clumsily, allowing the perpetrators ample opportunity to cover their tracks. It was a job that required painstaking surveillance and a willingness, where necessary, to break the rules.

None of this answered Merv's initial question. Did he hope that by proving Fran's innocence he would win her back? Little more than a week ago she had sat in this very chair, and he could not deny that he would do whatever it took to see her there again.

* * *

Chapter Seven

Two days later, Knight was sitting in Merv's van halfway up the street from Barbara Dawson's front door. He wore overalls and a hard hat, with a pair of goggles on his forehead ready to be pulled down over his eyes each time she came out. Completing the vision of white van man was a copy of *The Sun*, to be used as a shield if she walked in his direction. This was his third twelve-hour shift in the round-the-clock surveillance that Merv had agreed to share with him.

Knight enjoyed surveillance. He relished the cloak of invisibility in which he was able to wrap himself, and the possibility that something momentous might happen at any moment. It was like watching cricket, but with far higher stakes. He took pleasure, too, in the well-oiled logistical operation. The back of the van contained all the requisites of a comfortable camping trip: a twelve volt fridge full of supplies, a gas ring, a chemical camping toilet and an airbed. He had rigged up a motion detector by her front door to alert him via his phone should she make a move in the early hours while he was dozing. There was also a tracker on the underside of her car.

Thus far, the momentous had been in short supply. She had been to the hairdresser, the post office and twice to the supermarket. There had been a moment of panic when he forgot to take the newspaper on disembarking from the van in the supermarket car park. She turned back unexpectedly, forcing him to duck behind a car just as its owner returned with two small children. Disturbed by the sight of an elderly man in grubby overalls crouching beside the driver's door, the mother challenged him. When he concocted a story about dropping a pound she had insisted on helping him, and when the search proved fruitless gave him a pound of her own.

It was past nine thirty when Barbara Dawson opened the door and went to her car. This was the first time she had been out at night. He waited until she had turned the corner before following, content to track her on the laptop rather than risk being spotted.

He hoped he had played his cards right. Reluctant to return to the hospital, he had decided to concentrate his resources on the house. He had tried to make another appointment with a view to planting a bug, but she had given him short shrift. Breaking into the building was out of the question, exposed as it was to public view at the front and sealed off at the rear by the walls of neighbouring gardens. He needed her to lead him to her accomplice, and now perhaps she would.

On previous excursions, she had headed south to the town centre, but tonight she turned north onto the road that led to New Horizons, passing the speed camera that had caught her on the night of the murders. But when she came to the turning she continued straight on, and after a mile turned west towards the downs. Here the road climbed past rows of somnolent bungalows, pitch black except for the occasional flicker of a TV. A fox trotted by on the pavement, sparing him no more than a casual glance.

There were no other vehicles on the road now. When she pulled into a cul-de-sac three hundred yards ahead, he sped up and reached the turning in time to see her go to the front door of a house at the far end of the street. He watched through the binoculars as the door opened. It was the man from the dispensary.

He parked the van further on and hurried back. He had promised to call Merv if he succeeded in tracking them down together, but Merv had been exhausted after his last shift, conducted in the grip of a formidable hangover. In any case, he was perfectly capable of handling the situation alone, and slightly resented the implication that he needed nannying. His confidence was further boosted by the presence of a public path running down the side of the property.

A wooden fence separated the path from the back garden. Peering through a hole, he could make out a clump of bulrushes beside a small pond. The place would be easy to bug when its occupant was not present, but he was hell-bent on coming away with hard evidence that very night.

The fence was a little over head height. Further down the path was an abandoned recycling box, which he retrieved. He hung his stick on the fence and stepped up. Beyond the bulrushes was a conservatory where a light glowed from behind closed blinds.

It would be a simple matter, or so he thought, to pull the top half of his body over the ridge of the fence and slide down the other side. Yet having dragged his left leg over he found that the other would not follow, so that, instead of executing a smooth vaulting manoeuvre, he found himself perched shakily on the fence top. Try as he might, he could not raise the offending leg high enough to join its companion on the other side. It was if he were astride an impossibly anorexic horse.

He cursed the arthritic joints and enfeebled muscles that refused to do his bidding. As a young officer, he had revelled in the brutal challenge of the assault course, going at it with a frenzy that left him afterwards in a state of deep contentment. Well into his fifties he had scaled walls and drainpipes in the pursuit of commercial secrets. A garden fence did not qualify in his mind as a serious obstacle, though he could not claim to have climbed one recently.

It eventually became clear that he would have to take a fall. To his great relief, only a few feet away was a compost heap piled up against the fence. Placing one hand in front of the other and gripping tightly with his knees, he inched his way along. Despite the intense stabbing pain each time his perineum took the weight of his body, his spirits rose. He was at school, climbing over the back wall in the dead of night; he was in Borneo, creeping over slippery rocks behind a waterfall towards a camp of insurgents; he was in Armagh, crawling along a barn roof over the heads of unsuspecting Provos; and then he was at the compost heap. With a twist of his abdomen, he rolled down softly onto his back, unscathed apart from a small rip in his trousers. He had dared, and he had won.

At the pond by the bulrushes, he took out a strip of adhesive tape and a microphone transmitter in the form of a small metal disk. Stuck to a window it would pick up a conversation twenty feet away and send it in useable quality to his phone. The glass panels of the conservatory would be ideal if the targets were inside. A faint peal of laughter told him that they were.

He peeled the backing off the tape in order to attach the disk, but his fingers were sore from the fence. He was only aware that the disk had slipped through them when he heard the soft plop of it falling into the pond. For some reason the spares were not in his pocket. He remembered seeing them beneath the dashboard and making a mental note to transfer them to his jacket. Rather than fury, he felt the fear that always came when he forgot something of importance. Both his parents had succumbed to dementia, his father beginning the descent when only a few years older than he was now.

Thrusting the demon aside, he considered his options. He could go back to the van, but that meant crossing the fence again, twice. It would take at least ten minutes, during which the targets might move elsewhere in the house. Or he could use the stick. Leant against the conservatory it would not be flush with the glass, but it might pick up useable material. He was weighing the options when he noticed that a panel on the conservatory roof was a few inches open. If he could get the stick up there the sound quality would be excellent, and he would have video too.

He crossed the lawn to the side of the conservatory and pressed an ear to the glass. From within came a faint murmur of voices but they were muffled by the blind. Beyond him was a door leading to the back of the garage. Cheered that he had at least brought his bump keys, he took less than a minute to open it. His luck had returned, but would it hold long enough to provide what he was looking for?

Like a priceless treasure in a tomb, the ladder lay flat along a shelf. Scarcely believing his good fortune, Knight eased it down and carried it silently from the garage. He placed it against the brick wall where the house joined the conservatory and mounted slowly. Three rungs from the top he was able to slide onto the flat roof of the bungalow and drag himself clear. The roof was only a foot above the conservatory, which sloped downwards to the garden. Less than six feet away was the open panel.

There were distinct snippets of conversation now, among them Barbara saying something about the need for discretion. He switched the camera on and lay flat with his chest poised over the glass roof, but not touching it for fear that it would creak. He reached out with the stick, the crook foremost, but it was several inches short of the panel. Straining to stay above the glass he wriggled forward, his lower back complaining bitterly. He thought he heard a different female voice, which surprised him. Perhaps the conspiracy extended further than he had imagined.

He was inches away now. He strained forward again, but immediately felt his back giving way, obliging him, against his better judgement, to rest his spare hand on the wooden frame. Offered this slight respite, his aching back greedily took everything going. Even as his fingers detected the peeling paint and rotten timber, the front half of his body slumped onto the conservatory roof. He was aware of a loud crack as the panel and its near neighbours collapsed.

The jumble of images as he plummeted down included a candle on a table, a jacuzzi and, most strikingly, a mass of exposed human flesh. He heard a scream as the water engulfed him, breaking his fall. There was a momentary blur of legs and genitalia as he struggled to his knees to find Barbara Dawson standing naked before him with the man from the dispensary beside her. In the background several more naked bodies ran dripping from the room. He had just enough time to note her pronounced bikini line when her companion drew back his fist and punched him unconscious.

***

At first, all he could see was a cream-coloured tube, a few inches from his face. He reached out and touched it, feeling a hard metal surface.

'He's coming round.'

The tube revealed itself as the side bar of a hospital bed. Knight looked up to see two hazy figures sitting close by, with a blue curtain behind them. The blurred image resolved into his assailant, accompanied by Dawson. They were both fully clothed.

'Are you alright?' the man asked anxiously. Knight heaved himself up onto one elbow, scanning his surroundings for a handy weapon.

'Please, the doctor said you must not move!' There was a note of authentic concern, which was puzzling. Dawson sat stonily and said nothing. Beyond the cubicle he heard somebody ask about a trolley for upstairs. His mind raced, or rather limped, as he tried to make sense of the situation. Why had they brought him to A&E? They could have done what they liked to him at the house, killed him even, and passed it off as an accident.

'My name is Kemal Abduli. I'm sorry for hitting you, but I thought you were a burglar.'

'Don't apologise to him,' she snapped, then turning to Knight, 'I take it you're working for my husband. Or is it some disgusting newspaper?'

She had to be bluffing. He realised now that it would have been untidy to kill him at the house. There would have been a body to explain or dispose of, involving unwelcome risk. Far better to play the innocent by pretending to be concerned for his welfare.

Knight fixed Barbara with a stare he hoped was severe.

'Neither as it happens. I'm much more interested in the fact that you killed your mother and murdered two other women to cover your tracks.'

For a moment, she looked as if a unicorn had walked into the cubicle. But as he laid out his case, they both seemed to relax. By the time he had finished, far from being affronted or defensive they seemed positively relieved.

'Mr Atkins, or whatever your name is, let me put you straight on a few things.' There was a softness in her voice he hadn't heard before, bordering on pity.

'It's true that I told my mother I would help her when the time came. Maybe she'd got to the point where it would have been a good thing, I don't know. But I wasn't brave enough. And I'd never have got away with it, because of my history.'

'So, why did you lie about where you were on the night of the murders?' He knew it was a stupid question as soon as the words left his mouth.

She pursed her lips irritably. 'Do I have to spell it out for you? My husband is unable to have sex with me, and I don't wish to live without it. Kemal and I have… an understanding. My husband knows nothing about it.'

Kemal put his hand reassuringly on hers, but she withdrew it.

'I was at Kemal's house that night with…' she hesitated again. 'With some like-minded friends. They were there this evening too; if you don't believe me you can ask them.'

Knight did believe her. He lay back and shut his eyes.

'Mr Atkins, we will make an agreement with you.' It was Kemal now, conciliatory but quietly insistent.

'You will keep quiet about what you know, and we will not go to the police. We will not even make you pay for the damage. Do you accept, please?'

Knight nodded weakly. It was a fair offer, generous even. As they got up to leave, she fixed him with a withering stare.

'Just in case you were wondering, I didn't mean to kill that patient.'

Knight sank into a pit of self-loathing. He had been a fool, an old fool, building castles in the sky and taking outrageous risks that had won him nothing. Merv was right. He was out of control, a crazed, geriatric wolf howling uselessly at the moon.

A nurse put her head round the curtain and announced that a doctor would be with him shortly. Knight had no intention of waiting. He found his clothes and struggled into them. From his long history of mishaps he could tell that on this occasion, miraculously, nothing was broken. He took a taxi back to the flat; the van could wait.

He slept until early afternoon. It was only then that he noticed the flashing light on his phone signalling a missed call. It was from Fran.

* * *

Chapter Eight

Some hours before the events leading to Knight's plunge into the jacuzzi, Fran had been contemplating the safer challenge of choosing a book. It felt odd taking so much time to decide, but time was in ample supply and the prison library was a haven of peace.

The first few days had been a blur. She had been processed, informed of her rights and obligations, then left to settle into a monotonous routine of meals, exercise, TV, and sleep. And reading. In her old life, as she was beginning to see it, she might manage a few pages a night before drifting off. Here, where time slowed to a trickle, she had read three books in a week. It was a relief too that nobody insisted on her guilt. Her fellow inmates were broadly sympathetic, and apart from putting her on suicide watch for the first few nights the authorities were uninterested.

She was sharing a cell with Cindy, whose self-pitying story of drug addiction and confiscated children she now knew by heart. More troublingly, the solicitor remained unconvinced of her innocence, and her daughter was in a state of deep distress about which she could do nothing. She had implored her mother to accept Knight's offers of help, which arrived almost daily, but the very act of opening the letters conjured up once more the vision of the gaping gargoyle. She had not responded to any of them.

However, her mind had cleared. She was able to relive her downfall calmly, scanning the key moments for any insight that might help to explain what had really happened. For example, her alarm clock had not rung, which suggested that the killer had switched it off. Her solicitor had noted the point with little enthusiasm, for there was nothing to prove it. It also occurred to her that she might have been drugged. She usually woke up well before the alarm sounded, and she had not seen her water bottle in the office that morning. But it was too late for a blood test; any drug would long have passed from her system. As for the missing water bottle, it fell into the same unverifiable category as the silent alarm clock.

She felt sure there was some small yet crucial detail she had missed. The growing conviction that it existed gave her hope, accompanied by deep frustration at her inability to find it.

She was standing by a barred window that looked out onto a well between two wings of the building. The well was dark, so that the window acted as a mirror to the room behind her. A bulky outline was approaching. It was Shaz, whom she had been warned to avoid. Nineteen years old, Shaz had taken a butcher's knife to a rival gang member when he attempted to burn down the cannabis farm she was tending. He had not survived, and her claim to have acted in self-defence had cut little ice with the court in the matter of bail. She had a string of convictions for violent assault stretching back to her twelfth birthday, when she had opened her account by breaking a vodka bottle over the head of the classroom assistant who wished to confiscate it.

Shaz padded to a table on the far side of the room. She had a physique worthy of a Sumo wrestler and wore her hair drawn up tightly over her forehead, exposing a large, baby-like face with pale blue eyes. As she sat down she took a roll of Sellotape from her pocket and bit a piece off. Slipping behind a bookcase, Fran watched her reach down into her tracksuit bottoms, from where she produced a brown lump the size of a grape. She pressed the lump into the tape.

It was only now that Fran noticed Cindy watching from the doorway, peering round the frame so as not to be detected. She had not seen Fran behind the bookcase.

Glancing round again, Shaz extended her arm under the table top and held it there for a few seconds. Then she got up and ambled back to the door, from whence Cindy had now vanished. Fran's unease deepened when Cindy reappeared a few moments after Shaz's departure. She went to the table, reached underneath and removed the brown lump.

Wishing to avoid Cindy, Fran spent the rest of the afternoon in the library and didn't see her until shortly before supper. She was resting in the cell, mulling again over the missing incident, when Cindy entered in a state of uncharacteristic elation.

'Got a little treat for yer.'

She proudly produced a piece of hashish. It seemed somewhat smaller than the lump Fran had seen in the library.

'Go on, have a little nibble. Can't smoke it or the screws will know.'

Fran could readily see how it might relieve the tedium of prison, but the provenance of the piece filled her with dread, so she politely declined.

'Why not?!' Cindy flipped yet again into angry child mode. Fran had learned that the way to deal with her was to be calm but firm, nipping the mood swings in the bud before they spiralled into aggression.

'Because you nicked it from Shaz and I don't want anything to do with it.'

'How the fuck you know that?!'

Fran told her what she had observed in the library, reassuring her that no one else had seen the incident. This pacified her enough to explain how she had observed Shaz in the visitor's room engrossed in a kiss with a young man, which was odd given that Shaz made no secret of being gay.

'Oldest trick in the book, everyone does it. Quick snog and shove it in your fanny when the screws aren't watching.'

The recent whereabouts of the hashish did little to enhance its allure, but fortunately the dinner bell rang at this moment. Glad of the chance to get away from Cindy, Fran went to the door and made her way along the landing.

Coming towards her was Shaz, the pale blue eyes alighting on her with cold menace.

'Fuck off and don't come back,' she whispered, shouldering Fran off balance as she pushed past. Fran heard raised voices and a cry of pain. Her instinct told her to keep walking, but she found herself turning back, drops of sweat beginning to creep down her sides.

Shaz was holding Cindy to the wall by her hair. In her other hand she held a shard of glass bound in several layers of tissue paper, except for the final three inches which tapered into a sharp spike.

'You think you can sell my gear without me knowing? How fucking thick are you?!'

How thick indeed. Fran could scarcely believe that even Cindy would be stupid enough to sell some of the stolen lump to her fellow inmates. While Cindy whimpered that she had found the lump on the floor, Shaz pointed the knife at Fran.

'I thought I told you to fuck off.'

A voice inside Fran told her to go, now, but instead she held her ground and screamed for help. Like a rhinoceros debating which of two enemies to charge first, Shaz alternated her gaze between Fran and Cindy then pushed the point of the shard into the flesh below Cindy's eye.

'Where the fuck is it?!' she bellowed.

A droplet of blood appeared. Without thinking, Fran seized Shaz's wrist with both hands and heaved it away from Cindy's face, at the same time pushing herself between the two women. Shaz wrenched Fran aside and delivered a blow to her head that sent her sprawling onto the floor. She lumbered in pursuit, kicking Fran repeatedly as she tried to roll away.

Shaz was bending over Fran, deciding where to aim the knife, when a prison officer burst into the cell and pinioned her from behind. Though a man of adequate physique, he was unable to control her flailing arms, one of which broke free and delivered the point of the shard to the top of his inner thigh. Moments later two more officers entered. With a herculean effort they dragged Shaz kicking and screaming out of the cell and down the corridor past a crowd of equally noisy onlookers who had forsaken their meal to come and watch the spectacle.

Fran sat up unsteadily to find the concerned face of Mr Briggs looking down at her. Behind him she could see Cindy cowering in the top bunk.

'Are you alright, Haskell?' he asked with evident concern.

Briggs had been on shift for the last few days, a calm and patient man of about her age. As he helped her to her feet he frowned and put his hand to his thigh. He stared at her blankly, his breathing starting to labour and his face turning pale. He opened his mouth to say something, but before the words arrived he slumped to the floor.

It was only as he fell that Fran noticed the glass knife lying at his feet and the rip in his trousers. Now that the cloth lay flat on his skin, blood could be seen flowing out in a steady dribble. She ran to the corridor and shouted again for help, but was drowned out by the circus around Shaz.

Cindy in the meantime had climbed down from the bunk and stood gaping uselessly at the wounded officer as Fran undid his belt and peeled the sodden trousers down his leg. Blood was haemorrhaging from the punctured artery. She screamed at Cindy to fetch help, then tore a sheet from the lower bunk and tied it tightly around the wound. The bleeding slowed, though not enough to prevent a red blotch appearing quickly through the fabric.

From the other end of Briggs' body came a rattling wheeze, followed by silence. Fran put her ear to his mouth but could hear no breath. She held the face of her watch there, hoping in vain for it to mist over. Nor was there any sign of a pulse. She opened his mouth more fully to check that his tongue had not slid down into his throat. Struck by the whiteness of his teeth, for which she was grateful, she placed her lips over his and pinched his nostrils tightly shut before delivering five sharp blasts of air into his lungs, followed by fifteen thrusts to his ribcage. She was no stranger to the technique, having performed it several times at New Horizons, though on no occasion had the patient survived.

Losing track of time, she continued to alternate between his mouth and his chest, watching with dread as the red stain grew larger. Even after she had given up hope she went on, delivering whatever scraps of oxygen she could to his dying brain. At last a pair of officers arrived, followed shortly by the prison doctor. She and Cindy were hustled away as the doctor took over. She was sure she would never see Briggs again.

* * *

An hour later Fran was in the prison hospital having her bruises examined. She had been seen by the governor, questioned, thanked and assured that a full account of her actions would be read out in court. There was no word of Briggs, other than that he had been alive but unconscious when the ambulance took him away. A female officer entered.

'Fran Haskell?' There was a note of respect. 'I'm really sorry to bother you with this, but we haven't been able to find the drugs your cellmate had on her.'

Fran wondered what this had to do with her.

'It's just a formality, but I'm afraid I'm going to have to search you. Could you start by emptying your pockets, please?'

In other circumstances the prospect might have been distressing, but after the events of the day it felt no more than a minor inconvenience. While the officer turned away to find a pair of gloves, Fran reached into the pockets of her cardigan. She was removing a tissue when her fingers encountered a hard object the size of a large raisin. Any sense of triumph at having rehabilitated herself in the eyes of her keepers drained away. She remembered the moment when she had tried to squeeze between Cindy and Shaz. Cindy must have taken the opportunity to slip the hash into her pocket, doubtless hoping not only to avoid detection but also to save it for later. This was her repayment to Fran for preventing her face from being lacerated.

She thought about dropping it but dared not risk even the faint sound it would make on the bare floorboards. Instead, while the officer's back remained turned, she put it in her mouth and swallowed it.

That night she dreamed in a riot of dazzling colour and graphic detail. She was in Ibiza with the drummer, making love on the beach while seagulls urged them on with approving shrieks. The beach relocated to Eastbourne where they danced at a foam party. Joan was there too, with a blob of foam on her chin that needed wiping away as the party moved to the dining room at New Horizons. When Knight wanted to dance with her she left the room and ran to the first floor landing, conscious that he was following her. It seemed he was. Out of the silence came what she had been trying so hard to remember, the sound of a creaking floorboard.

* * *

Chapter Nine

The young man with the dreadlocks was staring at him, in flagrant contravention of the taboo against eye contact on the Tube. He pointed to Knight's face.

'Hey, what they do to you?' Two Chinese girls next to him looked away anxiously.

Not averse to flouting convention himself, Knight returned the stare, smiled and shrugged.

'Let's just say I lost one of my nine lives.'

The man got up and took the empty seat beside him.

'You see this?' He pointed to a scar on his cheek. 'That's where I lost one of mine.'

He jabbed his index finger energetically.

'But I make him pay, you know what I'm saying!'

It was hard to tell what he was on. There was no smell of alcohol, and he was too intense to be stoned. Acid, possibly? Or perhaps some laboratory concoction that post-dated Knight's experimental years. The effects of the smoke he'd had earlier still lingered sufficiently for him to feel a degree of kinship with the man.

'Let me see.'

Knight inspected the scar carefully. It ran from the corner of his right eye to just below the ear.

'That was close. Looks like we're both lucky to be here.'

His companion broke into a wide grin, exposing a pair of gold molars.

'Yeah bro, amen to that.'

He held out a clenched fist.

Remembering his London manners, Knight bumped his own fist gently against it. The Chinese girls watched in amazement, mystified by the city's endless permutations.

As the train drew into Mornington Crescent he stood up unsteadily. 'Take it easy, old guy. Don't be using up no more lives.'

The young man stumbled out, leaving Knight to reflect on the soundness of his advice. Despite a prodigious intake of painkillers, his body was still aching two days after the misadventure with the jacuzzi. The water had broken his fall, but in landing on his chest he had caused his head to jerk back violently and wrench his neck muscles. He had also hit the side of the pool with his elbow, and would have broken the bone had it not been for the padded sleeve of his jacket. As it was, much of his right arm was inflamed. This at least was hidden from view, unlike his face, which broadcast a message of victimhood to the world at large. Extending from his jawbone nearly to the top of his left cheek was the swollen and blackened aftermath of Kemal's blow. He hated the thought that people would assume he'd had a fall; far preferable that his disfigurement be recognised as a war wound by a fellow survivor.

The next stop was Camden Town, where he got out. Although he was tired, London had lifted his spirits. He rode up the escalator behind a trio of immaculately coiffured German punks and emerged into a hive of cosmopolitan enterprise. Between an organic Tibetan deli and a Vietnamese tattooist he found a pub where he ordered a large vodka and Red Bull from a Glaswegian barman, to whom his bruised face seemed nothing out of the ordinary.

Once more he replayed the message in his head. He knew it by heart now.

'Hello, it's Fran. I'm sorry I haven't replied to your letters but if you still want to visit I'd like to see you. I also have some information for you. Bye.'

Her voice had been flat, as if she had been changing the date of a dental appointment. Yet surely the fact that she wanted to see him indicated some small measure of forgiveness? It was a matter of regret that he lacked a trophy to lay before her. His trawl of the next-of-kin had produced nothing, and he was unsure what line of enquiry to pursue next.

The source of the heroin was one possibility. If the killer had bought it locally and was not a user himself, there was a chance that the antennae of the addict world would have detected the purchase. He also needed to find out more about the layout of New Horizons and its entry points. Then there were the other staff members to consider. Did one of them bear a grudge against the victims, or against Fran herself?

There was time for another vodka, but he could bear to wait no longer.

* * *

Fran was not looking forward to the visit with anything like the ardour of her visitor. It was her daughter who had insisted that she see him, after the solicitor had deemed her recollection of the creaking floorboard to be no more helpful than the silent alarm clock or the missing water bottle. It was the last fragment of hope and could not be wasted.

The prison officer escorting her to the visiting room stepped aside and politely ushered her through a steel door that shut behind them with a clang.

'Briggs came off the ventilator this morning. They think he's going to pull through, thanks to you.'

For a moment she forgot the uncomfortable reunion that lay ahead. That Briggs had survived elated her. Like a magician conjuring a rabbit from a hat, the world had come up with something good for a change.

'So, who's your friend?'

It took her a second to realise that the officer was referring to Knight.

'Oh, he's not a friend, he's a…'

What was Knight? Given the shortness of their relationship she could hardly describe him as an ex. Nor was he merely a casual acquaintance, or a person with whom she had a commercial agreement, as there was no possibility of paying for his services. There seemed to be no word for a man who had betrayed her trust but who represented her last chance of salvation.

'He's just someone who's trying to help me.'

'Well I'd call that a friend. Here you go.'

Knight was waiting for her at a table. She barely noticed how he sprang to attention as she approached, or the smart suit he was wearing. All she could see was the blackened swelling that had shrunk his left eye to a slit. If anything he looked worse than the grotesque vision that had haunted her since the evening in his flat.

To Knight her face looked thinner, bewitchingly so. Having rehearsed his apology repeatedly he found himself struck dumb, so that it was Fran who spoke first.

'My god, how did that happen?'

'It's a long story, maybe I should tell you another time. Look, I…'

'Are you sure you should be here?'

This wasn't the start he had envisaged. Ignoring her question, he forced the words out, woodenly it seemed to him.

'Look – I'm very sorry that I lied to you, it was a terrible thing to do.'

Fran had also rehearsed what she would say if he apologised. Her daughter had urged her to spell out calmly and clearly the hurt and disappointment he had caused, and then move on. In the event she couldn't find it within her to utter even a mild rebuke.

'That's alright. Please tell me what happened.'

She was shocked by the risks he had taken, and astonished that he should go to such lengths on her behalf. It was comforting, too, that someone apart from her children believed in her innocence. Nevertheless, when taken together with his appalling physical state, the account he gave did little to persuade her that freedom was close at hand.

'So… you're pretty sure that it's not the families?' She tried to make it sound positive.

'It doesn't look like it, which is why I have to start looking elsewhere. You said you had some information that might help?'

She told him what she believed had happened before she heard the creaking floorboard. The more she thought about it, the more convinced she had become that someone had spiked her water.

'I took the bottle from a pack in the kitchen. If it had been spiked already they would have had to do every single one to make sure they got me, and then everybody at the home would have been knocked out the next day when they drank the other bottles. So it must have been spiked later, in the office while I was upstairs. That creaking I heard was them going into the office.'

'Was the office locked?'

'No. Then when I was knocked out they came back for my car keys and planted the heroin under the front seat.'

He admired the lucidity with which she had marshalled the events, but could see the problem facing even the most creative of legal minds.

The account was entirely circumstantial, lacking a single verifiable fact to back it up.

'What about the key to the CCTV cupboard – where was that?'

'Hanging on a peg in the office. All they had to do was take out the hard drive and put the key in my bag.'

It defied belief that Fran would successfully dispose of the hard drive yet allow herself to be caught red-handed with the murder weapon, a point that seemed to have eluded both Bullock and the solicitor.

'Who had keys to the house?'

'Only Mrs Grayling and whoever was on duty, so that night it was me and Jana.'

'Is the front door the only way in?'

'No, there's a garden door at the back of the sitting room, but only Mrs Grayling has the key to it.'

It would, of course, be simple to make a copy of the key to either door. In principle, anybody could have one.

'Is there a Mr Grayling?'

'No, she lives alone.'

He asked about the other carers, but there was little she could tell him. Apart from Jana, the staff were women in their fifties and sixties, all of whom had worked at the home for five years or more, some of them much longer. There were no grudges and no feuds. Mrs Grayling ran a tight ship but, it seemed, a happy one. Nor was it plausible that she herself might have a hand in the murders. As the owner of the business she had no reason to deprive herself of three paying customers. Of the residents, the only two on the ground floor that evening were Brenda Newham and Susan Hillfield, whose mental and physical frailties ruled them out.

The prison officer who had escorted Fran put her head around the door to say they had five more minutes. It seemed to Knight that they had covered the facts exhaustively. However, he still craved some further reassurance that they had turned a corner.

'Fran, I meant it when I said I was sorry. I promise you I'll never do anything like that again, and I promise I'll do everything I can to get you out of here.'

Fran didn't doubt the sincerity of either promise, though she remained unconvinced that the second one would lead to her release any time soon.

'I'm sure you will,' she replied mildly. 'And I'm very grateful for what you're doing for me, I really am. Thank you, Tom.'

She managed a small smile, which fell like rain on a drought-stricken plant. As they stood up, he half-leaned over to kiss her on the cheek but thought better of it.

'I'll be in touch.'

He left the room and made his way back to the visitor centre, unsure whether in flunking the kiss he had missed a chance to move up another rung in the ladder of her affection. He was encouraged, though, by the rungs already ascended. She had asked to see him, she had been grateful, and she had smiled.

For her part, Fran had been relieved when he pulled out of the kiss, which she had seen coming. Yet there was no doubting the gratitude she felt, and she was glad to find she had forgiven him.

* * *

Chapter Ten

From a discreet corner of the chill-out lounge at Kalibanz, Bullock surveyed the midweek offering of office girls and shop assistants. On balance he was pleased with himself. Thanks to his efficient handling of the care home murders, his stock had risen markedly, albeit from an all-time low. He had recently been ridiculed by a defence barrister for the illiteracy of his notes in a fraud case, and had been ridiculed in the local paper for mistaking the church-going son of a local councillor for a similarly dark-skinned burglary suspect. By way of punishment he had been given the role of liaison officer to a social services enquiry into violence against the elderly. As far as he was concerned the elderly were a drain on taxes and a nightmare to drive behind; it was a waste of time that he bitterly resented.

That one blemish aside, life was good. He would rather have been sitting with a woman than with an informant, but this was technically a working night. Micky Hanrahan was a pawnbroker with a highly profitable sideline in stolen goods, whom Bullock had once caught in possession of some wheelchairs that had disappeared on their way to a charity. In exchange for the turning of a blind eye he had become Bullock's creature, feeding him information that occasionally led to clear-ups. Better still, he paid for the drinks.

'Will you be having another one there, Steve?'

Bullock acquiesced graciously to a fourth pint and scanned the room again as Hanrahan went to the bar. Some promising language students entered but on closer inspection were barely out of their teens. His preferred age range was twenty-one to twenty-eight. Much younger and there were parents in the background who might take a dim view of their daughter seeing a man in his late thirties, any older and they were looking for someone to have kids with. He'd had to dump his last girlfriend on these grounds, but to be fair he'd had a good six months out of her. He was assessing his chances with a pair of eastern European girls, often a good bet unless they were religious, when the girl from uniform came in.

Bev had just come off shift and wasn't working the next day. She looked around for her friends, two nurses who were likewise intent on letting their hair down. In contrast to Bullock's, her love life was on the up, thanks to a sports instructor she had met at the gym. They had been together for almost a year, and she was cautiously optimistic that he might be the one.

To her surprise she found Bullock standing in front of her.

'I know you, it's Liz isn't it?'

'No, Bev.'

'Alright, Bev then. Fancy a drink?'

She couldn't fail to catch the assertive exuberance that beer bestows on hopeful men. She was aware of Bullock only as a distant figure in CID. Canteen gossip among the younger female officers had it that he was adequate one-night stand material if you weren't too fussy, but otherwise best avoided.

'That's OK, I'm just waiting for my friends.'

'So, have one while you're waiting.'

'No really, I'm fine.'

'OK, let's have a dance then. Can't wait here all on your own.'

He was gesturing towards the stairs that led down to the dance floor. She found herself torn between her instinct to stay rooted to the spot and reluctance to offend a senior colleague. She would certainly have stuck with her instinct had she seen him directing a sly wink to Hanrahan at the bar.

They arrived halfway through a drum and bass track. She danced without looking at him, losing herself in the insistent beat and gradually relaxing. She was thus a little slow to foresee the hazards of the slow track that followed. In a transition honed by years of practice, Bullock slid his arms around her waist and drew her in.

'I think I should go and see if my friends have arrived.' She tried to make it sound pleasant and matter of fact.

75

'Don't be like that, we've only just got here.'

He held her more firmly, leaving her to choose whether to push him away or grit her teeth until the music ended.

'OK, just one more then I have to go.'

He was holding her close enough to ensure full body contact from her shoulders to her knees, exposing her to a reek of beer and tobacco. He moved his mouth from the top of her head down to her ear.

'You're a smart girl. I could make things happen for you if you wanted.'

She chose not to reply. But as she willed the music to come to an end he positioned a hand on her bottom, not as yet groping it but doubtless intending to if she left it there.

'Hey!'

She moved it away. She didn't shout, but said it loudly and sharply enough to leave no room for doubt.

'Just trying to be friendly.'

'I've got a boyfriend.'

Ignoring this, he moved his mouth back to her ear.

'I meant what I said. You need a bit of help in our business, friends who look out for you.'

Bev was thrown for a moment. What he said was perfectly true. Loners didn't get far in the force, and she had every intention of getting as far as she could. Before she could think of a diplomatic reply he replaced his hand, this time cupping her buttock and squeezing it gently.

She pushed him away forcefully. This time she shouted.

'Will you just fuck off?! I've told you I'm not interested.'

People were staring. She turned and walked quickly off the dance floor, praying he wouldn't follow. Part of her regretted having snapped. She could have taken his hand away again and laughed the thing off, or simply implored him to behave himself. But she had been seized by a physical revulsion that left her no more able to remain in his presence than put her hand in a naked flame. At least she hadn't slapped his face.

Bullock remained on the dance floor. Even when sober, he might not have considered his actions to be a significant breach of etiquette. Drunk as he was, his first reaction was one of savage resentment. Who did the stuck-up cow think she was? Wet behind the ears and full of human rights bullshit, what gave her the right to speak to him like that? As he watched the target of his wandering hand recede into the crowd, anger and lust joined in an unholy alliance.

To Bev's relief, her friends were waiting for her upstairs at the bar. Wishing to put the incident behind her, she didn't tell them what had happened. She would deal with the fall-out some other time, and only if she had to; Bullock might have no recollection of the event in the morning. The lounge was filling up, so she did not see him weave his way to a small table in the corner.

Hanrahan was quietly pleased when he saw the expression on Bullock's face. He disliked the condescension with which the younger man treated him, and it was good to see him take a knock.

'Give you the brush-off, did she?' he enquired cheerily.

'I don't do brush-offs, Micky, not my thing.'

'Is that so? Sure you don't want me to put in a good word for you?'

Hanrahan sat back, satisfied that he had made Bullock feel worse. He watched him brood, unaware that he had sparked the germ of an idea.

Bev was draining her second margarita when the Irishman in the shiny grey suit appeared. He was in his forties, with a jowly face and an over-sized smile. She wondered what he was doing in a place like Kalibanz.

'Can I be getting you a drink there, young lady?'

She felt a surge of annoyance at the second unwelcome approach in an evening that had barely begun.

'No thanks, I'm with friends,' she said curtly.

'You look all alone to me.'

One of her friends was in the scrum at the bar and the other had gone to the cloakroom. She was about to tell him this when, to her astonishment, he placed his hand on her arm, not quite holding it but making emphatic physical contact.

'Go on, just a quick one.'

She had her back to the crush around the bar, leaving little space to step away. With a sense of deja-vu she pushed the hand aside.

'I said no! Are you thick or something?'

'Now come on, that's not nice. Are you saying I'm not good enough for you?'

Unbelievably, he replaced his hand on her arm, this time holding it firmly. Without hesitation she pushed him, not especially hard but enough to make him step away. She was surprised when he staggered backwards and fell to the floor with a loud cry.

Hanrahan had been reluctant to engage in the charade until Bullock said he could keep a home cinema system from an up-and-coming schoolboy burglar he had betrayed earlier in the evening. Now, as he lay groaning on the floor with his head in his hands, he felt better about it. A grand for a few minutes' work was his kind of deal.

He bellowed again, like a wounded animal. Not having seen the confrontation, a compassionate bystander knelt down to assist him. Still clutching his head, Hanrahan allowed himself to be pulled to his knees, whereupon he pointed accusingly at Bev.

'Keep that woman away! She's a lunatic!'

Bev was outraged.

'You were trying to grope me,' she yelled back.

Any sympathy for Hanrahan among the onlookers evaporated, but now the bar manager arrived, providing a new audience for his refrain.

'This woman assaulted me – she pushed me over and I cracked my head on the floor! What are you going to do about it?'

'He's lying!' Bev produced her warrant card. 'I'm a police officer and this man was molesting me!'

Hanrahan rose to his feet. He seemed oddly triumphant.

'If you're a copper go ahead and arrest me! Then the judge can tell us what he thinks when he sees the pictures!'

He pointed to the camera in the ceiling above them.

Bev's blood ran cold. The CCTV would show her pushing him, followed by his spectacular crash to the floor. It would be impossible to see that she had not pushed him very hard, and the presence of his hand on her arm was not enough for her to claim self-defence.

'I'm calling 999!' Hanrahan took his phone out and jabbed at the keys. Public sympathy meanwhile was slipping away from Bev, at least among those onlookers who were in possession of forbidden substances and disapproved of her presence. A brave soul at the back of the crowd shouted 'pig'.

Bev was stupefied. Her friends had rejoined her by now, demanding to know what had happened, but all she could take in was the sight of Hanrahan apparently giving his name and whereabouts to the 999 operator.

She still hadn't seen the trap for what it was when Bullock sidled up to her.

'I can make this all go away for you,' he said softly. 'But you'll have to be nice to me.'

* * *

Chapter Eleven

Knight had always harboured a soft spot for Spiderman, having read the comics at school courtesy of an American classmate. The notion of darting effortlessly up the face of skyscrapers had enthralled him, in later years helping to inspire his efforts on the assault course. Now, looking at the poster in his grandson's bedroom, the possession of such a power seemed even more desirable.

He had spent the night at his son's house in south London, where there had been consternation at his appearance and his tale of slipping in the shower. A rubber bathmat was produced to forestall further mishaps, and he noted that the safety gate on the stairs outside the bedroom door was kept shut, even though Thomas had been moved downstairs to make way for him. Otherwise, the evening had been richly comforting, the tendrils of family entwining him in a tender embrace. He did not mention Fran.

Reinvigorated by a good night's rest, he had risen early and was sitting fully clothed with his feet up on his grandson's bed. He had thought of a way to see the inside of New Horizons, and it didn't involve climbing up buildings. With Jana's collusion he would pose as a home energy consultant and conduct a survey of the building at a time when Mrs Grayling was not there. Jana would simply write the appointment into the diary to confirm its legitimacy in the eyes of the other staff, and if possible she would be the one to let him in. Once under the wire he could search at leisure for any small clues the killer had left behind, it being safe to assume that Bullock's cursory investigation would have missed them. Pleased with his ingenuity at such an early hour, he had just called her, but her phone was switched off.

He turned his mind to the source of the heroin. He knew of a few pubs and housing estates in the hinterlands far behind the seafront, but Bev would know more. As soon as she answered he could tell something was wrong.

At first she was reluctant to reveal the extent of her dilemma, but eventually he got the story out of her. In her panic she had accepted Bullock's offer, but had managed at least to delay payment for a few days by persuading him that the time of the month was not conducive to what he had in mind. However, if she failed to keep her promise, the agreement Bullock had supposedly obtained from Hanrahan to drop the matter would be swiftly reversed.

Knight's instinct was that she should call his bluff, though the risks were intimidating should Bullock refuse to fold. If she fought and won she would place herself under a spotlight that would follow her for years. If she lost, it would be the end of her career. The chilling reality was that no one could predict which version of the story told by the camera a magistrate or jury would believe.

He could sense that, at the back of her mind, she was preparing to give in, which in some ways seemed a rational move. It was ingrained in him that pain was sometimes the inevitable price of gain, in which case it must be endured and forgotten. But with Bev it was different. He felt murderous towards Bullock. He was a boil that should be lanced. Having reassured her that he would try to find a way out he hung up and sat quietly until his heartbeat abated. He realised he had forgotten to ask about the addicts, but it could wait. There were forty-eight hours to get Bullock into a very small box and throw away the key.

'Grandad!'

The door opened, revealing Thomas in his currently favoured daywear of gladiator suit and cycling helmet. He stopped in his tracks and pointed with one of two rubber swords he was holding.

'What's that?'

He had gone to bed before Knight arrived and had not seen his grandfather's injuries.

Knight fixed him with a serious stare.

'Ah, well you see, Tom, I had a fight with Doctor Octopus, but Spiderman saved me.'

The boy grinned and leapt into Knight's lap, discharging what felt like an electric shock around his knee.

'No you didn't! Can we play swords again?'

'Not before I show you what Doctor Octopus did.'

Knight's arms became tentacles, which he wrapped around the happily squealing child while prodding his armpits with his fingers. The press of flesh and blood was galvanising. He swore to himself, as he always did, that he would make time to visit more often.

As they duelled he noted with approval that the lessons of their last encounter had been well remembered. Cut, parry, thrust, the boy was sharp. He wished Roz could see him. Of late Tom had begun to show the set of her mouth and the mischievous flash of her eyes when he laughed.

He found himself thinking of the night it happened. For a few weeks he had come out of semi-retirement to take on a case for a client who required the utmost discretion. Having triumphed, he had flown home earlier that day and was looking forward to telling Roz the good news when she returned from her sister's house in Bristol. Instead a pair of grim-faced policemen told of a conflagration on the motorway, and his life entered its ice age.

'Touché!'

He could not decide what was more impressive – that the boy had remembered the word or that he had landed the point of the sword on his chest. Had he really taught him that well? Or were his reflexes even worse than he feared?

It was Saturday, so there was no hurried exodus to work and nursery school. After a leisurely breakfast and a return bout which he won, Knight departed for Victoria Station. They insisted that he take a taxi. As it threaded its way through the prosperous terraces of Clapham and Wandsworth, his thoughts shifted randomly between Roz, Bev and Fran. Two women who needed his help, and one he had been powerless to prevent being snatched away. He mused again on the case he had finished that dark day, which for some reason was demanding his attention. When he realised why, he made a call and redirected the taxi to Chelsea.

* * *

82

Claire van Zyl was a high-class madame who ran a string of escorts from a flat in Sloane Avenue. She was high-class solely in the sense that her clients were CEOs and foreign princelings, for whom she procured women who had attended England's foremost public schools and universities, or could at least pass themselves off as having done so. She herself was of humbler origins, a show dancer from Johannesburg who had sought her fortune in London and found it not on the stage but in the bedrooms of the capital's leading hotels. She quickly grasped that the management of her new trade would bring even greater riches than its practice, and over time amassed savings of several hundred thousand pounds which for sentimental reasons she kept in the form of Krugerrands. Her one mistake was her choice of husband, a property speculator who eloped to Panama with one of her girls and all of the gold.

In her hour of need she turned to her most dedicated client, an MP whom Knight had once extricated from a blackmail attempt. The Honourable Member, as he was known among Claire's personnel, implored Knight to take on the case, going so far as to front the expenses. Posing as a senior MI6 operator, Knight convinced the errant husband that Colombian narco-terrorists would shortly abduct him and attempt to extort the Krugerrands as ransom from his girlfriend, who may or may not choose to pay. The husband's hurried departure from Panama was cut short when he returned to the love nest with the contents of his safety deposit box. On the stairs he encountered the friendly MI6 man with a cloth soaked in chloroform.

In addition to the stolen coins there was a large amount of cash. Claire offered to split the excess with Knight but he insisted on taking only his fee. It was a decision he later regretted, but he hoped she might consider that she owed him a favour. He alighted from the taxi outside a smart apartment block where a uniformed porter showed him to the lifts.

When she opened the door he was struck by how much and how little she had changed. A dark blue jersey dress showed off the same exquisitely lithe figure, and her hair was still cut in a platinum bob that accentuated her high cheekbones. But beneath her eyes there were deep, dark bags that hadn't been there before, and with them an air of bored resignation. That said, her rate of decline was mild compared to his own.

'Jesus, Tom, what happened to you?'

He repeated the fable of the shower as she led him into the sitting room. It was barely eleven o'clock, yet there was already a half empty glass on the large desk at the far end of the room. He didn't remember her drinking so early before. She poured him a vodka, a generous shot even by South African standards, and topped up her glass.

'As you can see I go easy on the tonic these days.'

At least she hadn't lost her sense of humour. The drink joined forces with what remained in his system from the night before, emboldening him as he outlined his request. He acknowledged the expense it would incur, which he had no way of meeting himself, and made it clear he would think no less of her if she refused. He had not intended to tell her about Fran, who played no part in the matter under discussion. But as many a man had discovered before him, she had a way of listening that made him glad to unburden himself, so that he told her the whole story including the lie about his age.

When he finished she shook her head slowly and looked at him in something approaching wonder.

'You're bloody mad, Tom, you know that?'

'Well I probably am. Just say the word and I'll be on my way, no hard feelings.'

She frowned, seemingly offended.

'What sort of woman do you think I am? Of course I'll do it, and it won't cost you a penny!'

He stayed for another drink and was pleasantly relaxed by the time he got up to leave. Doubtless for this reason he failed to detect the wistfulness in her demeanour as they parted. It might have pained him to know she had thought several times of calling him in the past two years, and was now regretting that she hadn't.

* * *

He called Bev from the train to explain what he had arranged on her behalf. She was uneasy to begin with, but the audacity of the idea grew on her until she happily agreed. He tried Jana again, but her phone remained switched off. Then he fell asleep.

When he awoke the train was passing through the South Downs. No longer befuddled, he considered how best to use the hours he hoped to spend at New Horizons. The office was a challenge, but a search of it was essential. The computer data had been rudimentary and in some cases incomplete. There was nothing, for example, about Susan Hillfield, presumably because she was a recent arrival and the system had not been updated. He hoped there would be paper records of the residents' medical histories and perhaps their financial affairs too. But it all depended on Jana. He resigned himself to more expense.

Her line was still dead when the train reached Eastbourne. Preferring not to draw attention to himself by calling or visiting New Horizons, he went straight to her flat on the off-chance of finding her at home. In a sense, she was. Her cousin informed him that Jana had been fired, and had returned with Milada for an extended stay at her parents' home in the backwaters of rural Slovakia.

* * *

85

Chapter Twelve

Mrs Grayling surveyed the room with a practised eye. The sink was spotless, as was the carpet, apart from a bleach mark where someone had once been sick. That was the trouble with beige, it showed everything. The floral print curtains were not ideal for a gentleman, but in her present position there could be no question of replacing them.

The business was haemorrhaging money. The loss of four residents, for another had left in the intervening fortnight, was forcing her to dip into reserves that were in any case sparse. On top of this she had been obliged to find immediate replacements for Fran and Jana, which meant paying through the nose for agency staff. She would have preferred to keep the Slovak girl, despite the occasional absences. She was hardworking and good-natured, not bad value for the minimum wage. But the CQC inspector, who was secretly not fond of immigrants, had hinted strongly that the future of New Horizons would be at even greater risk if she was seen to tolerate behaviour that so flagrantly breached the terms of her licence.

It had thus been a cause for modest celebration when a Mr Deakin had called seeking respite care for his elderly father. Deakin senior, eighty-six, was prone to falls. He lived with his son's family, who had sadly concluded that his condition had reached a point where they could neither take him with them on holiday nor leave him at home on his own. They required a safe haven for a week.

Deakin junior was evidently a devoted son and an exacting customer. He had carefully inspected New Horizons, recording every inch with a video camera so that his father might choose between the competing charms of local care homes without stirring from his armchair. To her delight the business had come her way. A week's rent at private rates wouldn't solve her problems, but it was money. Better still, they proposed to pay cash, in return for a small discount that she was more than ready to give. It surprised her that the son made no mention of the murders, and she found no reason to raise the matter herself.

She looked dubiously again at the myriad bouquets of pink roses on the curtains. They would have to do.

* * *

Wrinkling his forehead, Knight drew the make-up pencil lightly through the furrows between the raised folds of skin. He was getting good at it, possibly too good.

His first few attempts had merely made him look ridiculous, the spidery lines suggesting a poor effort to frighten children at Halloween. But with persistence the lines were becoming more subtle and the highlighting on either side of them more at one with the colour of his skin. He applied the powder, adding further pallor to a reptilian death mask.

The doorbell rang. It was Merv with the walking frame he had bought on eBay. He peered at Knight closely.

'I thought you said you were going to put on make-up.'

'Very funny. Come in and make yourself useful rolling something.'

He was glad Merv had regained his sense of humour. There had been an argument, first about the arrangements that Knight had made for Bullock, and then about the expense of the stay at the home. With regard to Bullock, Knight was adamant that the plan was not only watertight but an essential act of public service, while Merv took the view that he was provoking retribution from forces more powerful and more ruthless than he could possibly imagine. Merv feared the police, while Knight considered them a third-rate version of the army and was inclined to treat them as such. In the end they agreed to disagree.

The discussion about expense was more fraught. A week at New Horizons would cost five hundred pounds, and while Merv was not party to the detail of his friend's finances he expected it would have to be borrowed. In this he was correct, which added to Knight's irritation when the matter was raised. But with Jana gone there was no alternative.

The irony was that Merv had conceived the idea in the first place as a joke, only for Knight to hail it as a stroke of genius.

'You going to show us your moves on that thing, or what?'

The walking frame was lighter than he expected, and to his surprise more comfortable than walking with a stick. There was almost no pain in his knee, and if anything he seemed to move faster. He marched across the room and executed a smart U-turn. Merv shook his head in disbelief.

'Slow it down a bit. You'll stick out like a dog's balls going round an old folk's home like that!'

Knight decelerated to a crawl. He leant more of his weight on the frame, half dragging his feet behind him.

'Much better. That's proper coffin-dodger walking.'

Knight found the prospect of life in the crawler lane disconcerting. As a hunter he could be as patient as a cat stalking a mouse, but for the mundane act of getting from A to B he found delay intolerable.

'I think this is tearing the arse out of it. They can't all be that slow.'

'Look mate, those old biddies are in there for one of two reasons, they're either doolally or they're crippled. You've got to be one or the other.'

The description struck Knight as harsh but he couldn't argue with the logic. The chance of detection was not outrageously high, but in every undercover operation the golden rule was to minimise unnecessary risk. If that meant shuffling around like an ancient starfish then so be it.

'Let's see how good your memory is. Who lives where again?'

They ran through the names of the residents and their whereabouts. There were five women on the top floor: Penelope Savage, Amy Brown, Gwyneth Williams, Sheila Tovey and Dorothy Flowers. On the first floor were the three rooms where the women had died. He had chosen the one previously occupied by Joan Baldwin. The other two were still vacant, so he would be in splendid isolation. On the ground floor were Brenda Newham and Susan Hillfield. Down in the basement were the kitchen, store rooms and laundry.

'What about the fuse box?' Merv asked. 'The plan's fucked if you can't find that.'

This was the one item Merv hadn't found. They had watched the video several times but had seen no obvious cupboard or compartment where it might be hidden. Merv wanted to go back for a second inspection but

Knight had vetoed it. There came a point where filial devotion might look obsessive.

'It has to be there somewhere. I'll just poke around until it turns up.'

'I still think you should have a plan B.'

'I'll make one up when I get there, then. Now stop fretting and pass that over before you smoke it all.'

Merv gave him the joint, somewhat against his better judgement. He felt responsible for his friend in a way he hadn't before. Their various collaborations up to now had mostly been a laugh, with little threat to life or limb. Knight had always seemed in control of events, able to conjure rabbits out of hats more or less on cue. But now his appetite for risk seemed out of control. Since the jacuzzi incident it had begun to occur to him that Knight might actually die in pursuing this case. It didn't help that, with his present appearance, he would look perfectly at home on a mortuary slab. He took back the joint and inhaled deeply, then stubbed it out even though there was still half an inch left.

'Come on Dad, it's time to go.'

* * *

If not a buzz, there was a frisson of anticipation at New Horizons as the hour of Mr Deakin's arrival approached. The announcement that a man would be joining them had been made at lunchtime, since when there had been speculation ranging from the genteel to the ribald. Not one to mince her words, Amy took the view that a man of eighty-six would be no use to anyone, so she couldn't see what the fuss was about. Penelope stated rather too pointedly that she hoped the new arrival would be capable of intelligent conversation. Amy took offence, as was the intention, and it was left to Mrs Grayling to pour oil on troubled waters. Brenda announced that the new arrival was a lover she had invited to spend the night with her, but then forgot about him.

It was Mrs Grayling who spotted the car drawing up, which was not surprising since she had been watching from the window seat on the first floor for some twenty minutes. She hurried downstairs to greet her new source of income.

Ready for action, Knight already had the car door open when Merv spotted Mrs Grayling at the window.

'Hold your fire, landlady's watching.'

He made a show of assisting Knight from the car, first by helping him to swivel his legs out, then seizing him under the armpits and hauling him to his feet.

Knight contemplated the house with mixed emotions while Merv went to get the frame. It heartened him to feel he was moving closer to Fran, entering the space where she had breathed the air and touched the furniture. Yet the home also inspired fear. Although he could not count himself as young, he shrank from the possibility that he might be old. The old were another country, a place he tried not to think about and certainly did not wish to visit.

'Now, don't go tearing across the road like a bleedin' Jack Russell.' Merv set the frame down and slipped his arm under Knight's.

'For god's sake, I'm perfectly capable of crossing the road.'

'Not if you're supposed to be half dead. Watch it, she's coming out.'

Smiling beatifically, Mrs Grayling waited at the kerb as father and son crossed the road together. It was a touching sight. She knew from first-hand experience that there were not many sons as dedicated as Deakin.

'Albert, how nice to meet you. Your son's told me so much about you.'

Knight beamed in return and held out his hand gallantly. Mrs Grayling wasn't a bad-looking woman. She was a little thick around the middle, but otherwise her curves were well-proportioned in a sub-Rubenesque way.

'Ah well, I hope some of what he said was good. It's very kind of you to put up with me.'

'It's my pleasure. Shall I show you in while your son gets your suitcase?'

Knight hadn't reckoned on losing Merv quite so soon, but Mrs Grayling had already clasped his forearm and was steering him across the small, gravelled car park towards the front door. He calculated it would have taken less than thirty seconds to slip out, plant the heroin in Fran's car and slip back in again.

'Do you have a lot of pain in your legs when you walk?'

In truth he was feeling no pain at all. The combination of the smoke and the modest uplift provided by Mrs Grayling enabled him almost to glide across the ground.

'It's my right knee. Gives me a bit of gip from time to time, but it's no big deal.'

'Well, that's the spirit we like to see in here. It's all about positive thinking, isn't it? Now up we go.'

A portable ramp had been laid to save him mounting the steps to the front door. It wasn't strictly necessary, nor indeed routine. But Mrs Grayling was well aware that first impressions counted for a lot. As for the impression he was making on her, she liked what she saw; he was the type who would want to do as much for himself as possible.

As they crossed the threshold he quickly confirmed the layout he had seen in the video. To his right was the glass-fronted office, one door of which faced into the hallway and the other to the dining room that lay beyond. Directly in front of him was a folding partition that likewise opened onto the dining room, while to the left in the far corner a corridor lead to the two downstairs bedrooms and their shared bathroom. Also to his left was the staircase that went up to the first floor and down to the basement.

'Now then, would you like to join us for some tea?'

Before he could answer, the partition slid open and Brenda came through, making a steady two knots on her walking stick. She stopped and peered at him.

'Are you the husband?'

Mrs Grayling instinctively moved between them.

'This is Albert, Brenda,' she declared, enunciating each word clearly. 'He's come to stay with us.'

Knight held out his hand once more. Mrs Grayling felt uneasy at the prospect of physical contact between them, but in the event all went well. With a coquettish gleam that had something of a hungry bird spying a worm, Brenda took the proffered hand.

'How do you do, Brenda?'

'How do you do?' She slightly prolonged the second 'do'.

She was a tall woman whose flesh enfolded her in three well-defined rings like a slightly deflated Michelin man. From her prominent jaw sprouted several curly silver hairs, one of which got caught in a ray of sunlight.

'Brenda used to be an author, didn't you, Brenda?'

Ignoring her, Brenda's eyes fixed themselves piercingly upon Knight's. They had a wild but shattered intelligence he found disconcerting.

'Did you bring the boy with you?'

91

She was still holding his hand firmly, despite the gentle tug that signalled his wish to withdraw it.

'I'm afraid I didn't. I stand before you in humble solitude, Brenda.'

Taken by such eloquence, she clasped his hand even more tightly. Mrs Grayling was steeling herself to intervene when one of her agency staff came through the partition and escorted Brenda on her way. Knight had been forewarned of the resident author and was not unduly alarmed, though it did little to improve his state of mind. For her part Mrs Grayling was relieved that Brenda had behaved well by her standards.

They proceeded through the partition into the dining room. He felt the knot of tension in his stomach that always preceded the first moments of action.

* * *

Chapter Thirteen

When he was very small, Knight had been the only boy at a birthday party in the course of which the girls had amused themselves by tying him up with the clothes line and dragging him around the garden. Other than that he had never found himself outnumbered by the opposite sex, and had sometimes lamented their absence from his male-dominated world. Now, however, as five ancient female faces turned towards him as one, his lone male status weighed heavily, as did the memory of the clothes line.

'Everybody, I'd like you to meet Albert Deakin. He's going to be with us for a week, and I'm sure you'll all make very good friends with him.'

A squat, dark-haired woman with a mole on her chin broke the silence.

'I told you he'd be clapped out.'

'Please, Amy, that's not how we greet newcomers.'

Mrs Grayling glanced apprehensively at Knight, but he did not seem to have taken offence.

He remembered Amy from Fran's description, and that her deficit of social grace was a source of regular friction. He chose to take the remark as a compliment on his skill as a make-up artist, but was pleased that Mrs Grayling had reserved a place for him at the other end of the table. The slight, blue-rinsed woman beside the empty chair he took to be Penelope, while the severely hunched one on the other side must be Dorothy. Mrs Grayling took his frame and Knight sat down between them, making a point of steadying himself on the chair before easing himself on to the cushion.

'Mr Deakin, how very good to meet you. Would you like a sandwich?'

With a trembling hand, Penelope picked up a plate and 'held it precariously in front of him. He took the nearest one, which exhibited a faint streak of something vaguely pink that he took to be salmon.

'Thank you, that's very kind. And good to meet you too.'

'Penelope Savage. May I say how very nice it is to have a man about the house.' She had a delicate, patrician voice that reminded him faintly of the Queen.

'Hark at her, she's worse than Brenda.'

In the absence of Mrs Grayling, who had departed to the kitchen, Amy clearly felt emboldened to make her presence felt again. Penelope grimaced.

'Pay no attention to that dreadful woman, Mr Deakin. I'm afraid you just have to ignore her.' She made a point of saying it loud enough for Amy to hear.

'Piss off, you silly cow!'

Through gold-rimmed spectacles Penelope fixed Amy with a laser-like stare, then hissed at her like an angry mamba.

'That is disgusting language, Amy, and you are a disgusting woman! Kindly remember where you are or return to the gutter where you belong!'

Amy was instantly cowed. She sat back abruptly in her chair with her arms folded and her head bowed. Taken aback by the outburst, Knight took refuge in the sandwich he was still holding, which to his dismay contained jam. The others paid no attention whatsoever.

Penelope turned back to him as if nothing had happened.

'Now then. The lady on your other side is Dorothy Flowers.'

Dorothy was wearing a lilac smock and black tracksuit bottoms. Her head was hanging at a right angle over her chest. She rotated it a quarter turn towards Knight, which was as far as it would go, and looked up at him sideways through misty eyes.

'Hello,' she said timidly.

'It's a great pleasure to meet you,' Knight responded charmingly. 'May I pour you some more tea?'

She nodded once and rotated her head back again, so that her face disappeared from view. Knight filled her teacup, to the approving looks of the assembled company, except for Amy who continued to gaze into her lap.

'A proper gentleman, that's nice.'

This was Sheila, who sat two places away next to Gwyneth. Penelope introduced them both, plainly seeing it as her duty to appropriate the role of hostess when Mrs Grayling was absent. It occurred to Knight that Susan Hillfield was missing. She must have been the woman he saw leaving the home the day he damaged the two cars. He wondered again if the small one was theirs. He hadn't taken the number and there had been no response to his note.

'So, is that everyone Mrs Savage? Or do you prefer Penelope?'

'Oh, Penelope please. And may I call you Albert?'

'Yes, of course.'

She smiled with a radiance that made her recent performance all the more extraordinary. Her eyes darted round the table.

'No, there's one more.'

The partition slid open and Brenda reappeared. Penelope sighed.

'And here she is.' Sotto voce she added, 'I'm afraid she's another one you might prefer to ignore.'

Brenda made her way to the empty chair opposite Knight. She moved with relative ease on her stick and was steady on her feet.

'Who are you?' she asked, frowning.

Knight identified himself once more and reminded her that they had just met in the hallway. There was a glimmer of recognition.

'Yes of course, you're the husband.'

Penelope smiled patiently.

'No, Brenda, he's not your husband.'

Brenda looked at her as if she were utterly dim-witted.

'Not *my* husband, *hers*, the woman. What was her name?'

There was an air of resignation around the table, and no attempt to explain who the owner of the husband might be.

'Sometimes,' Penelope ventured diplomatically to Knight, 'Brenda thinks about the stories she used to write.'

Brenda was staring at him again. It was unnerving, but he was curious now.

'Who was the husband in your story, Brenda?' he enquired.

'*Her* husband,' she replied, as if it were obvious.

He persisted gently. 'I see. And who else was there?'

Brenda's face lit up.

'The boy!' she exclaimed, as if undergoing an epiphany. 'The wonderful boy! The one she fucked!'

There were a few muffled groans of disapproval, discouraging Knight from further enquiry. He noted that Penelope did not attempt to censor Brenda as she had done with Amy, presumably because it had no effect. Rather, she shook her head sadly and turned back to Knight.

'I'm afraid some of the language is a little fruity, Albert, but I expect you're a man of the world.'

'There she goes, she's chatting him up again.'

Amy had recovered sufficiently to risk another tongue-lashing, but at this point Mrs Grayling reappeared to announce that Mr Deakin junior was waiting upstairs. Rightly suspecting that a fresh cycle of insult and recrimination was about to begin, Knight gratefully took the chance to excuse himself. Reunited with his walking frame he shuffled out of the room on the arm of his hostess, uncomfortably aware that Brenda was watching him every inch of the way.

They crossed the hallway to the staircase. Fazed by this first encounter with his new housemates, Knight suffered a lapse of concentration and had already mounted the first stair before Mrs Grayling could hold him back.

'Careful dear, we don't want you having a fall!'

He set aside his aversion to any form of physical restraint and allowed her to ease him off the stair.

'Have you ever used one of these?'

Relieving him of the frame, she placed one hand on his lower spine and held his shoulder blade fast with the other, as if she were leading him in a tango and expected him to plunge backwards. Instead she deposited him in the stairlift and fastened the safety belt.

It took off with a jolt, but then ascended smoothly, albeit at the pace of an unhealthy snail. Mrs Grayling followed behind with the frame.

At first the experience was perfectly agreeable, like riding a slow-motion ski-lift. He was relieved to be away from the front line, even though he had not spent more than a few minutes there.

There was one consolation in the form of Penelope, with whom he could at least hold a rational conversation. She might also be a source of useful information. As the chair inched upwards he realised that she reminded him of the show jumper. She exhibited the same magisterial authority with an accompanying hint of wild hinterland that had tantalised him as a young man. He had been shocked, when, bored by the inconvenience of army wifedom, she had abruptly left for another man. With the passing of time, and above all with the advent of Roz, his disappointment had changed to profound relief at what he came to see as a narrow escape. They had no children and few friends in common; it had not taken long to lose contact. He wondered what she looked like now, whether she remained brusquely hearty or whether time had ravaged her.

The chair meanwhile had only just reached the halfway point and was creeping round the bend where the stairs doubled back towards the landing. He was not in any particular hurry, but the novelty had worn off and the grinding pace was becoming unbearable. It did not seem to trouble Mrs Grayling, who followed patiently with the frame.

'Nearly there,' she called cheerfully, in blatant disregard of the facts. 'And there's your son waiting for you.'

Merv was standing at the top of the staircase, smirking.

'Alright, Dad?'

It struck Mrs Grayling as odd that they spoke so differently. She wondered what accident of family fortune might lie behind this, whether at some stage the son had been cast into a humbler social milieu. It happened easily enough. However, it was of no consequence. What mattered was the fat envelope containing five hundred pounds that pressed consolingly against her thigh. She assumed there were tax-related reasons for the cash payment, similar to the reasons for which she would not be mentioning it to her accountant.

At last the chair reached the top and stopped with another jolt.

'You enjoyed that, didn't you, Dad?'

'Enormously. I'm sure you can't wait to try it yourself.'

He was at one end of a corridor with doors on either side. At the far end was a bathroom. Joan Baldwin's old room faced the street. Supported by his two escorts, Knight approached his new abode.

'And I've asked for a commode so you don't have to walk to the loo in the night.'

Merv was taking the piss now, but there was nothing he could do about it. Mrs Grayling opened the door, revealing the welcoming committee of pink roses.

'Look at that!' Knight exclaimed brightly. 'They're just like the curtains you had when you were a boy!'

'Ah,' cooed Mrs Grayling fondly. 'How old was he then?'

'Eighteen,' replied Knight. 'Timmy has always liked pink.'

* * *

Chapter Fourteen

The room was about twelve feet by ten, furnished with a bed, a chair and a small wardrobe. Knight forced himself to look on the bright side; it was no smaller than the room he had shared at Sandhurst, and as a base for operations it was clearly more comfortable than Merv's van. Décor aside, the most discordant note was the grimly symbolic commode.

Together they had scoured every inch of the space, removing the drawers from the wardrobe and turning up the edges of the carpet. If the murderer had deposited any trace of his presence it was no longer here, Mrs Grayling having ensured that every nook and cranny was spotlessly clean before their arrival. With Merv keeping watch at the staircase Knight also blitzed the rooms where Denise and Lotty died, but these too had been sanitised.

When it was time to leave, Merv had grown serious again.

'I don't give a shit if it blows your cover, if anything goes wrong you call me, right? I don't want you back in that soddin' hospital.'

Knight was unaccustomed to hearing orders from Merv, but chose to make light of it.

'Have no fear, my finger shall be poised faithfully over the dial button at all times.'

'Yeah, and make sure you press the fucker. Will you promise me you'll do that?'

Before Knight could object, Merv put his arms around his shoulders and hugged him tight.

'Just look after yourself, you daft bugger.'

And then he was gone. Knight was moved by his friend's evident concern but irritated by the way he had begun to fuss over him. In the present circumstances it seemed even less appropriate. What on earth could go wrong in an old people's home?

There was a knock at the door, followed by a woman in her late forties with her hair tied back in a ponytail. She was chewing gum.

'You alright, Albert? Want to come down for a bit of telly?'

This was Dawn, whom he had seen earlier in the hallway with Brenda. He had no burning desire to rejoin his fellow inmates and had been putting it off for the past half hour, content to adjust his make-up while he considered his next step. The first task was to find the fuse box, but this would have to wait until the early hours. In the meantime he might usefully find out what he could from Penelope.

He forgot himself again and was on his feet before Dawn could assist him. Fortunately she seemed content to let him take the frame and move unaided towards the door.

'You fittin' in OK?'

'Excellent, thank you. Everybody's been very kind.'

'I'll take you down the lounge then.'

She said this in a perfunctory way, signalling the end of the conversation. When they reached the stairlift she took his frame and left him to get into the chair on his own. Her indifference was a bonus, he decided. It would take a significant indiscretion to arouse suspicion.

Chewing vacantly, Dawn followed the chair down, content for the minutes to tick away until going home time. She was trying to decide between frozen pizza and ribs when she became vaguely aware that her charge had asked her something.

'What's that, Albert?'

'I said what happens to this thing if there's a power cut?'

Fresh as she was from a training course for the long-term unemployed, it was an event she had never witnessed.

'I dunno, I expect it stops.'

'I heard about it happening to someone once,' he persisted, 'and they were stuck there for hours because nobody could find the fuse box.'

It was beginning to strike her how easily old people found something to worry them and then went on and on about it. It was one of the many things she disliked about her new occupation, having much preferred lying on the beach and spending afternoons in bed with her boyfriend, who had done a far better job at convincing the authorities he was unemployable.

'I always know where the fuse box is in my house. I wonder if you know where it is here?'

Who cared where the fuse box was? It felt like she was taking her exam again.

'Don't worry about it, nothing's going to happen to you.'

When they reached the bottom he followed her across the hallway to the sliding partition. He took in more clearly now the glass panelled office, which straddled the threshold between the hallway and the empty dining room. Two desks, one with a computer, faced out through the glass. Along the back wall were shelves crammed with box files, above which he could see the CCTV cupboard.

On the far side of the dining room was a second partition. This one was made of transparent plastic panels, through which he could see about a dozen armchairs arranged around a large TV set. As Dawn opened the connecting door, a thought that had been quietly assembling itself in the recesses of her otherwise unoccupied mind bubbled up into a short but useful life.

'I know where I seen the fuse box, it's by the freezer in the basement.'

She left him and returned to the office to fetch her coat. Her replacement had not yet arrived for the night shift, but she meant to be ready.

Knight's satisfaction at having extracted something of value from such an unpromising source was dimmed when he saw that his quarry was not among the occupants of the armchairs. Nor, thankfully, was Brenda. Dorothy was asleep, which left a choice between Sheila and Gwyneth. On the basis that Sheila sat furthest from the television and did not seem to be paying it much attention, he chose her.

'Ah, Sheila, do you mind if I join you?'

Her glasses were attached to a string around her neck. She held them up to her eyes and peered at him for a moment before beaming in recognition.

'Oh hello, it's the new fella. Yeah, course you can.' She allowed the glasses to fall again.

He sat down beside her, encouraged that she knew who he was.

'It's a lovely place, this.' It wasn't the greatest chat-up line, but these were early days.

'Oh yeah, it's ever so nice.' She said it with something approaching fervour, as if he had illuminated a profound truth for her.

'Have you lived here long?'

Sheila had been nodding enthusiastically, but now she stopped and looked thoughtful.

'Here?' she asked. 'Do I live here?'

Knight's instinct was to beat a hasty retreat, but it would be cowardice.

'I believe you do, Sheila. I think you've lived here for eight years.' He felt a glow of achievement at having remembered this. Or was it five years?

Her face lit up in wonder.

'Have I?'

She held her glasses up again and looked around the room.

'Have I really? That's good, isn't it?' She cackled like a contented crow.

'I've just come back from a course at the Home Office. That's where I work, you see.'

It seemed unlikely, as she was well into her eighties.

'But I'm going to retire now, put me feet up. Next time they ask me I'll say sorry, chum, you'll have to get someone else!'

She cackled again, evidently finding pleasure in the defiance of authority. In the midst of her delusion there was something about her he liked, an innocent delight in the moment that carried him with it. Up to a point.

He wasn't betting she had any useful information, but it did no harm to ask.

'Very sad about those murders, isn't it? I read about them in the papers.'

Her cheerfulness suddenly evaporated.

'What murders? Was there a murder somewhere?'

He already regretted asking, but there was no going back.

'They were here, two weeks ago. Perhaps you don't remember?'

He said it as gently as he could, but her face fell as if she were receiving the news for the first time, which in a way she was. She put her hand to her mouth, clearly distressed.

'What – here!? Oh my lord, was it really?'

She looked around the room again, this time with palpable fear. But after a moment, having seen no evidence of lethal violence, she became calmer.

'Did they catch him?'

'Yes, it's all over now. Best thing is to forget all about it.'

It pained him to treat her like a small child, but she was instantly reassured and did not seem to mind in the least when he excused himself.

'Lovely to see you, take care, dear.'

She gave a little wave and sat chuckling to herself as he made his way to Gwyneth. The TV was on an ad break, which she had sensibly chosen to mute.

'Hello again, Gwyneth, is this chair taken?'

At the tea table she had not seemed much smaller than the others, but in the armchair he could see that she was barely five feet tall. She looked up at him alertly and nodded.

'He's going to call it off,' she announced in a husky voice as Knight sat down. He recognised the ravaged vocal chords of a heavy smoker and was heartened that she had survived so long.

'I'm afraid I'm not quite with you there. Who's going to call what off?'

'The wedding. He's found out what she's up to.'

He wondered for a moment if she shared Brenda's affliction, but presently the ads ended and the next segment cast light on her meaning. Never having watched the programme, Knight was confused by its legion of characters and soon bored by their concerns, though he could at least grasp that the wedding in question was a non-starter. He experienced a flicker of interest when the cuckolded fiancé attacked his rival with a garden spade, but noted with professional disapproval that he chose to use the flat of the blade rather than the edge. He was unmoved when the incompetent assailant suffered a heart attack shortly afterwards.

Gwyneth, by contrast, had a flawless understanding of what was afoot. She watched with her mouth half open, sometimes repeating a line to herself or pursing her lips at moments of what Knight took to be tension. After a while he found it more interesting to watch her than the screen.

When it was finished she pressed the mute button.

'That's him gone,' she rasped. 'She'd been on at him about going to the doctor but he wouldn't listen.'

'Well, I'm afraid men can be like that. I'm not too keen on the doctor myself.'

'He thought it was the doctor she was having her affair with. That's why he wouldn't go, and when the doctor heard he was going round accusing him he found out who it really was and told him.'

Before Knight could think of a suitable interjection she had launched into a labyrinthine retelling of the comings and goings of the soap's vast cast of characters. He recoiled and marvelled in equal measure at the detail with which she recalled events that went back months, if not years. With a memory like this, might she not still harbour some small snippet from the events of two weeks ago? The only question was how to get a word in.

The commercial break finished, but to his horror he now discovered they were watching an omnibus edition, which meant he was condemned to sit through another ten minutes at least. The bride-no-longer-to-be sat weeping by the bedside of her stricken fiancé, mesmerised by the bleeping of his life support machine. Knight willed her to switch it off. As soon as the ads started again he jumped right in.

'You have a remarkable memory, Gwyneth. I expect you can remember everything that happened the day those poor ladies died here.'

She fixed him with her bird-like stare again.

'Oh yes, I can remember everything.'

She paused, re-assembling the day in her mind.

'They kept us in our rooms all morning. All we had for breakfast was a bit of toast that Mrs Grayling brought up, and it was cold by the time it got there and if you wanted to go to the loo she had to take you. But she wouldn't say what the matter was and we didn't know what had happened until the big detective came up and told us.'

She wrinkled her nose in distaste.

'I didn't like him, he was ignorant.'

This came as no surprise, but what she said next did.

'Proper arrogant he was, horrible man. That's why I wouldn't tell him.'

Knight nodded judiciously, as if it were the most normal thing in the world.

'Tell him what, exactly?'

'About the argument. He wanted to know if there'd been any arguments.'

Out of the corner of his eye he could see that the ads had given way to a trailer for a celebrity game show, which meant that the next segment was only seconds away. She was already reaching for the remote, which she kept on the small table between their chairs.

'Here, let me get that for you.'

He fumbled convincingly and it fell to the floor out of her reach. He apologised and leaned over to get it.

'Who was the argument between?'

'Mrs Grayling and her gardener, outside.'

'Did you hear what they were arguing about?'

'She wouldn't give him an advance on his wages. Have you found it yet?'

'I think it's gone under the chair. Hang on.'

She was becoming agitated, trying to peer over the side of the armchair while glancing back repeatedly to the screen where the next scene had begun.

'What's his name?'

She tutted with impatience.

'Ryan! Why do you want to know his name?'

It seemed a good moment to bring the discussion to an end. He restored the sound, rendering her oblivious to his presence. He felt mildly deflated. For a moment he had seemed on the brink of a major revelation, perhaps a quarrel involving one or more of the victims; an argument with the gardener was not in that league. He filed it away under miscellaneous and made ready to move, happy to pass on a passionate reunion between the guilty lovers in a hospital storeroom.

Beyond the television was a drawn curtain, behind which were French windows leading to the garden. It was only seven o'clock, and the faded brown fabric was framed by thin lines of golden light. The end was billowing softly in the gentle breeze from outside, which told him that the door was open.

It was the easiest of retreats. Dorothy was still asleep, Gwyneth was held fast by the television, and Sheila remained staring into space. It felt oddly liberating to be thus invisible. He could have stood on his head or danced a Highland Reel, no one would have noticed. He settled for the more achievable feat of nudging the curtain aside with his frame and slipping discreetly through, noting as he went that the door showed no signs of forced entry.

* * *

Chapter Fifteen

A patchy lawn extended some ten yards from the back of the house to a wooden fence at the rear. In one corner stood a chestnut tree. Opposite it was a raised slab of concrete that was home to some cheap garden furniture. He set off towards the hedge that ran alongside the building, dividing it from its neighbour.

He did not expect to find the hard drive from the CCTV, but it was on his list of tasks and relieved a craving for physical action. He turned down the gap between the hedge and the house, working his way methodically, poking bits of hedge aside with the frame to afford a better view of what might lie within.

About halfway down was the window to the ground floor bathroom. It was slightly ajar, and without thinking he looked in. A member of staff he had not seen before was leaning over the tub, at the far end of which he could see Brenda's head and shoulders rising above a mountain of bubble bath. She screamed when she saw him.

Knight flattened himself against the wall. From inside he could hear Brenda insisting frantically that 'the husband' was outside, intent on viewing her naked body, while her carer tried to reassure her that he most certainly was not. As a sop to her imagination, the window was closed.

Knight breathed out. Reproaching himself for such carelessness, he continued his inspection of the hedge. Reaching the front of the house he crossed the car park, which was separated from the pavement outside by a low wall. It was a sterile space where nothing grew apart from a few weeds that had heroically forced their way through the gravel. There were no hiding places here, so he continued to the hedge that ran along the other side of the building.

He looked longingly at the open gateway and the street beyond, where the shadows from the trees were lengthening. It was an evening for supper on his terrace, sipping red burgundy while the starlings performed their vanishing act over the pier. He pictured a row of langoustines turning bright pink on the barbeque, a bowl of panzanella on the table, and Fran lazing while he cooked.

Afterwards they would go indoors. He would put on a guitar concerto, or a sitar raga. The music would draw them into a state of dreamlike contentment, their minds entwining and then their bodies, until eventually they would saunter down the corridor together, their arms around each other like teenagers ambling back from the beach at the end of a hot day. They would stand kissing at the foot of the bed, in no hurry to move, until she slowly began to undo the buttons of his shirt. And then…

'Albert! Have you lost something?'

He had not noticed Penelope on leaving the house, obscured as she was behind the chestnut tree. Now, on completing the circuit, his angle of view gave him a clear sight of her in a chair she had evidently removed from the concrete patio.

'Uh, no.'

He cast around for a suitable explanation. Why else might one be poking at a hedge with a walking frame?

'I'm afraid it's, er, a sort of obsession I have, going round looking for bits of litter.'

He could not think which was worse, that he should be believed, or not. A look of distinct disappointment on her part told him that he had succeeded. No matter. If she thought he was odd he could ask her odd questions and get away with it.

'Well, it's good to see that somebody bothers. Will you join me?'

He fetched another chair and made a show of dragging it awkwardly behind him while holding the frame in one hand.

He had as yet no reason to eliminate Penelope as a suspect. She was frail, certainly, but she had her wits about her, not to mention an edge of sharp steel.

'I've been thinking,' he said, after pleasantries about the weather, 'this wouldn't be the place where those murders happened, would it?'

She looked at him incredulously.

'You mean you didn't know!?'

'No. I read about them in the papers, of course, but I'd forgotten the name of the place until now. Well, fancy that!'

He gave a wry chuckle. Penelope seemed taken aback by such insouciance.

'Doesn't it bother you at all?'

Knight shrugged. 'Well, you know what they say about lightning striking twice in the same place. On that basis I'd say we're probably pretty safe, wouldn't you?'

She confessed she hadn't seen it that way before.

'Of course, I understand it must have been very traumatic for you. I didn't mean to be frivolous.'

'Not at all. As it happens, I was fortunate enough not to be here.'

'Oh, I see. Where were you?' It was indiscreet, but not inexcusably so. She smiled with an air of resignation.

'Oh, the usual, in hospital. I have this very boring heart condition and every now and then they have to whisk me in.'

Knight was sorry to hear it, and said so. She elaborated no further on the subject, and he didn't ask. She had an old school reluctance to discuss medical symptoms, of which he approved. He was also pleased to strike her from his list of suspects.

'I did think about leaving, of course. One of the other ladies went, though she was only here for a sort of trial. But then I thought one could quite easily end up jumping from the frying pan into the fire, so why bother?'

That explained the absence of Susan Hillfield.

'Did you know her well, the woman who left?'

She shook her head sadly.

'No, but I felt sorry for her. She was absolutely terrified of everything around her. Some kind of deep-seated depression apparently, it seemed to have taken over her mind.'

This matched Fran's description. It would do no harm to check her whereabouts at some stage, but it was not a priority.

Penelope was looking up at a wisp of passing cloud, as if she might happily exchange places with it. She turned back to Knight.

'But do you know who I feel sorriest for of all in a way? It may sound a wicked thing to say, but the one I feel worst about is the woman who did the killings.'

Knight was astonished to hear this. He had Penelope down as Old Testament, not lacking in compassion but most unlikely to take the side of a cold-blooded killer. Could she think Fran was innocent?

'Why, do you think someone else did it?'

'Oh no, I'm sure it was her. But it's so tragic. Such a wonderful lady, and she was driven to do such a terrible thing.'

Knight was confused now.

'Something drove her to do it?'

Penelope nodded grimly.

'I don't know all the details, but from what I understand there was a man who treated her very cruelly.'

Knight was not anxious to pursue the topic, but she had alighted on a theme about which she had more to say.

'From what I can gather he told her a dreadful lie of some kind, and I believe it unhinged her. To be so badly betrayed, to find out that someone you trust is capable of such deception. It's...'

She paused, casting around for words that would do justice to the injury, but in the end she concluded quietly, 'It's a terrible thing.'

He sensed she spoke from personal experience but was not about to ask.

'I'm afraid the male of the species has a lot to answer for,' Knight ventured uncomfortably. 'Mea culpa.'

She allowed herself a brittle laugh.

'I'm afraid it has, Albert, though I'm sure you're a perfect gentleman. Now please tell me something about yourself. I've a sneaking suspicion you're a military man.'

He found himself giving a potted and mostly truthful account of his army career, which prompted her to reveal that her husband had likewise served as an officer and risen to the rank of colonel. A light went on in Knight's head. He had never crossed paths with Colonel Savage, but he remembered his widely-reported downfall. On leaving the army he had joined an investment company that subsequently went down in a blaze of publicity. There was talk of embezzled funds and Cayman Island orgies, though it was never made clear how much responsibility he had borne for either. What was not in doubt was that, before the start of his trial, he had shot himself with a hunting rifle.

Penelope said nothing of the scandal or its aftermath, stating only in the briefest terms that her husband had passed away some thirty years ago. Knight tactfully claimed never to have heard of him. Reading between the lines, it was not hard to conclude that she had been left penniless, a misfortune she bore with a fortitude he found admirable.

The talk of his career allowed him to steer the conversation back to its original purpose.

'Well, Penelope, as an army wife I'm sure you're an expert on fitting in to new places. You'll have to give me some tips on fitting in here.'

She snorted with good-humoured derision.

'There isn't much to fit into, I'm afraid. One just plods on from day to day.'

'No villains to watch out for? No vendettas to be wary of?'

She laughed again, this time with a peal of amused delight.

'Really, Albert, what an imagination you have! There's no one here but a bunch of batty old ladies, as I'm sure you've seen for yourself.'

He assured her that he was far from forming such an impression, and certainly not with regard to present company.

'I was really thinking about the staff. It's a bit like being back at boarding school, getting a line on teachers and prefects.'

She shook her head. The amusement had passed now.

'No. Nothing like as much fun as boarding school.' She gave a little sigh. 'The staff are very good on the whole, they do what they can, but really...' She shrugged, as if conceding a defeat of some kind. 'Let's just say it's all a little dull.'

They sat in silence for a few moments. Then she frowned.

'Actually, there is one little piece of advice I'll give to you. If you have any valuables, keep them locked up.'

She held out her left hand and pointed to the empty ring finger.

'My wedding ring disappeared a while ago. Of course, they all thought I'd dropped it somewhere but I know I didn't. I always kept it on my bedside table at night and I'm sure someone took it.'

Knight began to say how sorry he was, but she stopped him with a little wave of her hand.

'It really doesn't matter,' she sighed wearily. 'I don't know why I bothered wearing it to tell you the truth.'

Pulling herself back smartly from any chance of self-pity, she fixed him with an earnest look.

'But do be careful. I'm pretty sure I wasn't the only one.'

* * *

Chapter Sixteen

It was the second time the small, dark-haired one had smiled at him, then whispered something to her friend. Bullock couldn't decide which of the two he fancied more. The dark one had the better arse, but the stacking on the tall curly blonde was phenomenal. Now she was looking at him too.

There was no sign of Bev yet. He had originally told her to come to his place, but she had insisted on meeting at Kalibanz first. It seemed odd that she should want to revisit the scene of her humiliation, but she had joked about getting a couple of drinks inside her before seeing the doubtless filthy state of his flat, which he realised would be no bad thing.

When the dark one smiled at him a third time, he felt he had no option. Nothing would come of it tonight, but it was a golden rule to keep the pipeline topped up. If Bev arrived while he was talking to them it was tough shit; it wasn't as if she had a choice.

'All on your own? Something can't be right.' He delivered the line with a confidence born of frequent practice.

They looked at each other as if deciding whether to let him in on a secret.

'No, something's not right as a matter of fact. We've been stood up, I'm Caro by the way.'

This was the blonde. She sounded posh, well out of his league, but she was sizing him up with interest. So was the dark one.

'And I'm Lucy. Are you going to buy us a drink?'

It seemed they were down from London for a hen party, but the hen had been taken ill and neglected to let them know that the party was off. Rather than return they had decided to make a night of it anyway. Caro was wearing Versace jeans and a small leather jacket over a white T-shirt, while her friend wore tight fitting silver shorts with a sequined black singlet. He was intrigued to learn that they were in the movie business. This, however, was divulged with a certain amount of reluctance and barely suppressed giggles, as if some indelicacy were being withheld.

Further questioning secured the coy admission that they worked not only in the adult sector of the industry but in front of the camera. Bullock reeled. He was in the presence of porn actresses, real ones.

Not wishing to be considered dull he told them he was a lawyer, and when further pressed claimed to represent musicians and film stars accused of drug offences, though he could not possibly divulge their names. Becoming over-confident, he nearly came to grief with the assertion that he had studied at Oxford. To his dismay they revealed they were fellow alumni and demanded to know which college he had attended. His blood running cold, he said the first thing that entered his head, Saint Sebastian's, having been there once on a ferry to Spain, and to his immense relief this impressed them no end. His previous encounters with posh totty had been uniformly unsuccessful but with these two it seemed he couldn't go wrong. Caro laughed helplessly at his jokes, while Lucy would put a hand on his arm or a finger on his chest when she spoke to him, looking up attentively through dark brown eyes. Which of them should he go for? He was Pavlov's dog, caught between two competing bells.

'So Stevie, where's the action in Eastbourne?' Caro arched an eyebrow in a way that suggested he might be joining in. Yet he found himself at something of a loss to suggest alternative venues, Kalibanz being the nearest thing to a high spot in otherwise low-lying terrain. As he described a couple of bars and clubs he felt their interest slipping away. Ignoring Bullock for once, Lucy turned to Caro.

'Don't really fancy any of those. Maybe we should be thinking about tomorrow.'

For a moment it seemed the miraculous bubble would burst, but Caro turned to him with an amused twinkle.

'We've got a couple of scenes to rehearse. Maybe you'd like to come back to our hotel and help us?'

It was as if destiny had tapped him on the shoulder. He had always known that this was meant to happen, that he should be whisked away by beautiful strangers who had stepped out of the websites that passed for his spiritual home and entered the real world where they so plainly belonged. The sense of well-deserved serendipity was further enhanced by the arrival of a text from Bev, blaming her absence on a stomach bug.

He would have been less optimistic had he noticed Merv behind a pillar on the far side of the room, and bitterly disappointed to know that until a few moments ago he had been on the phone to Bev. Merv watched them leave together, then texted the good news to Knight.

* * *

Knight read Merv's text with satisfaction. He had been confident that Bullock would take the bait, and with Merv on the ground to coordinate the timing of Bev's text there had been no danger of him leaving in disgust before the girls could get to work. If anything rankled it was the thought that the treats he had arranged for Bullock were far too good for him, short-lived though they would prove to be. But it was better to err on the side of caution.

He checked the battery level on the document scanner and replaced it in his dressing gown, glad of the deep pockets. It seemed odd to be going into action in his pyjamas, but one did what the operation demanded. If he was caught he would claim to have lost his way on an expedition to the bathroom. Reuniting himself with his stick, he made for the door.

He crept silently down the staircase, rejoicing not to be in the hated stairlift. At the bend he peered over the banister towards the office. A night carer had her eyes fixed on a computer screen. He would be in her line of sight if she looked up, so he continued on his bottom, easing himself down like a cautious toddler. When he reached the hall he checked her again, noting that at this angle her face was completely obscured by the screen, allowing him safe passage.

The kitchen was dimly illuminated by a light from the laundry room in the far section of the basement, which is where the freezers were. From the laundry room came the muffled dialogue of a film; a thin strip of light flickered beneath the door. The unofficial deal was that one staff member stayed in the office while the other took their ease in front of the TV, or slept.

Outside the laundry room stood a chest freezer beneath a run of storage cabinets attached to the wall. Beyond them was the fuse box, which Merv's quick pan around the basement had missed.

He was about to open the cover when he heard a door handle rattle. He dropped to his knees beside the freezer a split second before the laundry door opened and the light went on, momentarily blinding him. His neck and back stung viciously as he curled his body into a ball, listening to the approaching footsteps. They stopped inches short of his hiding place and the freezer lid creaked open. After an endless twenty seconds the lid closed and the footsteps retreated to the kitchen, where a microwave hummed, then they returned to the laundry room. The light went off and the door clicked shut.

At length he hauled himself up on his stick, taking the strain through his arms and shoulders. The mains switch was housed above a row of fuses, each printed with the parts of the house they served. After carefully identifying the ones for the basement, which would be removed last, he quickly pulled out all the others. Taking a firecracker from his pocket, he made ready to light the fuse.

* * *

In the hotel room, Caro poured champagne while Lucy explained the plot of their forthcoming epic. A handsome young traveller is stopped by two female customs officers and taken aside for a strip search which soon involves all three parties removing their clothes. It was unquestionably cheesy, but no more so than any of the other films they had appeared in to boost the already considerable income they earned from Claire. From what Knight had told them of Bullock, the story ticked all the right boxes – the male protagonist possessed overwhelming sexual allure that awakened uncontrollable lust in subservient female characters who found themselves in thrall to his every whim. Caro always said that Lucy over-intellectualised the scripts, but then Caro didn't have the benefit of a third class honours degree in English. She was the money brains, having failed economics.

Bullock listened with the expression of a dog waiting to be fed. The gullibility of men in the face of easy sex no longer surprised them, though it had been a while since they had come across anyone as naive as this.

'So the bit we're trying to work out is when he's doing one of them from behind and the other one's sort of doing him from underneath. We're not quite sure how it's going to work, so what we need to do is improvise a bit.'

Caro handed him a glass of champagne and took a gulp from her own.

'Let's get Stevie in the mood first.'

She performed a languid striptease in front of him. Bullock's sense of rightful destiny gave way to a state of rapture as one miraculous event succeeded another. Next Lucy was disrobing too, then they were undressing him and leading him to the bed, past a dressing table on which a ceramic shepherdess observed the proceedings with an air of innocent delight. First they massaged him, then they arranged his body between theirs in a number of complicated permutations, though never quite leading him to the consummation he now urgently required. They assured him that this would follow shortly.

'We just need to work out how you do the charlie.'

Caro retrieved a small envelope from her bag. Lucy meanwhile rearranged herself in the crab position, facing upwards on all fours so that her torso offered a level surface. Caro sprinkled some white powder between her breasts and coaxed it into a straight line with a credit card.

'Don't snort it whatever you do, it's not the real thing.'

Too right it wasn't, there was no question of wasting coke on the likes of Bullock. Given the circumstances, he wasn't complaining. He took the rolled up twenty that Caro had prepared and followed her instruction to kneel between Lucy's legs. Caro meanwhile wriggled under the arch of Lucy's body until her head was in striking distance of his nether regions, but still the promised delights did not quite materialise.

'OK, see if you can reach it.'

Steadying himself with one hand on the bed, Bullock inserted the banknote in his nose and leaned forward to position it over the powder. Through the valley formed by her breasts Lucy was grinning at him.

Beyond her was a small clock attached to the wall. It was half past midnight; he would remember this moment for the rest of his life.

'Now make like you're hoovering it up.'

Bullock's last attempt at acting had been a lacklustre interpretation of a sheep in his primary school's nativity play, but encouraged by Lucy he affected a series of facial contortions intended to convey pleasure of a high order.

'Darling that's wonderful, you're a natural,' she purred. Her praise was evidently sincere, for she collapsed into fits of giggles with each new expression that he contrived until it was finally agreed that the job was done. And now, surely, he would be rewarded. There was no longer any question of which of the two he should choose, for plainly he was going to have them both; the only decision left was which to have first. He knew that his life was approaching a peak that it might never reach again, but he didn't care.

'I think we've all earned another drink.' Caro poured more champagne, taking care not to let him see what else she was putting in his glass. A few moments later he was sleeping like a baby while they packed their things, including the clock and the shepherdess containing the cameras.

* * *

In the office, Knight lifted down another box file and rifled through its contents. Downstairs, the two night staff would be scrabbling for the fuses he had scattered over the floor to mimic the result of a small explosion. There would, of course, be some detritus from the firecracker, but he was betting they would be too preoccupied with restoring the power to dwell on this. They would struggle to find the basement fuse, which he had pulled out immediately after the bang and placed behind the freezer. Then he hurried back through the kitchen, conscious of the laundry door opening as he reached the staircase. At the top he watched the woman in the office fumbling in the desk drawers and hid in the corridor outside Brenda's room while a beam of torchlight crossed the hallway. Once it had disappeared down the stairs he made his way to the office and set to work.

The first few boxes were filled with reams of regulations and guidelines, followed by welfare records that went back several years. It seemed that Mrs Grayling's efficiency did not extend to pruning her files. He scanned in the pages pertaining to the victims and the current residents, conscious of the seconds ticking by. His calculation was that they would find the basement fuse last, and remain downstairs until they had done so. The lamp on the desk was his early warning system. When they succeeded in restoring the power on the ground floor it would come on, at which point he would retreat with whatever he had found.

The next sequence contained staff records that he recognised from the memory stick, but now he was opening an unmarked box in which the first item was a folder bearing his name. Inside was a sheet of paper with the contact details supplied by Merv, fictitious save for an untraceable mobile number. Beneath this folder was one for Susan Hillfield, and several more for names he did not recognise. He scanned the skimpy details in her folder and opened one of the others at random; its last entry was over a year old. There seemed to be a parallel system at work, segregating a small minority of residents from the rest.

At the bottom of the box was a cash book. As he opened it he became aware for the first time of an electrical hum. Looking round for its source, he saw that the computer screen had come to life. Why had the desk lamp not done likewise? On closer inspection he saw that the switch was off. The woman must have toggled it when the power went down and left it as it was.

Light was shining from the stairs and now a torch was ascending from the basement. Replacing the box, he crawled through the door to the dining room and reached the sitting room as the light in the office went on.

He squeezed himself behind an armchair, irritated that he hadn't checked the lamp. Twenty years ago, ten even, he was sure he wouldn't have missed it. It wasn't the end of the world, but now he had to find a way of crossing the hallway to the staircase without being seen from the office.

Craning forward, he looked through the panels that divided the sitting room from the dining room. In the office, the woman was opening a packet of biscuits, her reward for dealing with the emergency downstairs. Eventually, he hoped, she would go to sleep. There was nothing to do but wait.

The chair was the one that Sheila had occupied earlier. He pictured her asleep upstairs and wondered what she dreamed of. Was she at work, or talking to her husband, or perhaps playing with her children? She would wake to another day of staring blankly into space, content to be back from the Home Office, just as Gwyneth would spend another day in the virtual world of soaps and reality shows. What were the chances that he would become like them? His assumption had always been that he would simply keep going on all cylinders until he dropped, yet there were no guarantees. It was by no means impossible that he would end his days in a place like this.

He tried to put his finger on why the thought appalled him. The physical decline he could handle, or so he told himself. But he had never seriously contemplated the prospect of entering a world such as the one that, say, Sheila inhabited. On the surface she was perfectly content, he would go as far as to say happy. What was so bad about floating in a state of medicated serenity, as if permanently stoned?

Then he thought of Brenda, marooned and baffled in fragments of her stories, and Amy in a cloud of anger and scorn. This was what he feared, an unending bad dream over which one had no control. It was how Fran had described the Hillfield woman, trapped in a dungeon of anxiety, hell without the brimstone. How did you avoid that? Only by being prepared to quit while you were ahead, and doing it while you still had your wits about you. Everyone here had left it too late.

Except perhaps Penelope. He wondered if she had a syringe of something tucked away at the back of a drawer, and flirted briefly with the notion that the dead women had been part of some long agreed suicide pact, in which the last member to retain her mental faculties did for the others and then herself. But why take the trouble to frame Fran?

The thought of Fran spurred him to step off the morbid path his mind had taken. The woman in the office must have settled down by now. As he leaned forward to look, he heard a sharp click.

He ducked back, conscious of cool air from the garden. Raising his head above the arm of the chair, he saw the curtain moving, pushed aside by the garden door. From behind it a shadowy figure emerged and stood still, as if assessing whether it was safe to continue. As far as Knight could see it was a male, wearing a balaclava.

Knight shrank behind the chair again while the visitor padded across the carpet and opened the dining room door. It struck him as foolhardy, but then he realised that from within the brightly lit office everything outside would be in total darkness. When he dared to look again the figure was a dark blur skirting around the dining room. Reunited with her magazine, the woman in the office remained oblivious.

Knight pictured the far side of the dining room. There was a dumb waiter that brought the food up from the kitchen, and beside it the door to a cupboard. The latter appeared to be the object of interest.

The silence was broken by a ping from Knight's phone, which even inside his pocket was loud enough to alert the intruder. He turned and fled, failing to spot Knight in the act of recoiling behind the chair, and vanished through the curtain into the garden. With a glance to confirm there had been no reaction from the office, Knight crawled out and followed. Outside he heard footsteps running down the side of the house. An engine spluttered to life, followed by the whirr of a small motorbike taking off into the night.

He returned to the garden door and peered cautiously round the curtain. The woman had still not stirred, and would not see him even if she turned in his direction. He moved silently to the door between the two rooms and followed the intruder's tracks to the cupboard.

Inside it were buckets, mops and a pair of vacuum cleaners. But this was not what interested him, for at the back he could just make out the form of a second door. He inched through the clutter, aware that the slightest miscalculation could send something crashing to the floor.

The door opened silently, revealing the corridor that contained the two ground floor bedrooms and the bathroom where he had surprised Brenda. He had seen both doors in the video, but it had not occurred to him that they might be linked. As he stepped out, a floorboard creaked.

The woman in the office did not look up. Shielded by the darkness, he crossed with impunity to the staircase, remembering Fran's account of the noise she had heard before the killer struck.

He was back in his room before he thought of the phone, which he had still failed to mute. His irritation passed as he opened a picture of Bullock framed between a striking pair of breasts, his eyes crossed and a twenty pound note in his nostril.

Knight allowed himself a moment's rejoicing before turning his mind back to the enormity of his discoveries. Anyone with a key to the garden door could be assured of safe passage from the garden door to the foot of the stairs. It must have been the route used by the killer.

Had he returned to seek fresh victims?

* * *

Chapter Seventeen

Knight rubbed the brickwork vigorously with a cloth. It had to be dry, or the glue wouldn't set. In the narrow passage between the house and the fence, unobserved but damp from the drizzle, he applied a light coating and pressed the small black box into position. It was a treasured piece of kit, made for him by a talented ex-colleague. To a casual observer it would pass as a phone junction on the external wall of the house, just like the one he had already attached on the other side.

He was betting on the chance that the intruder would return. The unexpected sound of a phone should not be enough to scare away a determined assassin permanently; the phone could easily have been forgotten on a chair, it happened all the time. With hindsight he would see that and try again. To reach the garden door he would have to pass along one or other side of the house, where he would be greeted by a motion detector. Moments later, Knight's phone would vibrate.

The scans from the previous night had revealed nothing new. He regretted not having taken the cash book when he fled. That alone required a second visit. But what he wanted most of all at this moment was to be a fly on the wall in Bullock's office.

Had such a metamorphosis been possible, he would have seen a man in a state of existential despair.

Bullock had awoken an hour late for work, roused finally by the repeated missed call alerts from his phone. He made a feeble excuse about food poisoning and limped into work via a quick shave at his flat. At first there seemed nothing sinister about the package awaiting him, although some sixth sense told him not to open it in front of the sergeant. When he saw the photos he came close to being sick in his cubicle. The message accompanying them could not be more explicit. 'Tell Hanrahan to back off,' it said, in letters stencilled on a card. It was obvious that Bev had set him up, but impossible to prove. He put the pictures through the shredder while he called Hanrahan.

The author of Bullock's misfortunes meanwhile returned to the sitting room.

'Albert, you're wet!' Penelope was sitting a few chairs from Sheila, a book in her hands. Gwyneth was watching a shopping channel, Amy and Dorothy were asleep. Brenda, he knew, was having her hair done.

'Thought I'd have a breath of fresh air, but I got caught.'

She asked him to sit down. He couldn't tell if it was an invitation or a request and was happy to accept either way. They had sat together at breakfast but conversation had not thrived in the disorderly exchange of misunderstandings and catcalls around the table, which had only abated when Dorothy was quietly sick into her cereal. He descended a little too easily from the frame into the chair beside her.

'I was thinking about what you told me,' he said casually. 'The ring that went missing, how long ago was that?'

She looked at him in alarm.

'Don't tell me you've lost something already?'

He assured her he hadn't, adding that there was nothing of value in his room.

'But it set me wondering about the security here. If someone had a key they could easily come in from the garden in the middle of the night, and no one would be any the wiser.'

She sat back, shaken.

'I'd never thought of that, I'd always assumed it was one of the staff.' She cast her mind back down a timeline that was low on meaningful landmarks. 'It must have been about three months ago.'

'You thought you might not be the only one – do you know of anyone else?'

He was aware that what had begun as a fishing trip was already veering towards an interrogation, but for as long as the answers flowed he would press on.

She shuddered. 'It was one of the ladies who died. Mrs Brewer lost some earrings.'

Denise Brewer was Barbara Dawson's mother. She hadn't mentioned the earrings, but why would she?

'And what happened?'

'Nothing. Her daughter kicked up a bit of a fuss but everyone thought she was just a daft old lady who had let them fall off somewhere. Which is exactly what they thought when my ring went.'

'You didn't consider reporting it to the police?'

'Well, what could they have done?'

She gave a shrug of resignation, then frowned as a new thought occurred to her.

'But if it was a burglar, he must have come at night. There are too many people here during the day.'

He could sense fear creeping into her, and sought to offer some reassurance. There was almost certainly no burglar, his speculations were pure nosiness, a bad habit acquired from his time in military intelligence. She seemed to accept this so he chanced one more shot.

'I'm afraid I was just as nosey with Gwyneth. She was telling me about Mrs Grayling having a row with someone out in the garden.'

He let it hang. If she had seen the incident she would say something. It was not especially important, more the habit of leaving no stone unturned.

'I saw that, I was there.'

He waited for her to say more, but she let it hang too. There was something wrong about the way she was looking at him.

'Really?' he laughed. 'Now you've got me wanting to know what happened. You see how incorrigible I am, it's an appalling affliction.'

She was staring at him intently now, not exactly in the eye, but a fraction to one side. It wasn't so much suspicion as bewilderment, but laced with amusement.

'It was with the gardener. I was sitting where you saw me yesterday. I couldn't quite hear what they were saying, but I think money was mentioned. Do you mind if I ask something a tiny bit nosey now?'

Knight was knocked off his stride.

'By all means, how could I possibly refuse?'

'I was wondering why you're wearing make-up. You got it wet in the rain and its running down your face.'

Without thinking he put his hand to his cheek. It came away smudged with lining pencil. He imagined, correctly, the dark smear left behind.

'Ah, well…' he produced a handkerchief and dabbed at his cheek and temple, casting around desperately for an explanation.

'I'm afraid that's my other little weakness.' His mind was approaching blankness, but somehow the words kept coming. 'I'm a bit vain, you see, and it's my way of keeping the years at bay.'

'I see.' She nodded understandingly, which he took to mean he had got away with it. 'The only thing is, as far as I can tell, you've made yourself up to look older than you are, not younger. I'm not sure you're who you say you are, Albert.' She said the name with a trace of irony.

He began to invent a bizarre psychological compulsion, to do with preparing himself for the end by confronting the degradation to come, but she cut him short.

'You also don't need your frame. I saw how you sat down just now, and when you were fetching a chair in the garden yesterday you had no trouble holding the frame with one hand. If your leg was that bad you'd have fallen over.'

He saw that he had completely underestimated her. Beneath the genteel exterior she was like a bird of prey, fastidiously observing every detail. There was no hostility as yet, or any indication that she meant to betray him immediately. He made a snap decision to trust her.

Knight told her the whole story, including the lie to Fran about his age. Her face hardened at this point, but softened as he described the various trails he had followed and how they had so far led to nothing. She was plainly shocked when he confessed to the true cause of his facial injury, and at the end she suppressed a burst of laughter when he recounted the events of the previous evening. She didn't revise her opinion that he was slightly mad.

She remained silent for a few seconds, studying him sternly yet with a certain warmth.

'Well, Albert, or should I say Tom, I can see you've been working rather hard to put things right. Not that it's for me to pass judgement.'

Knight sensed that she had indeed passed judgement. He might only have achieved a C plus, but he felt he had redeemed himself sufficiently to avoid exposure.

'You can rely on me to remain discreet,' she added, as if reading his thoughts. He wasn't prepared for what she said next.

'So please tell me, how can I help you?'

* * *

Brenda admired her hair in the mirror. Ten minutes later she would have forgotten the pleasing flow of warm water over her scalp and the friendly commentary of the visiting hairdresser. Next time, in a fortnight, the experience would be almost as good as new. She would not recognise the hairdresser, but the process and its near-identical commentary would be reassuringly familiar, leading to the same temporary sense of well-being.

She was sitting at the sink in the downstairs bathroom, half-facing the window where Knight had surprised her not twenty-four hours ago. She no longer remembered the incident, save for a feeling that the window was somehow charged with significance. Each time she looked at it she tried to fathom what this significance might be, and each time the association that came to mind was the husband, followed by the hazy notion of a boy. Here her train of thought would end, leaving her staring blankly at the window until it began to acquire significance again.

There was a reason for this, although, of course, she did not know it. To everyone else her repertoire of explicit carnality consisted of randomly occurring, unconnected scenes. In truth they shared a home of sorts, in the last story she ever wrote. Like much of her canon it portrayed a woman of a certain age rediscovering the sexual magnetism of her youth: Graziella Budd, tediously married to a rich businessman, is cast away on an uninhabited island when their yacht falls foul of a tropical storm. The only other survivor, or so it seems, is a strapping young crew member with whom she has already exchanged flirtatious glances. Having retrieved him from the surf and saved his life by means of tenderly administered mouth-to-mouth resuscitation, she nurses him back to health, whereupon he becomes her adoring and attentive lover.

All is well in their island paradise until the husband reappears, having been rescued by a passing freighter. The logistics of his survival were blurred, though the readers of *Hot Sand* – had there been any – would barely have noticed given the dramatic climax that followed. Faced with the choice between husband and lover, Graziella defies convention by deploying her reinvigorated allure to win them both. On the beach she disrobes and dances before the pair, sending them into a state of erotic nirvana from which they emerge as her devoted partners in a life-affirming *ménage à trois*.

Brenda believed it to be the breakthrough piece that would finally lead her to the sunlit uplands of literary reputation; at the very least it deserved recognition for its feminist perspective. Sadly, she never found out. Her editor, faced with a reading pile that was mostly worse than Brenda's oeuvre, merely skimmed the first hundred pages before signing it off. As a result, the first reader to reach the end was the publisher's new American owner, a devout Baptist who failed to see the merits of Brenda's vision and insisted she be removed from the roster.

She never wrote again. For many years the wound festered, until dementia arrived to wipe away the facts. What remained was a nagging feeling of unfinished business, an urge to get to the heart of something that bothered her but which she could not identify. The place this feeling always tried to reach was the scene on the beach. She imagined odd flashes, random jigsaw pieces offered up from the rubble of her memory, but the pieces would never stick together. She did not know they were part of a story.

However, the presence of a man in the house had nudged her mind in a certain direction. Each time she saw Knight the notion of the husband arose, and the more the husband entered her thoughts, the more she had flashes of the boy. But where was he?

Dawn came and escorted her back to the sitting room, complimenting her mechanically on her hair. Brenda remembered the image in the mirror and felt buoyed. Perhaps this release of endorphins was why, when she saw Knight, two of the jigsaw pieces joined up.

Knight was deep in conversation with Penelope when he noticed Brenda speeding towards them.

'I know where the boy is!' she boomed. 'I know where to find him!'

Before Knight could speak Penelope tutted irritably and asked, 'Where, Brenda?'

'On the beach!' she shouted joyfully. 'He's on the beach!'

* * *

Chapter Eighteen

Knight waited until the staff had done their rounds before spiriting himself downstairs. At the bottom he turned left and made for the bathroom at the end of the corridor. The same woman sat in the office, conscious only of the online auction she was following.

He put the plug in the basin and stuffed the overflow with toilet paper. Then he ran the cold water tap, restricting it to an inaudible trickle. Having experimented earlier in the day, he knew that the basin would take ten minutes to fill, after which the water would run down the sides and into the wooden floorboards. By four in the morning, or thereabouts, a steady stream of water would be pouring through the ceiling of the kitchen below. Vandalising a retirement home did not come easily, but the kitchen ceiling was in a poor state and the insurance would pay.

More to the point, when the occupant of the laundry room discovered the leak she would be fully occupied for a good half hour. His original assumption had been that her colleague in the office would be called down to help, but he could not guarantee it, and in this respect the plan was far from perfect. With Penelope's assistance the odds had improved significantly. At four o'clock she would press her personal alarm and draw the woman in the office up to her room, enabling Knight to complete his search. Until then he had to go into hiding.

He opened the bathroom door and crept into the corridor. Susan Hillfield's old room was locked, presumably to prevent Brenda from wandering in. After squeezing past the vacuum cleaners in the cupboard he took up his old position in the sitting room, with its view of the office and the garden door. He checked that his phone was receiving the signal from the motion detectors and settled down to wait.

Penelope had volunteered with polite insistence, almost hinting that this was the price of her silence. Although never keen to work with amateurs, he had felt obliged to consider what role she might play, and the sight of Dorothy being sick at breakfast had inspired the beginnings of an idea. Penelope had acquiesced readily, suggesting refinements and alternatives that struck him as highly practical. At tea they spirited away a napkin's worth of cake, tomato, fruit and – a stroke of good fortune – tinned diced carrot, which she later took to her room and mixed together. A boy at his school had used this minestrone of supposed stomach contents no less than three times to get off games before being found out.

At four o'clock he watched to see what the woman in the office would do. She was asleep now, her feet up on the storage box and her head slumped to one side. From where he sat the display unit for the personal alarm system was just visible on the desk beside her. Ten seconds went by, twenty. He was having second thoughts about the wisdom of involving Penelope when one of the lights began to flash.

The sound was inaudible through two closed doors, but the effect on the woman was galvanising. In one neat movement she sat up and swung her feet to the floor, then turned off the alarm and spoke briefly through the intercom to her downstairs colleague before hurrying to the stairs.

Knight moved into the dining room and re-entered the cupboard. Any moment now the carer in the basement would discover the flood. Craning his head around the door, he saw a sudden glow from the staircase as the kitchen light went on, followed by a string of expletives and hurried footsteps.

He retreated to the dining room in case she opened the cupboard door in search of a mop and bucket. There were further expletives from the bathroom and he heard her calling Brenda's name, clearly holding her responsible for the deluge. Her footsteps sounded on the stairs again as she went up to find her colleague, then she was hurrying back down to the basement. Now was his chance.

In the office he took down the box file, keeping an eye on the staircase. On the top floor, Penelope would have smeared herself and her bedclothes with the foul looking concoction. It lacked an authentic stench, which was what had eventually given its inventor away, but on a first performance the risk of detection was low; the carer's attention would be focused on giving Penelope a bath and changing the sheets.

He flicked through the cash book. The most recent entry showed his own initials and the sum of five hundred pounds. Before that came two entries for S.H., also for five hundred, dated a fortnight and three weeks ago respectively. The other pages showed entries with different initials, going back over several years. Mrs Grayling had a dirty little secret: she kept a separate account of cash payers and hid the money from the taxman. There were also outgoing payments, no doubt to tradesmen in return for a discount. One pair of initials appeared regularly: R.C.

He felt he had advanced a step but could not see where it took him. Low level tax evasion didn't give Mrs Grayling a motive for murder unless, implausibly, she was being blackmailed by one of the victims. He scanned the pages and rifled through the remaining boxes for an answer. He was getting nowhere slowly when the phone vibrated in his pocket.

Arranging the chair and its footstool so that his face could not be seen from the dining room, he waited.

There was absolute silence. The intruder had been wearing dark clothing the previous night, so it would be impossible to see him until he approached the staircase, and even then he would just be a blur. Only now did it occur to Knight that he had left Brenda out of his calculations. Her door was opposite where he would exit from the cupboard, and it was well over a minute since the detector had been activated. Knight was about to break cover when a dim figure shifted in the darkness and disappeared up the stairs. There was no time to check on Brenda. He crossed the hallway and mounted the staircase, propelling himself with the stick.

If this was the killer, the rest of his potential victims were at the top of the house. He would find Knight's first floor room empty and pass on, but would then hear sounds from Penelope's room or the top floor bathroom. On last night's showing he would then turn and flee, straight into Knight's path. It wasn't necessarily what he wanted, but he would have the advantage of surprise, a snake seen too late by the wayside.

It didn't come to that. As he reached the first floor he saw that his door was ajar. He flattened himself against the wall and eased one eye around the frame. The man had his back to him and was rifling through the contents of the wardrobe. He was slim and wiry, about the same build as Colin Boyle. It had not come to a fight in the Grand Hotel, but here it almost certainly would, and he knew he would lose if he failed to strike first. The door, thankfully, did not creak. He nudged it open and took a tiny pace into the room. The challenge was to walk without the stick, which he held with both hands by the end of the shaft as if he were taking strike with a baseball bat. In a game of grandmother's footsteps he approached a few inches at a time while the figure inspected the contents of the drawers.

'Psst!'

Knight swung as the man spun round. The metal crook caught him just below the ribcage, sending him staggering back into the wardrobe. He slid to the bottom with Knight standing over him, ready for another blow.

'If I as much as see you twitch, the next one's on your head.'

The man held his hands in front of his face.

'No, don't!' he wheezed.

'Take the balaclava off.'

With trembling fingers he obeyed, revealing a boy in his late teens. He had a pointy face that played host to a thriving community of pimples and cold sores. He was plainly terrified; the longer he stayed that way the better.

'What's your name?'

The boy hesitated.

'John.'

Knight swung again, deliberately missing his shin by a couple of inches.

'Don't hit me!' he cried. He had a whiny, nasal voice that sounded like it complained a lot.

'Then tell me your real name.'

'Alright, it's Ryan – Ryan Carter – just don't hit me!'

R.C., the recipient of multiple cash payments.

'Why did you kill those women? Did Mrs Grayling pay you to do it?'

The boy gaped at him, bewildered.

'You what?'

'You heard me!'

Knight threatened another swing.

'I never killed no one, I'm the gardener.'

Knight shuffled a little closer, the stick over his shoulder.

'What were you doing here that night?'

The boy hesitated, just as he had when asked his name, and looked at Knight as if he were a ghost.

'I wasn't here, I was at home!'

'Liar!'

Knight swung again, this time within inches of Ryan's ankle. He jerked it away and pulled his feet up under his knees, requiring Knight to move closer to stay in range. He edged forward, raising the stick again. Something in his caution must have signalled opportunity, for Ryan thrust a foot with surprising force into his shin, enough to make him sway. Emboldened, he propelled his body from the wardrobe and lashed out with his other foot. Knight swung hard as he went down, and felt the stick connect with something soft.

Ryan lay semi-stunned, his hands clutching his cheek. Knight heaved himself from the floor, knowing that his advantage now hung by a thread. He needed a holding pen where he could continue the interrogation without fear of attack.

Ryan felt himself being dragged across the floor by his hair and the back of his belt. Before he could struggle free his head and shoulders were thrust into the gaping mouth of the commode and a heavy weight came down on his back.

'Let's try that again. What were you doing here?'

He was sitting astride Ryan with one hand bearing down on the back of his neck, using the other to steady himself with his stick. The reply was muffled; it took a few repeats before he could make it out.

'I was nicking stuff, but I saw who done it!'

Knight felt the heady buzz of the case breaking open, but he had been here before.

'Start from the beginning. You won't like it if I don't believe you.'

He put yet more weight on Ryan's neck, eliciting a torrent of unintelligible obscenities, then released the pressure enough for him to speak clearly.

'I come in through the back like I always do. I got a copy key.'

'Who gave it to you?'

'No one. There was a key left in the door one day with a spare on the ring, so I took it.'

This seemed plausible enough. Knight invited him to continue.

'I gone through the cupboard in the dining room and saw the woman in the office was asleep. I done one of the downstairs rooms, it was empty, then I gone up to the first floor.'

'Which rooms?'

'I can't remember! I was doing one of them when I heard someone downstairs so I run down again and that's when I saw her. There was another woman in the office.'

'How do you know it was a woman?'

'I think it was a woman, I can't remember.'

It was shaping up to be another lie. Knight increased the pressure.

'It's true! She was standing over the one who was sleeping, holding a handbag. I thought she was nicking stuff, like me.'

'And then what happened?'

'I went in the cupboard and legged it back to the garden.'

Knight regretted never having used the commode in the normal way, for he felt an urge to force Ryan's head down as far it would go. If the story was true, Ryan had known all along that Fran must be innocent.

The question was, what to do with him. Bullock considered the case closed and would resist anything that undermined its success. It would be too easy for him to cast doubt on Ryan's evidence and allow it to slip quietly away. There was only one solution: Ryan had to make a statement in front of a lawyer. Before that could happen he needed Merv.

The phone was in his dressing gown, which meant he had to choose between releasing his prisoner's neck and letting go of the stick. Opting for the latter, he put the stick down and reached across his waist to the pocket.

Ryan had been alternating between further obscenities and pleas to be released, but now he was quiet. He tentatively drew one foot forward. The ancient madman on his back didn't appear to notice, so he continued until his thigh was coiled like a spring.

Knight was willing Merv to answer when his mount suddenly bucked. Too late to push his head back into the commode, he fell to the floor with Ryan on top of him. The boy sprang to his feet and lashed out. The second kick struck the side of his right knee like a sledgehammer.

Ryan fled. Frantic to escape his tormentor, as he turned the corner on the landing he missed a step and fell, twisting his ankle and cracking his head on the stairs and banisters. When he reached the bottom he lay still.

Knight hobbled precariously out of his room. His knee had ceased to cooperate and would take no weight at all. Peering down the gap between the banisters he saw Ryan sprawled below. His spirits rose. If he could get to him fast enough he could continue his questioning from where he left off. There was still no sign of the two night staff. The one attending to Penelope must still be in the bathroom, though it was odd that the one in the basement had not heard the crash on the stairs. He remembered that she had been wearing earphones earlier; he hoped she was wearing them now as she mopped the floor.

Steadying himself on the banister, he eased his left foot down then brought the stick level with it. But with the next step he felt his body swaying and had to hug the rail to stay upright. It was impossible. Half an hour ago he had made the same journey with minimal discomfort; now he was stuck. As the prospect of failure mocked him anew, he found himself staring at the stairlift. If Ryan stayed down for another three minutes he had a chance.

* * *

The only other person to have heard Ryan's fall was Brenda. She had been awake for some time, ever since a woman had stood in the doorway, accusing her of causing a flood. Soon she forgot about it, but was left with her customary feeling of a nagging, unfathomable question. On this occasion, however, the succession of thumps from outside invited her to seek an answer.

Not bothering with her dressing gown, she rose and took her stick from the foot of the bed. She opened the door and looked out into the corridor. Someone was groaning; it was coming from the staircase.

When she saw Ryan, her mind started off down its usual track, but now it was charged by the restoration of the missing character. Here at last was the boy. And here was the husband, descending on the chair lift. Admittedly they weren't on a beach, but they were together. Yet something was wrong. When the husband got off the chair he started tying a dressing gown cord around the boy's ankles. She had only a vague idea as yet of what was meant to happen, but she was sure it was not this.

'Leave him!' she barked, advancing rapidly.

'Go away!' hissed the husband, glaring at her in an unfriendly fashion. Now, intolerably, he was tying the other end of the cord around the boy's wrists. Without upsetting her balance in the slightest, she raised her stick and aimed a series of blows at the husband's head. He crawled away clutching his eye.

134

Brenda had an intimation of something arriving, something ancient and long overdue. As another piece of the jigsaw fell into place she was filled with a glow of understanding and then joy. Setting the stick aside, she started to remove her pyjama top.

One of the blows had clipped Knight's eyelid. His breath taken away by the sting, he forced his hands away from his face and took stock. A Baconesque vision emerged. Brenda had by now removed her pyjama bottoms as well, exposing a sagging gut above which her breasts drooped like two crinkled marrows. She started to dance, or rather to sway from side to side, shifting her feet like an elephant attempting dressage.

This was the sight that also greeted Ryan as he came to. Unlike Knight, he had seen very few naked women in the flesh, certainly none of this age or shape. Beset by a terror nearly as strong as what he had experienced upstairs, he glimpsed the front door only feet away. His ankle gave way when he tried to stand, so he dragged himself across the floor, acutely conscious of the madman crawling after him.

Brenda was gripped by a euphoria she had not experienced for many years, not since she had written the scene on the beach and been convinced of its perfection. Yet something jarred again, for her audience seemed to be leaving.

Knight was within inches of a trailing foot, but it retreated beyond his grasp as his quarry hauled himself up at the front door. Using Ryan's belt as a grab handle he rose on his serviceable leg and wrenched the boy's hands away from the door latch. The sleeve of Ryan's sweatshirt rode back, revealing a cluster of festering track marks.

Before he could take him down, something hard wrapped itself around Knight's neck and pulled him violently backwards. He tried to wrench it away, his fingers burrowing between his skin and the crook of Brenda's stick. He was already toppling as Ryan pulled his arm free and jabbed an elbow hard into his chest.

Knight fell on his back and found himself looking up at the lower extremity of Brenda's stomach and beyond it two frenzied eyes staring down at him. The front door slammed.

'You've scared him away!' she wailed.

The lights went on.

* * *

Chapter Nineteen

A dejected assembly of the unlucky and the imprudent thronged the waiting area at A & E. They were resentful of the teenage clubber who had been copiously sick in their midst only to be rewarded with an invitation to jump the queue. A small boy with a bandaged finger continued to wail deafeningly at his mother for denying him a fizzy drink from the vending machine. None of it improved the mood of the two policemen sitting either side of an angry giant with a gashed forehead, his England shirt stained with blood.

Deemed not to be at the point of expiry, Knight had been left in a wheelchair to wait his turn. Feeling underdressed in his pyjamas and gown, he reflected unhappily on what might have been.

He had been tantalisingly close to getting his man and with him bail for Fran. As Brenda was hustled away he was helped to his feet and placed in a chair, powerless to prevent the carers from calling an ambulance.

It was compensation of a sort that the scanner and the phone in his pockets went unnoticed, and that his story about falling off the commode and coming downstairs to look for help was instantly believed. It tallied with the chaotic scene in his room, while Brenda's account of him trying to harm the boy was naturally disregarded. Mrs Grayling, arriving shortly before the ambulance, likewise suspected nothing. Her main and ill-disguised concern was that he would press charges, and when it appeared he would not she was deeply grateful, doubly so when he insisted on going to the hospital unaccompanied.

As he was wheeled out he saw Penelope watching unhappily from the stairs before being told sharply to return to her room.

The angry giant was now swearing loudly at his captors, distracting Knight as he tried to marshal his thoughts. It seemed unlikely that Ryan was the murderer. He had not been carrying a syringe or any other means to kill apart from his bare hands, and his interest in Knight's possessions suggested that his sole business in the house was theft. But the track marks on his arm made him the prime candidate for a link between the home and the supply of heroin. There was a chance the police would have his address, which was why he had already left a message for Bev.

The problem that so far defied solution was his inability to put any weight on his leg. It meant he was confined to the wheelchair, which was not even the type he could push himself.

There was something else. Among the staff on duty he had already noted one or two faces from his previous visit; it was only a matter of time before someone recognised him and discovered that he wasn't Albert Deakin.

'Sorry, fry-up was off.'

Merv was back from the vending machines with a breakfast of coffee and crisps. By an unhappy coincidence a flooded villa had curtailed the family holiday, leaving him available to join his father at the hospital.

A nurse came through from the assessment area behind the reception counter and spoke to the receptionist. Knight remembered the cheerful Irish lilt and heard it again now, but was too slow to turn away when she happened to glance in his direction. The receptionist pointed to something on her screen that the nurse appeared to find interesting. She looked over at him again and frowned.

'Merv,' he said quietly, 'I'm afraid we need to leave. Now.'

Merv had so far resisted the temptation to take Knight to task over his fresh round of injuries. He no longer wished to sound like a nagging wife, having suffered one for a number of years, but the unexpected demand set him off again.

'You are fucking joking, mate. We're staying here until we find out what you've done to yourself.'

Given that he needed him to push the wheelchair, Merv took the view that there wasn't much Knight could do about it except complain. He steeled himself for an angry outburst, but to his surprise Knight remained icy calm. The nurse meanwhile had been joined by a young Asian woman.

'Over there is the nurse and the doctor who saw me last time.'

'So?'

'I checked in as Albert Deakin this time. The names don't match.'

The doctor was staring too.

'I'd give it another thirty seconds until they come and talk to us, and a minute after that before they get those two coppers over. Any suggestions?'

He didn't like to play on his friend's aversion to the police, but it was only a slight exaggeration of the threat. If things got that far, he had no idea how he might explain his dual identity.

The suggestion had the desired effect. For a moment the view from the counter was blocked by the mother of the bandaged child demanding that they should be allowed to jump the queue too. Without further discussion, Merv propelled the wheelchair to the exit.

They had made about fifty yards before the nurse and the doctor came out. There was a flurry of pointing and shouting, whereupon they hurried inside again.

Merv turned the corner into the car park, rolling the wheelchair at a steady canter despite the uphill slope. Knight clung tightly with both hands as they sped to the van.

'In the back!' he shouted. 'You'll never get me into the front in time!'

The van was facing down a grass slope that overlooked the roadway along which they had just retreated. Merv opened the rear door and all but threw Knight in.

'Hang on to something!'

Along each side were fold-down metal benches. Knight pulled one down and heaved himself onto it as the van reversed. With one hand on the back of Merv's seat he craned his head and looked through the windscreen. Ahead of them was the barrier, but through the passenger window he could also see the doors of A & E. One of the policemen was staring at them.

Merv had seen the policeman too. At the barrier, he thrust the ticket with trembling fingers into the machine. The machine bleeped, apparently offended, and the barrier remained down.

'What's the problem?' Knight asked, trying to sound calm.

'I forgot to pay the fucking ticket!'

Merv pounded the dashboard.

'What have you got me into!?' he bellowed. 'We can't get out now and that bastard's going to nick us!'

The policeman waved at them to wait and started walking towards them.

'Drive through it!'

'You what? Are you insane?!'

The policeman was a hundred yards away. The van's rear number plate was kept deliberately filthy for occasions such as these, but from twenty yards he would be able to read enough of it to find them.

'Back up and drive through it, I'll pay for the damage!'

Resigned to whatever fate might befall him, Merv put the van into reverse. Knight heard a crash and felt the van judder.

'What was that!?' he shouted.

'I hit the fucking wheelchair!'

In the wing mirror Knight saw it rolling slowly away towards the slope. Merv threw the van forward into the barrier. It bent back, but not enough to let them through.

The policeman broke into a run. The van was squeezing through now, the maimed barrier scraping along its side. In a moment it would turn towards the main road and the rear plate would come into view. He took out his notebook, ready to write down the number. As he did, he heard a rattling sound and looked round too late to avoid twenty kilos of speeding wheelchair.

* * *

Bullock surveyed the reception area of the Norfolk Terrace with distaste. Despite the grandeur of its name, it was a smallish hotel on the seafront beyond the pier, with a glassed-in section where, for want of anything better to do, guests could sit and watch the cars passing outside. A coachload of pensioners had arrived, from Wales by the sound of it, cluttering the place with their cheap suitcases. He disliked the Welsh. He disliked the Scots and the Irish too, indeed there were few nationalities for whom he did not have a bad word, except perhaps Americans. He had been to Las Vegas once, they had proper hotels there, not like this knackered old dump.

He elbowed his way to the front of the queue, eliciting some sharp protests which he ignored. Lippy bastards the Welsh, you'd think they'd show a bit of respect in someone else's country. The receptionist scowled at him disapprovingly as he produced his warrant card.

'Hi Steve, nice to see you again,' she said, with undisguised sarcasm.

She looked vaguely familiar to Bullock, though he couldn't recall seeing her before. He had not taken in his surroundings on arriving with the two girls, and his exit in the morning remained a blur. The accent was foreign, but no surprise there.

'It's about the two women in room 301 who were here the night before last. Can I see the reservation?'

'So you not come to see *me*?' she asked mockingly.

Not before time, he recognised her as a woman he had taken back to his flat from Kalibanz about a month ago. Having entrusted her with the administration of a condom, he had been sharply rebuffed when she noticed it was past its sell-by date and refused to proceed further.

'Oh yeah, it's er...' he peered at her name badge. 'Ivana. How you doing?'

She fixed him with an Arctic stare.

'I get manager.'

She gave a finely judged shrug of contempt, plainly visible to the waiting queue, and disappeared into the office.

His rage that night had scared her, reminding her of the cops at home. She had fled the apartment, fearful for her safety and annoyed at her lack of progress in finding a serviceable English boyfriend.

She hadn't been on duty the previous evening, but she remembered the two girls checking in during the afternoon and thinking they looked tarty.

Bullock repeated his request when she returned with the manager. He vaguely recognised this man; an uncomfortable memory swam up of him smiling indulgently from behind the counter.

Having no animus towards the detective and little interest in the legalities of the situation, the manager obliged cheerfully enough.

'I saw you come in with them. Very nice-looking young ladies they were too, if I may say so.'

It was news to Ivana, who sensed an opportunity to inflict punishment.

'They weren't hookers were they?' she asked, in a tone of shocked concern.

There was a murmur of interest from the queue.

'He was here with a hooker!' said a lady in the queue disapprovingly.

'Well, you've been here with two full backs and a scrum half,' said her friend, invoking a ripple of laughter that Bullock disliked. It made him uneasy when people laughed near him, unless he had told the joke. He turned and growled at them,

'I'm here on police business, if you don't mind.'

'Sounds like you've already done the business,' called a man, which was followed by another round of laughter.

The reservation record bore nothing of use. The payment had been made in cash, and he doubted the names were real.

'Did you see them talking to anyone?'

'I did see them talking to a gentleman with tattoos,' Ivana offered with relish. 'Do you think he was a client too?'

There was a ragged cheer from the few male pensioners present, swiftly drowned by scandalised tutting from the women.

'You've got competition, boyo!' shouted one of the men.

'You should get a tattoo yourself,' added another. 'You'll only feel a little prick.'

Bullock could take no more. He pushed his way to the exit, making a point of kicking a suitcase that was blocking his path. The crowd booed.

His mood did not improve when he arrived back at the police station. An officer had been hurt by a wheelchair at the hospital. The news had finally reached his desk on the basis that one of the suspects might be traceable through Bullock's survey into violence against the elderly. It was an old man with leg and face injuries.

* * *

Chapter Twenty

Bev was on the afternoon shift and didn't call until well after two, for which Merv was grateful. Knight was still asleep, awash with painkillers. He took down the address she gave him and fobbed off her questions, promising that Knight would call her back. He had recovered his composure since the meltdown in the car park and had decided that getting Ryan's address was a good thing. If they could catch him, the whole headfuck would be over.

He had to hand it to the old man. Fran had obviously unhinged him, but he was good in a crisis. There was, of course, the matter of the number plate, but Knight had convinced him that the policeman was too far away to read it.

He went into the bedroom and shook him gently awake. Even though the make-up had faded he looked more cadaverous than ever.

It took Knight a moment to get up to speed. At first he thought he was at New Horizons, then the hospital, before the events of the night came rushing back. His mind snapped into gear when he grasped that Bev had come up with the goods.

Beside the bed lay a pair of crutches Merv had acquired from a charity shop. Refusing the offer of help, he used one to steady himself on his good leg then tucked the other quickly under his right arm. As a veteran of skiing accidents in more prosperous times he knew the drill. As long as his foot remained clear of the floor he could move almost as fast as with his stick.

'Get some coffee on, I'll be ready in five minutes.'

'You might want to think about having a shower first, you smell like an Arab's jockstrap.'

The Arabs that Knight had met had been scrupulously clean, as far as he knew, but there could be little doubt that he stank. On returning from the hospital he had collapsed into bed, still in the pyjamas he'd been wearing at the care home.

With the prickle of hot water came a renewed sense of urgency. Even assuming that Bev's intelligence was accurate, there was no guarantee that Ryan would be present at the address she had given them. The trail could be going cold even as he stood there. He shaved and cleaned his teeth, giving a wide berth to the tap on which he had broken his crown.

Lying on the bed he inserted the toes of his good leg into a pair of ancient boxer shorts and shook them onto his ankle. Now came the challenge of getting them onto the other foot. He flipped them repeatedly in a game of hoopla, but when he at last prevailed his back would not bend enough for him to reach them. Instead he jerked his good leg to slide them up to their destination. He imagined Fran seeing him like this, his leg twitching as if afflicted by some bizarre tic. Finding the thought unbearable, he called Merv back to do the rest.

The bed and breakfast was in a sullen patch of rundown terraces east of the town centre, where no tourists came unless they were lost. The pointing was crumbling and a window at the top was cracked. It was a last chance saloon for those who had reached the bottom of the welfare safety net but not yet fallen out of it into parks and doorways.

'So, how exactly are we going to convince our junkie mate to come with us? We can't just drag him out on his arse in front of everyone.'

They were sitting across the street in the Skoda, with Merv at the wheel. A lawyer was on standby; all they had to do was get Ryan in front of him.

'We won't need to.'

Knight flipped open the lens cover on his stick, which he had brought in addition to the crutches.

'I get him talking about what he was doing last night, and you record him. Then we show him and tell him we'll call the police unless he repeats it to the lawyer.'

'And if he does, what do we do with him after that?'

'We take him to the police anyway.'

Merv was partially soothed. Stitch-ups appealed to him, as long as someone else was the kipper. He helped Knight from the car in a repeat of the display outside New Horizons, only now there was no pretence. Before he could get the crutch in place Knight tottered and winced loudly as his foot touched the ground.

'You alright?'

'I'm fine. Give me the bag and bring the stick.'

Before Merv could intervene he was across the road, swinging his dead leg with the ease of a pirate, a supermarket bag looped round his fingers. At the steps Merv went in front and scooped him up to the door.

It took two rings before a young Asian man in a kurta appeared and considered them uncertainly. He didn't like the ingratiating smile of the younger one with the tattooed biceps, and the old one on crutches looked to be at death's door. He didn't want him passing through it here.

'I'm sorry,' he said, pointing to the no vacancies sign, 'all full.'

Knight feigned confusion followed by amusement.

'No no, it's not a room we're after, it's Ryan Carter. I'm his grandfather and this is his cousin.'

The man relaxed, reassured by the notion of wholesome family bonds, which were in short supply among his residents.

'He's not here,' he offered in a friendlier tone. 'He went out a while ago, I don't know when he'll come back.'

At least the address was right.

'Oh dear,' Knight sighed, taking a gift-wrapped parcel from the bag. 'It's his birthday today, and I was hoping to see him.'

'You want me to give it to him?'

'Do you think I might leave it in his room? I've never actually seen it, you know. I'm Peter Carter, by the way.'

The man took Knight's outstretched hand and identified himself as Waheed. He knew full well his uncle's rule that visitors could only enter if the resident was present, but somehow a different code seemed to apply here. He decided he could see no harm in it, and besides, his uncle was on business in Lahore.

He watched with approval as Merv hoisted Knight up the staircase, then went to fetch the master key. They were decent people, he had been right to let them in.

Knight's quarters at New Horizons were an extravagance compared to the desolation that greeted him. A scrap of nicotine-stained net hung limply over the window and the unmade bed clothes were smeared with the residue of things he didn't want to think about. As his imaginary grandfather, Knight felt an unwelcome jolt of pity for Ryan. Merv felt nothing of the sort. Self-preservation was a cardinal virtue in his eyes; what he saw here was a profound heresy.

Waheed was hovering, waiting for them to leave the present and go.

'It's a bit of a mess, isn't it?' Knight said quietly.

'Cleaning once a week,' Waheed replied with scant regard for the truth. He flicked the light switch but the room's only bulb had long given up the ghost. 'This one gone again, new one tomorrow.'

Knight shook his head sadly.

'Do you think we might spend a few minutes and make it a bit nicer for him?'

Waheed could not help but be touched.

'Please, go ahead. I will be downstairs.' He closed the door behind him, leaving it on the latch.

'You could get a fucking disease in here.'

'You probably wouldn't be the first. See if you can find his heroin.'

Knight was already scouring the room for hiding places; their negotiating position would be vastly improved if they found the boy's stash and withheld it. The floor was strewn with Ryan's meagre possessions, mostly music and games. While he rummaged through them Merv engaged warily with a broken-down chest of drawers.

Knight was inspecting a box of DVDs when there was a knock at the door. He put it aside quickly as the door opened without invitation. He had been expecting the Asian man, but it was a girl in a grubby tracksuit. She had lank, greasy hair and dark bags under her eyes. It took him a moment to recognise the prostitute Colin Boyle had brought to the Grand Hotel.

'Who are you?' she asked, with no great curiosity. Knight was thankful now for the broken bulb; she had evidently not recognised him.

'I'm Ryan's grandad,' he replied, apparently delighted to see her. 'Are you a friend of his?'

Ignoring the question she took a couple of steps into the room and looked blankly at Merv.

'I'm his cousin,' he explained, failing to disguise an instant aversion. By rights she should have been a looker; what he saw was an inexcusable waste.

'Have you seen him, dear?' Knight enquired with grandfatherly concern.

'I thought you was him coming back, I heard you through the wall.'

He detected disappointment, tinged with impatience.

'Are you waiting for him too?' he enquired. 'I hope he's not been keeping you too long.'

'Our Ryan's never been much good at timekeeping,' Merv added, as fondly as he could.

Her hollow eyes flicked nervously between the two men. Knight feared she had recognised him.

'Is something the matter?' he asked solicitously.

She hesitated a moment longer.

'Can you lend me some money?'

It wasn't a welcome request, given the state of his finances, but it was an opportunity. He saw Merv's expression sour.

'I'm afraid I don't have a lot of money. How much do you need?'

'Fifty quid. Ryan'll pay you back, he's getting money now, he's getting loads.' She said it quickly, with a new assertiveness.

'Is he?' Knight sounded pleased to learn of his grandson's entrepreneurial spirit. 'Has he got a job then?'

'Yeah. So can you lend us it? He'll pay you soon as he's back.'

There was no attempt at charm, only a cold impatience to seal the deal. He had no intention of giving her any money, at least not yet, but he also had to get her on the hook before she lost interest. He guessed that under the tracksuit her arms were as scabbed as Ryan's.

'I might be able to, but we'd have to go to a machine.' He detected a glimmer of interest. 'Are you his girlfriend?'

'Yeah, sort of,' she said, then corrected herself, 'I mean yeah, I'm his girlfriend.'

Knight didn't believe her for a moment; at best, she let Ryan sleep with her sometimes in exchange for a fix.

'I just need fifty quid, OK?'

He had to gamble on her being prepared to trade. If she walked away because he refused to come up with the money immediately he would learn nothing more, but he knew she'd be gone the moment the cash was in her hands. He took out a ten pound note and passed it over.

'I'll tell you what,' he said, as one might indulge a fractious child. 'You can have this now, which is all I've got, but before we go and get the rest I want you to tell me what Ryan's doing. I'm sure you'd understand that.'

It was touch and go. She looked at the note with disappointment then put it quickly in her pocket.

'He's working in a cafe.'

Not impossible, but he wasn't buying it yet. He looked at her sorrowfully.

'I'm sorry dear, but I need to know the truth. Please.'

She sighed irritably, her patience clearly wearing thin.

'Alright, he's seeing this woman. He saw her once before and he sold her something, and now he's gone to see her again. That's all I know.'

'Selling her drugs, was he?' Merv blurted out. Knight shot him a sharp glare.

'It doesn't matter if it was,' he cut in. 'It's just that we're worried about him. The last thing we want to do is get anyone in trouble, especially his friends. And I do want to help you.'

The promise of cash resumed its sway over her.

'It might have been,' she said quietly.

'Please, tell me.' He injected a tremble into his voice.

In fits and starts, he teased out a jumbled account of his newly acquired grandson's activities. Reading between the lines, it seemed that Ryan was an occasional dealer who bought and sold in small quantities to fund his own habit. But the money he made was never enough, hence his other careers as part-time gardener and burglar.

There had, however, been a bright spot in Ryan's recent fortunes. About three weeks ago he had sold a large amount of heroin, at least by his standards, to a woman he had never seen before. He had met her in a pub Bev had mentioned, a favourite of dealers and junkies. The woman was old and not short of cash. He had followed her home on his moped to see if there were further pickings to be had. She lived in a posh house, but he had not said where.

'And did he ever go back to the house?'

'Yeah, but there was a burglar alarm so he didn't bother.'

'So why did he go back today?'

'Cos he'd run out of money,' the girl snapped. 'He said he was going to find her and make her give him some.'

'Why would she give him money?'

'I don't know! Can we go and get mine now?'

She was getting twitchy, the craving intensifying as the promise of relief beckoned.

'Just one more thing. I'm not sure I like the idea of Ryan and this strange woman. You couldn't just phone him and ask him where he is could you?'

She stared at him incredulously.

'You want me to call him!?'

'I'd just like to know he's safe. But don't say I'm here or he'll think I'm checking up on him. I know he wouldn't like that.'

Knight sensed he had crossed a line, but he had to keep pushing.

'And as you've been so very helpful to me, I'd like to help you with a bit more money. Why don't I lend you a hundred?'

He avoided looking at Merv, but a hundred was dirt cheap for the prize of finding Ryan together with his mysterious client. He had speculated about the existence of a new face in the junkie netherworld, and now it seemed there was one.

She produced a phone in a case dotted with smiling faces and called Ryan's number.

'Would you be a dear and put him on loudspeaker? I'd love to hear his voice.'

The ringing reverberated around the room. He was getting his money's worth so far, but it all depended on Ryan answering. They couldn't stay at the house much longer without incurring Waheed's suspicion, and if the girl saw Ryan before they did he would almost certainly take flight on hearing of his fake grandfather. He sounded stressed when he finally answered.

'Jen? What you want?'

Knight realised he hadn't even asked what her name was, nor offered her his.

'Just wondering how it's going. Where are you?'

'By the woods outside East Dean.'

'Why aren't you at the house?'

'Because she wasn't there, it's her sister's house.'

The note of irritation was unmistakeable. Knight was mouthing at Jen to get the house address, but she ignored him, her curiosity evidently aroused.

'So what are you doing by the woods?'

'I'm waiting for her! Her sister called her and she said she'd meet me here.'

'So you talked to her?'

'No, that's what she said to tell me. Why you asking all this shit?'

She looked at Knight questioningly. He mouthed at her again to ask where the house was.

'So, where was the house, then?'

'Fuck's sake, Jen! She's bringing money, that's all that matters!'

The line went dead. She shrugged.

'Can we go now?'

Knight agreed readily. There was nothing to stay for.

* * *

Jen went to her room and hunted for her trainers. She had been asleep when Knight and Merv arrived, and would have slept through the noise had she not been desperate for Ryan to return. Times were hard; Colin Boyle had not called of late. On seeing the old man and his companion her first reaction had been disappointment, followed by hope when she identified an alternative source of funds. Sleepy and befuddled, she had made no connection between the frail creature sitting on the chair in the dingy bedroom and the vigorous though clumsy interloper at the Grand Hotel. But her mind was clearing now.

The two men were nearing the bottom of the staircase when she came out. It wasn't the sight of Knight being helped down the stairs that triggered the memory, but the stick with its distinctive handle that fell from under Merv's arm as they reached the hallway. She had seen that stick before, lying on the floor at the Grand Hotel when the old man tripped over in front of them. Now that she recognised him she was overcome by fury.

'You bastard!' she screamed down the stairs. 'You're not Ryan's grandad! Who the fuck are you?'

Knight had been preparing himself for this moment, thankful that it hadn't happened earlier. Dropping all pretence of grandfatherly concern, he barked back at her,

'It doesn't matter who I am, young lady, the offer still stands. If you want your money come with us and I guarantee you'll get it!'

'Why should I believe you?' she shrieked.

'Because I'm a better bet than Ryan. Ask yourself – who's more likely to come up with the goods, him or me?'

Anger at this point was giving way to desperation. She knew that Ryan was flaky and miles away pursuing some vague quest she didn't understand, whereas Knight was standing in front of her.

'I promise you, you will get your money,' he was saying. She followed them into the street, watched by a mystified Waheed. Recalling the time she had offered him sex in lieu of rent, he wondered if he had misjudged the men and thanked god for sending the stomach bug that had forced him to decline.

* * *

Knight surveyed the whimpering figure in the passenger seat next to Merv. She had switched her tracksuit top for a loose-fitting blouse that revealed a finely wrought chain around her neck. It was attached to a pendant in the shape of a leaf and looked incongruously adult on her, not something she would have chosen. Perhaps there had once been a grandmother or an aunt fond enough to give it to her. He was only able to guess what she was going through. As part of his programme of experimentation he had smoked heroin once at Sussex University. It was only the entry level version but the effect had been a euphoric contentment that left him wanting more without delay. Unlike Jen, he was fortunate that none had been forthcoming.

'Just tell me you're not going to be sick,' Merv demanded with a marked absence of tenderness. Even though it was Knight's vehicle and not his own he would inevitably have to clear it up.

Jen groaned and shook her head. She had not noticed that they had passed several cash machines but now she spotted one.

'Where the fuck you going?' she protested shrilly to Merv. 'You're supposed to be getting my money, turn the fucking car around!'

'After we find Ryan,' Knight growled from the back seat.

'No, I want it now!'

'Well you can't have it, can you?' Merv was nearing the edge with her.

It infuriated him that she was taking Knight for a small fortune. 'Just sit there and keep your mouth shut.'

She rounded on him viciously.

'You piece of lying shit! Who the fuck are you anyway? Fucking toerag, I hope you die of cancer!'

Merv erupted. 'So what do you think you're going to die of then? Old age? You won't even get past thirty will you? Fucking junkie parasite!'

She leaned over and tried to slap him. When that failed she attempted to bite him on the arm. With one hand on the wheel he fended her off roughly while Knight pleaded with them to calm down. None of them saw the woman until they were nearly upon her.

They were approaching the woods along a winding road with open land on one side and trees on the other. Still engaged in battle, Merv was drawing level with a wayside car park when she came out of the trees less than thirty yards ahead. He braked hard and swerved round her onto the other side of the road. Thrown violently into his seat belt, Knight glimpsed her for a fleeting instant as she leapt to safety and ran to the car park. She was wearing sunglasses, in itself not surprising on a bright day, but she had a thick winter coat and heavy duty gloves. What concerned him much more was the car bearing down on them with its horn blaring.

There wasn't time to swerve back. Merv ploughed into the grass verge beside the trees, narrowly missing one as the car swept past in a blaze of flashing headlights. Still it wasn't over. An abandoned moped lay on the verge directly in their path, forcing him to swing back onto the tarmac as a second car sped by, missing them by inches. At last he brought the Skoda to a halt under the trees.

'You stupid fucking cow! You stupid, useless fucking nutjob! If you were a bloke...'

He couldn't find the words to describe what might have befallen her had her gestation taken a different course. His face was drained of colour and the upper half of his body was trembling. Jen was curled into a ball, moaning to herself. At least she hadn't thrown up.

Nor had Knight, not that he hadn't come close. Shaken though he was, he had the presence of mind to look in the door mirror. A small car was pulling out of the car park and driving away in the opposite direction. He thought he saw something roll away from it, possibly a wheel cover.

'Nice bit of driving,' he said quietly to Merv, aware that his voice was shaking. 'That could have been all of us.'

'Too fucking right it could. And who left that sodding bike in the way?'

Merv blew out a long breath, intent on avoiding another meltdown. He helped Knight out and onto his crutches.

'For Christ's sake stop provoking her,' he whispered. 'Can't you see the state she's in?'

Merv bit his tongue, and extracted the limp girl from the passenger seat. She scratched feebly at his face as he half-carried, half-dragged her along the verge, but he didn't retaliate. She was staring in bemusement at the moped when Knight caught up with them.

'Jen, listen to me, is this Ryan's bike?'

She nodded weakly. Knight peered over the road at the Downs, bare of human form as far as the eye could see. Ryan had to be in the woods.

They set off, Merv supporting the girl. Knight veered away from them to widen the angle of search, picking his way tentatively through the sparse undergrowth. He crossed a dirt track. The trees were in full leaf, blocking out all but a few shafts of sunlight that pierced the gloom at intervals.

He could remember enough of his jungle training to read the basic signs. A sapling had been trampled by a deer, or so the nearby droppings suggested; feathers around a gap in the gorse indicated a foxhole. The map on his phone showed that the area was bounded on all sides by open land that contained no buildings. He was sure Ryan was in the woods; it was not a place you went through to get to somewhere else.

At first he thought the object was a fungus growing from a tree stump, but it was too white for that. As he drew closer it resolved into a baseball cap with the letters NYC emblazoned in shiny silver thread. Ryan had not worn a hat to their previous encounter, but in its meagre assertion of glamour it looked like something he might own. He waved to Merv and waited as he propelled the girl to where the cap lay, beside a dense thicket of bramble.

She identified the hat with a nod, her face betraying no emotion.

'So which way from here?' Merv scanned between the trees; if Ryan had heard them this could be the moment he chose to break cover.

The line from the bike to the cap suggested a direction of sorts. As they skirted the bramble, Knight saw a patch where the branches had been bent and broken; it was not to his eye the work of a deer or a fox. He rested on one crutch while Merv used the other to pull the spiky tendrils aside. Inside the dark hollow lay Ryan, his mouth slightly open, staring up at them through glassy eyes. Knight's energy drained away as the case crumbled before him for a second time.

'Merv, can you get in there? Don't touch him whatever you do.'

It was worth a shot, but he knew what the answer would be. Merv ripped aside enough of the bramble to make a kneeling space beside Ryan's head. Using a leaf to cover his finger, he checked for a pulse then held his watch over the boy's mouth to see if condensation would appear. He shook his head.

'What's the matter with him?'

They had almost forgotten about Jen. Distracted for a moment from her own troubles, she gazed dumbly at the lifeless body, unwilling or unable to grasp what it meant.

'I'm afraid it's what it looks like,' Knight said gently, 'he's dead.'

He waited for her to become hysterical, but she simply stood and watched quietly as Merv used the crutch to turn the body over. He inspected the back of the head for signs of injury, of which there were none, then reverting to the leaf he rolled up the sleeve of Ryan's sweatshirt. In amongst the tiny scabs was a new mark, the blood still fresh.

'There's your answer, he OD'd.'

It was more than plausible. Bathed in serenity, the pale face could have been from a painting of a saint beholding the Almighty at the moment of martyrdom. Would a heroin death not have the same ecstatic intensity?

Further conjecture would have to wait. If a rambler or a dog walker saw them they would be sucked into a police enquiry, leaving his own investigation even more broken than it was.

'Check his pockets and we'll go.'

The pockets revealed a few pounds, a lighter and Ryan's room key. There was no syringe. Merv removed himself and pulled back the bramble as best he could.

'Are you going to leave him there?' It wasn't a protest, more an acceptance of the inevitable.

'Just for now. I'll call the police in a little while.' He heard himself adopting the consoling fatherly tone for when pets or elderly relatives died.

Since the outburst in the car she had remained sullen and withdrawn, barely reacting to the sight of Ryan's body. Now it was as if a tectonic plate shifted inside her, giving vent at last to something other than her craving. Tears ran down her face and she began to cry. Knight's heart went out to her, but for Merv the effect was devastating. The sight of women crying unnerved him, unleashing some primal instinct he wished he didn't have. He suddenly felt a profound sense of shame for the way he had treated her.

Knight tried half-heartedly to squeeze more information from her as they drove back to Eastbourne: who was Ryan's supplier, and was Colin Boyle part of the chain? She stayed silent, oblivious to everything except the approaching moment of relief. Merv remained in the grip of severe remorse, yet unable to find a form of words that would comfort her. He felt grateful, too, that she had not been sick. Gradually he conceded the possibility that she was not a bad person.

They found a machine and Knight counted the money out. A voice told him they should take her to a hospital, that he was consigning her to the same fate as Ryan; a louder one said it was futile.

'I'm very sorry about everything,' he told her truthfully. 'And thank you for your help. Good luck.'

He felt sickened by the choice he had made. Merv was still tongue-tied, aware that time was running out to make amends.

Before she went, she pulled the chain and pendant from her neck.

'He nicked it from an old person,' she said. 'Take it, I don't want it.'

Knight slipped it into his pocket as she turned to go.

'Jen, wait!'

She eyed Merv coldly.

'What?'

'I just wanted to say…' What did he want to say?

'I'm sorry too, and…' He searched desperately for something positive, something to send her on her way with a shred of comfort. At last it came to him, a tribute he had read about a mountaineer who had succumbed to an avalanche.

'At least he died doing what he loved.'

Jen stared at him in disbelief. She opened her mouth to say something, but her knees were giving way and she was falling. Merv swooped and caught her. As he held her steady, her face resting on his shoulder, she was copiously sick on him.

* * *

Chapter Twenty-One

Knight inhaled deeply, relishing the hot rasp on his throat, indifferent to the consequences.

The sea and the sky had merged into inky blackness, so that all he could see from the terrace were ragged lines of white foam advancing and vanishing in an endlessly repeated cavalry charge.

He hobbled to business class and reclined the seat until it was nearly flat, then gazed into nothingness, mulling his troubles. Chief among them was the body that still lay in the woods a few miles away, although it felt as present as if it were on the sofa in his sitting room. There was an extremely uncomfortable encounter to be endured before he could finally report it.

He had at least attended to basic housekeeping. Merv had called Mrs Grayling to say his father would be recuperating at home for a few days, and he had written a reassuring letter to Penelope. He'd also agreed with Merv to go to a different hospital the next day to have his leg examined.

Hardest had been the letter to Fran, telling her he was making progress. It was strictly speaking true, in that he had uncovered a seam of criminality that he was sure led back to the murders. He was convinced that the woman they had nearly run over was Ryan's killer. Why else wear a coat and gloves on a summer's day if not to protect herself against the brambles when she hid the body? She had planned his death, there could be no other explanation. Had she also planned the deaths of the three old ladies?

He pictured the face again, or what little he had seen of it around the sunglasses. He wouldn't have said she was old, as Ryan had described her, but anyone over forty might seem ancient in his eyes. Her skin was not wrinkled and she had a full head of dark curly hair; then again, with a wig and make-up she could pass for any age at all.

What puzzled him most was her relationship with Ryan and the role of her sister. It wasn't hard to imagine a prosperous family with an addict for a black sheep. It made less sense that she should appear out of nowhere and buy a large amount of heroin from a source she had never used before. Unless she wished to remain anonymous.

An insomniac seagull landed on the wall on the far side of the terrace, its view of Knight obscured by the table that stood between them. Emboldened to consider the terrain its own, it descended to the ground where it foraged for the scraps it knew were sometimes present. Knight watched through the legs of the table, enjoying the bird's ignorance of his presence. It was the invisibility he felt on a stake-out or wearing a false identity. The woman would have felt invisible too, but who was she?

She was without doubt a highly capable operator. She had engineered Ryan's killing more or less on the spur of the moment, if the story about the telephone conversation between the two sisters was true. But was there even a sister? Could Ryan have failed to recognise the person who opened the door to him – could it have been the killer herself, someone he had met in a different guise, who had tricked him into going to the woods and then followed him as the version he knew? Perhaps he was dealing with a consummate shape-shifter, one even better than himself. He ran through it again. Ryan had gone to the woods in the expectation of money, even though he had nothing to sell. There was only one way of getting cash that might also lead to his death, and that was blackmail. Had he threatened to expose his wealthy buyer for money to buy more heroin for himself and Jen?

The seagull flapped up onto the table, where it was greeted by a half-eaten ready meal and the sight of Knight sprawled on the seat. It had seen this creature before and knew it to be slow. When it waved its stick the bird held its ground. When the creature got up it watched dispassionately, stabbing calmly at the lasagne. Only when its upper section swayed and fell with limbs outstretched onto the table did the bird fly away, evacuating its bowels to gain altitude quickly.

Aware of something warm on his neck, Knight heard the doorbell ring.

* * *

'Jesus Christ, Tom!'

Bev stared at him with mounting alarm as the implications of Ryan's death sank in.

'I get his address for you and a few hours later he's dead. How am I meant to explain that?'

Knight shifted uncomfortably on the sofa.

'That's why I'm telling you before I call it in. I'm really sorry, Bev, if I'd had any idea this might happen I would never have got you involved.'

'But I *am* involved!' She saw him flinch and checked herself. She had already embarrassed him by insisting on wiping his neck clean when he had tried to ignore it.

'I don't mean to sound ungrateful after what you did for me, but I'm in deep shit here! What am I going to do?'

'There might be a way out. Did you spend any time alone during your last shift?'

She took a moment to think about it.

'I was on my own in the car for about twenty minutes when my partner went for chips and got chatting with the owner. Why?'

A weight fell from Knight's shoulders.

'Then here's what you can say.' She arched an eyebrow. 'It's a suggestion anyway. You saw Ryan acting suspiciously, sizing up a car maybe, and went to have a word with him. You didn't ask for his address at the time because you decided he was harmless, but afterwards you had second thoughts and decided to check him anyway.'

She turned the story over in her mind. Their car had been parked around the corner from the kebab shop, so her partner would have no way of knowing it was a lie. As to why she had not mentioned it to him, she could say she had not thought it important at the time, and in any case they had more pressing things to talk about. It was thin, but adequate. Thankfully there was no record of her calls to Knight, for which she used one of his stock of untraceable phones.

'Alright. What will you say when you call it in?'

'I'll say I'm a junkie who was shooting up with him. That way they'll be less suspicious when they can't find me.'

Bev turned that over too. She knew Knight had software that made his voice unidentifiable, even to sophisticated analysis; there would be nothing to link him to the call. With no compelling evidence of foul play there wouldn't be a murder investigation, at least not to begin with. The coroner would record an open verdict and the file would eventually be elbowed aside by more pressing cases.

'So all you have to do if anyone asks about the address is play the innocent. There's nothing else that can link you to him.'

Her fears abated somewhat. The situation wasn't great, but she could live with it.

'Alright. Now tell me the rest. Every single thing.'

'Are you sure you want to know? The more I tell you, the more you're implicated.'

A cautionary voice told her to back off. By the time he'd finished she wished she'd listened to it. There was more than enough to end her career if she could be shown to be even slightly involved.

'So, let's get this straight, first you trash an exit barrier and injure a police officer, then you withhold evidence about a possible murder, and to top it all you interfere with a witness. Anything else I should know?'

'No, that's about it. I'm very sorry.'

'What happens if they speak to Jen? Or the guy at the bed and breakfast?'

This was the part that worried Knight the most. If linked, the colourful performances he had given in the past two days spelt nothing but trouble.

'It depends how hard they try to find Ryan's grandfather. The risk is that they link him to the hospital. If that happens they'll get serious about tracking him down.'

Bev felt the water deepening. All it needed was one CCTV image to be seen by the wrong person for Knight to be dragged under, possibly taking her with him. She shared Knight's opinion that the woman at the woods had killed Ryan and quite possibly the old ladies too. The problem was, the theory couldn't be investigated officially without exposing Knight's involvement and her own. She took another step down the career ladder.

'OK,' she said, 'this woman, are you sure you've never seen her before, or anyone like her?'

'As far as I could tell she was about five foot six and medium build. There must be millions of women answering that description.'

'What about recently?'

More to humour her than anything else he ran back through the women he had met since the day of the murders. Barbara Dawson and Mrs Grayling fitted the bill approximately. The shape of the face was wrong but prosthetics could fix that. Carol O'Brien was much larger, and Antonia Baldwin far slimmer, though the coat was bulky.

'Sorry, no one.'

'What about the car?'

'I told you, it was small, blue probably. Maybe missing a wheel cover.'

'And have you seen one like that anywhere?'

Knight felt a stab of impatience. She meant well, but this would go nowhere.

'I expect I've seen hundreds.' He tried not to sound dismissive. 'I'm not sure this really helps, Bev.'

'It's called basic police work. Have a think.'

He felt he owed it to her to honour the request, so he attempted to envisage small blue cars. He could recall none at the bank where he had paid Jen off, or outside the B&B, or at the hospital.

He went back methodically over the past fortnight, to his surveillance of Barbara and his visits to the other next of kin. The car that had nearly hit them was a Mercedes, he still remembered that, but before that everything became a blur of metal. He was on the point of giving up when he came to the encounter with the rubbish truck. The large car that had taken his mirror was some kind of SUV, a Range Rover possibly, but what was the one he had scratched before that, a few doors up from New Horizons?

'What was it, Tom?'

It was small, certainly. And it was blue.

'What make was it?'

He tried to picture the badge on the bonnet. It was an animal of some kind. A lion.

'A blue Peugeot then? See what a bit of plodding can do?'

Bev was pleased with herself. Knight was caught between gratitude and irritation not to have thought of it himself. He remembered now that he had not seen the car again when he came back round the block in search of the Hillfields. It could have been theirs.

'Bev, I have to find that wheel cover before I report the body. If the police find it they'll take it away.'

Bev was shocked. 'For Christ's sake, Tom, it's evidence!'

'Evidence that will mean nothing to them, so it'll go into storage and get forgotten about. I need to know what car that woman was driving.'

Bev slid to the bottom of the ladder.

'OK, I'll go and look. But only if you stay here.'

* * *

It was well after midnight and the seafront was quiet. They took the back roads to the Downs, avoiding the places where her colleagues would be waiting with breathalysers. Even then they came upon a police car in a lay-by and endured an agonising minute until they were sure it had not followed them.

In the end he had been reduced to pleading with her to let him come, promising like a delinquent child to do exactly as he was told. In the empty parking ground opposite the woods there was a further discussion about whether he should come with her or remain in the car. After heated exchanges he prevailed with more promises of strict obedience.

It was only when they had crossed the road that Knight realised he had left his torch behind. Not disguising her irritation, Bev instructed him to stay exactly where he was and went to fetch it.

Fully intending to comply, Knight gazed up at the stars. Normally it would have soothed him, only now he recalled that the torch was not in the side compartment where he had told her but in the glove box behind the manual. It would not improve her mood. It disturbed him that she had more or less accused him of being obsessive. He was wondering whether she had a point when he thought he heard a voice.

It was no more than a murmur and then gone. Knight peered through the trees and saw a dim flicker of light. The murmur again. Probing the undergrowth with a crutch, he took a cautious step through the tree line. The ground was level and he'd negotiated it easily enough with Merv. There was still no sign of Bev; a little further would do no harm.

His first thought was that the killer had come back to remove the body. When the light flickered again he glimpsed a rectangular shape that could have been a vehicle. He remembered the track they had crossed earlier – it would be simplicity itself to steal in under cover of darkness and spirit Ryan away.

He was taking out his phone to call Bev when something rustled away to his left. It couldn't be her, it was the wrong direction. He racked his brain to think if he could possibly have been spotted, and wished he had brought the Browning. As he attempted to get behind a tree he was caught by torchlight.

'Think I can't see you there?'

It was a woman's voice. Knight steadied himself on the tree, ready to swing with a crutch if he needed to.

'Who's that?' he growled, with less menace than he would have wished.

The approaching torchlight redirected itself onto a woman at least as old as him, with close-set eyes beneath a jutting brow. Incongruously, she was wearing a tie-dyed smock.

'Maggie,' she said. 'You're in a bit of a state. Have we met?'

Could she be taunting him? She was the same height as the woman who had crossed the road. Before he could see if she was holding a syringe the light shone back on him.

'We might have done.' He made it sound casual. 'I heard Ryan might be here.'

He watched for her reaction, ready to strike if she suddenly went for him.

'We'd better go and see then. You sure you can manage?'

If it was a trap she was playing her hand beautifully. He followed her cautiously, rehearsing his next move.

'I'm one of his customers,' he said. 'Are you one too?'

This time she did react, turning sharply and examining him anew.

'Well, you're a dark horse.' She cackled softly to herself. 'He wasn't rough with you, was he?'

Knight was mystified.

'So if you're not a customer, where did you meet him?'

'I never said I did. People don't use their real names, do they?'

Knight's confusion deepened. Was there some other web of connections around Ryan that he didn't know about? Or was she being deliberately ambiguous to keep him on the hook?

As they reached the track the light grew stronger, revealing a battered Transit van. Gathered at the rear was a small group of people shining torches through the open doors. They weren't how he imagined grave robbers, not that he had any point of reference. There was a man in a string vest, another with a studded collar round his neck and a woman sporting a feather boa over an ill-fitting French maid's dress. None of them looked much under seventy, nor did they pay the slightest attention as Knight and his guide approached.

'Sorry we're late,' she whispered, as if squeezing into the stalls five minutes after curtain-up.

She led him to the second row where his view was partially blocked by the feather boa, though not so as to obscure the narrative. On a mattress in the back of the van was a restless mound of human flesh, jerking and swaying in the unflattering torchlight.

Knight must have recoiled, or it may have been that the feather boa shifted position to get a better view and nudged him off balance. His weight came down heavily on the bad leg causing him to discharge an angry expletive.

'Are you alright?' Maggie enquired anxiously. The other spectators turned their attention to him, the performance having hit a slow patch.

'Absolutely fine,' he reassured her. 'It's just I think I might be in the wrong place.'

'You not ESDP then?'

The man in the string vest was looking at him dubiously. He had a slightly officious demeanour that was at odds with the nipple piercing showing through the string.

'I'm afraid I've never heard of it,' Knight answered politely. 'And I'm so sorry to have disturbed you, but I really must be going now.'

'Doesn't he have a lovely voice?' the feather boa said, to no one in particular.

The string vest wasn't having it.

'If you're not ESDP then who are you?'

Knight stared at him blankly.

'ESDP. Eastsussexdoggingpensioners.' It rolled crisply off his tongue as if he were answering the phone.

'He's looking for Ryan,' Maggie offered helpfully.

'You sure you don't want Seasidegaydogs?' the studded collar asked. 'They're under the pier tonight.'

There was a commotion at the rear of the van as the two occupants removed themselves, wishing to know why they had lost their audience. Knight had no appetite to see more of them, save for an idle curiosity about their faces which made him hesitate for a fatal second. The man appeared to be entirely hairless apart from a goatee that reached almost to the foothills of his impressive stomach. Not that Knight was impressed. His eyes were riveted on the woman, and hers on his. It was Carol O'Brien, the Tarot card reader.

He turned and fled down the track at a reckless pace, the risk of falling trumped by the entranced expression on Carol's face, as if she had been picked for the Rapture. Heedless to the stones and sticks that might lie in his way he hurtled along at a steady three miles per hour.

The mystery confounding Carol was that the cards had suggested nothing of this. But the question of how she had misunderstood them would have to wait. She knew she had provoked a jealous rage in her chosen one, and he was slipping through her hands.

'It's not what you think!' she howled, 'I swear, he means nothing to me!'

Knight veered off the track. Among the trees the ground hazards multiplied. Behind him he could hear low level chatter and another cry from Carol, demanding his immediate return. He flew on, dreading the prospect of explaining himself to Bev.

Torchlight raked the tree trunks. Risking a look back he could make out a cluster of silhouettes advancing slowly from the direction of the track. There was a shriek, suggesting Carol's bare feet had encountered something sharp. It was still fifty yards to the road. He bellowed for Bev.

Afflicted as they were by the ravages of age and in some cases bulk, his pursuers were by no means fleet of foot. Like a zombie apocalypse filmed in slow motion, hunters and hunted crept through the woods in their varying states of decrepitude. Slowly the hunters gained ground with Carol at the fore urging them on.

Knight could see the edge of the woods. Carol was no longer calling his name but wheezing heavily as exhaustion overtook her. The road came into view. Bev would be there. Giving thanks for his deliverance, he put on a final spurt. As he reached the tree line, one of the crutches slid on a smooth flat stone and he crashed to the ground.

It had not occurred to Bev that Knight would be so stupid as to go into the woods. Thinking he must be somewhere along the grass verge she had patrolled a fair distance up the road. When she heard him shout she doubled back. A dark blur of bodies appeared, accompanied by a female voice testifying loudly to the hand of destiny. It seemed a naked woman was kneeling over Knight while two other people held him down. She was removing his trousers. Despite the risks involved in identifying herself, Bev felt she had no choice. She took out her warrant card and shouted 'police'.

For the second time in twenty-four hours Knight was afforded a close-up vision of the female form that left him wanting less. He had been debagged once before, though not with the same intent, in the officers' mess after a drinking session. There he had fought back fiercely; here all he could do was kick feebly with his good leg, which if anything sped the removal of the garment. Then suddenly his tormentors abandoned him, the man in the string vest dragging the hysterical Carol away while the others ran into the woods.

He scrabbled for his trousers, desperate to pull them up before Bev arrived.

'Are you hurt? Tom, talk to me!'

'I'm OK. Just a bruise probably.'

His shoulder throbbed where it had hit the ground. The knee at least appeared to have escaped further injury. He raised himself slowly onto one elbow.

'Who were those people? What did they want with you?'

'Never seen them before in my life. If I were you I wouldn't bother going after them.'

Any sympathy Bev might have felt drained away.

'Don't fucking lie to me, Tom, that woman was shouting your name! What else are you mixed up in that you haven't told me about?'

The inference horrified him.

'Bev, I swear...' he spluttered.

'Forget it, I don't want to know. We're getting out of here – now!'

She hauled him up only to realise that he couldn't stand without his crutches. She let him down again and went to where they had fallen. He could hear her muttering under her breath.

As Bev picked up a crutch her torch picked out the obstacle that had brought about Knight's downfall.

It wasn't a stone, it was a Peugeot wheel cover.

* * *

Chapter Twenty-Two

Fran chewed absently on the dried crust of the pasta bake, burned black by the neglect of its cooks. That it should be served on her birthday seemed appropriate, for she was in no mood to celebrate. There had been cards and gifts from her children, but they had been opened and inspected before they were given to her, which somehow sullied them. She had at least succeeded in keeping her fellow inmates in the dark.

Opposite her, Cindy was complaining once more about the inadequacy of her treatment after the attack. In her view, the small scratch on her neck had merited a trip to hospital rather than a plaster, and for this she intended to sue the government. Her litany of victimhood had become a source of profound boredom, rivalling the leaden food and daytime TV.

The letter from Knight had done little to lift her spirits. It was understandable that he could not go into any detail for fear of the prison censors alerting the police to his activities, but it added to her sense of helplessness not to know what he had achieved, if indeed he had achieved anything. She was therefore surprised and not a little excited to receive a second letter from him twenty-four hours later, urgently requesting a meeting.

Deciding that suet pudding wasn't worth the price of listening to Cindy, she rose and made her way to the cells. On the landing, the officer who had taken her to the interview room for Knight's last visit was approaching. It surprised Fran, as he wasn't due for another hour. The officer was beaming for some reason.

'You're popular, Haskell. There's someone else wants to see you too.'

She couldn't imagine what the officer meant; her daughter's next visits were already booked and the solicitor wasn't coming again for a fortnight.

'Mr Briggs is out of hospital and he wants to come and thank you for what you did. Monday afternoon, if you're free?'

At least some of them had a sense of humour; it would help if she never got out.

'I'll have to check my diary, but I'm sure it's fine.'

There was a spring in her step as she continued to the cell. The visit from Briggs was an unexpected gift, which for some reason seemed to cheer her more than the others.

* * *

The Glaswegian barman nodded to the old guy on a stick making his way towards the gents. He was going downhill, but who wasn't?

Knight felt better than he looked. He was convinced he had enough to secure a not guilty verdict for Fran when her case came to trial, and with one more push he believed he could stop it coming to trial at all. He would have considered himself on a roll had it not been for his stomach, bloated from a late-night takeaway with Merv.

He locked the door of the cubicle and undid his trousers. It was stiflingly hot. Above him, London baked in a heatwave; here in the bowels of the pub it felt like a sauna. He took out a small syringe case and paused, putting off the disagreeable task for a moment.

The Hillfields had disappeared. The mobile number was untraceable and the address was a commercial mailbox that had never received any mail. He regretted again not having taken the number of their car, but even if he had there could be little doubt they would have covered this track too. Far more effectively than he himself had managed to do, the Hillfields had slipped into New Horizons to achieve their objective and slipped out again without leaving a trace.

Yet it was still scarcely credible that the woman crossing the road was a miraculously rejuvenated version of the frail, ancient creature he had seen outside the home. He had barely glimpsed Susan Hillfield's face, and who better than Fran to describe it to him?

Balancing the case on his lap, he removed a sachet of antiseptic gel which he wiped on the side of his kneecap.

Knight was unsentimental about injections. They were a form of running repair, much as one might patch up a jeep to get it back to base.

He had kept his promise to Merv and gone with him to another hospital, where it came as no surprise to learn that he required a new knee. It would have to wait. In the meantime there was the morphine he'd acquired from a private doctor he knew who didn't ask too many questions. He'd had the odd dizzy spell but otherwise it did the job required of it, so much so that the crutches had been abandoned and he was back on his stick.

As he inserted the needle he felt an odd kinship with Ryan, whose body remained as yet unclaimed in the morgue. According to Bev there was no great urgency to establish his identity.

He waited while the knee grew numb. Apart from his churning gut he felt nothing whatsoever when he stood up. He was good to go for another two hours.

* * *

Holloway looked as bleak as ever, as if in mourning for itself. The prison's life was drawing to an end; in a few months it would close down to make way for a housing estate. Knight felt no sympathy. He let the taxi go and took a moment to compose himself.

He was picturing Fran's face as she heard the good news when the discomfort in his stomach raised itself to a piercing ache that could no longer be ignored. Further running repairs were required, but he had not seen a chemist on the way from the pub. He went through his pockets on the off-chance of finding an abandoned strip of tablets. His search was rewarded in the back pocket of his trousers, though not in the form he had imagined.

The discovery of forgotten weed, even a very small bag like the one he held in his hand, was always an uplifting experience. Moreover, they had smoked the last of Merv's supply over the curry. He felt honour-bound not to throw such a godsend away, even though this was what common sense demanded.

He decided to hide the weed and retrieve it later, but the busy street offered no obvious opportunities and he didn't want to be late. Stepping into a bus shelter, he secreted the bag in his underpants.

The reception area was a cheerless affair. Knight queued patiently behind a woman of uncertain age trying to cheer up a small girl. She was the girl's aunt, he speculated, or her grandmother. He wondered what crime would be enough to justify depriving a child of its mother, whether there had been violence or death. He wondered too if he had been rash not to jettison the weed, but other than a cursory pat-down the visitors were being let through unhindered. Of more concern was the pain now spreading through his pelvic region. He looked around for a toilet, but the queue had built up behind him and it was nearly his turn. There was nothing for it but to face the pain down.

He took slow, deep breaths and focussed on the strip light in the ceiling. With steely resolve he dragged his mind away, imagining himself on a beach with the sun on his face. Somewhere out on the edge of his consciousness there was a mild flurry of comment. Someone new had joined the crowd at the seaside. It was another prison officer, holding a spaniel on a lead. Knight liked dogs. Holding the line against the tumult below, he thought of dogs from his childhood, his first girlfriend's dog, the commandant's Labrador at Sandhurst.

It was only when the spaniel started sniffing its way down the queue that he fathomed the reason for its presence. As the dog approached, his tenaciously achieved grip on the situation evaporated in an instant. The gas imprisoned in his lower abdomen burst forth with the urgency of a genie exiting a cramped bottle after centuries of confinement. The woman looked at him with unease and the officer with profound distaste. The girl was instantly cheered.

The dog pricked up its ears at the noise but was otherwise undeterred. It thrust its nose into Knight's groin and inhaled deeply, heedless of his attempts to push it away.

'That's disgusting!' the woman shouted at the officer as a second genie made good its escape. 'Get him off, you stupid wally!'

It wasn't clear whether her sympathy lay with Knight or the dog, but she was evidently no fan of authority. Under her withering gaze the officer pulled the animal away.

'Is everything alright, dear?' she enquired. Then dropping her voice to a conspiratorial whisper, 'I've got some of them pants here for my dad, I can let you have a couple if you like.'

'Could I really?' Knight asked plaintively. 'I meant to buy some this morning, but my pension hasn't come through yet.'

As the woman took a pack of incontinence briefs from her bag the officer thought better of it and moved on. She broke out a few pairs for Knight.

'Is that going to be enough for you, my love?'

Knight was sure that it would and thanked her warmly. Viewed with pity and disgust in equal measure by the onlookers, he completed the entry formalities and was shown the way to the men's room.

* * *

The first thing he noticed was that Fran was pale and had lost more weight. But the warmth of her voice as she greeted him was genuine. He felt thrice blessed. The pants had proved unnecessary and the pain had cleared; now it seemed he had already taken a stride towards rehabilitation.

'So, what is it you wanted to tell me about?'

He realised he was staring at her. Despite her changed appearance she was as desirable as ever.

'Quite a lot, as it happens.' He had wondered what to tell her first and decided against modesty. 'I think I know who did it.'

Fran seemed astonished, as he had hoped. Even more so than on their last encounter, she listened to his story with mounting incredulity, at times wondering if he was pursuing some deranged fantasy. She thought of the feeble, locked-in woman who lived in terror of the world and the daring killer who sprinted across the road; they could not possibly be one and the same. Yet the perfectly managed disappearance spoke for itself.

'The problem is,' Knight concluded, 'I only saw her face for a split second. What I need you to do is describe it to me in as much detail as you can remember.' He had not mentioned the second visit to the woods.

Fran tried to picture Susan Hillfield, but struggled to put meaningful detail on the vague image. In its withdrawn, anxious sadness it was a face that asked you to look the other way and leave it be.

'I think she had brown eyes. She wore thick glasses, though, so you couldn't really see them that well.'

Which meant, if she was wearing coloured lenses, you wouldn't know.

'What about her complexion? Was it wrinkled or smooth?'

Fran conducted a mental identity parade. All the women at the home were wrinkled, some gouged by deep trenches, others etched with spidery lines like maps of river deltas. Susan Hillfield did not belong in the first camp, that much she could remember, but no more.

'I suppose she must have been a bit wrinkled, but then she could have been wearing make-up. I never really looked.'

Knight was not surprised. Nobody had looked hard enough at him to see that he was wearing make-up, and if it hadn't been for his carelessness even the observant Penelope would not have noticed.

'How about the shape of the face? Would you say it was more round, or more square?'

'I'd say it was a bit more square, definitely not a round face.'

A tenuous link was better than none, though it barely justified the urgently requested meeting. It was time for something that did.

'I've written an affidavit,' he said, as if it had just sprung to mind. 'It states everything I've told you and you can use it in court as evidence. It's not enough to get you bail, but it'll damage the prosecution at the trial when they can't produce the Hillfields.' He added, rather gravely, 'It's with my solicitor, in case anything happens to me.'

The news dumbfounded her. She had come to the meeting with low expectations, only to be handed what was almost a get out of jail card. Nor had she missed the more sombre implication.

'What do you mean, in case anything happens to you?'

He savoured the concern in her voice like a hungry bee tasting nectar, then affected an unconcerned shrug.

'It's a normal thing to do, but I don't think anything *will* happen to me.' At this particular moment he believed it, although he had never written such a document before. Ryan's fate had led him to make a sobering risk assessment; whoever was responsible would not hesitate to kill him too if necessary.

'Tom, I don't want you putting your life on the line for me. What you've done already is amazing – give them the affidavit now and I'll take my chances.'

He had thought she might say this; in fact, he had imagined it several times and what he would say in reply.

'It's my choice. I've no confidence in the police getting to the bottom of this even if they wanted to. The only sure way to get you out of here is to do it myself.'

'But it's too much, you don't owe...'

'Don't worry about me,' he cut in, 'I promise I'll be fine.'

Fran saw that his determination allowed her no say in the matter. In other circumstances she might have objected, but now she accepted with good grace. Perhaps this was a birthday she would wish to remember after all.

A birthday. What was it about a birthday? Something was tapping at the door of her memory, something that had happened in her other life before the murders.

'I took a picture of her!' she exclaimed.

Basking in the glow of her approval, Knight was slow on the uptake. 'A picture of who?'

'Susan Hillfield! I took a picture of them all on my phone at Lotty's birthday party. The police took the phone but I pinned the picture on the noticeboard.'

Knight pictured the cork board on the side panel of the staircase. He was sure he would have noticed the picture if it had been there.

'I think it must have been taken down before I arrived. But if you printed it from the office computer it'll be on my copy of the hard drive.'

She confirmed that she had. The picture itself would not solve the case, but to have it in his possession was a coup of sorts. The glow intensified.

When it was time for him to go, she leaned over and kissed him unbidden on the cheek, thanking him profusely and urging him to take care of himself. He walked on a cloud back to the prison gates, convinced that he was within an inch of winning her back. Perhaps he had done so already, if the tenderness of her farewell was anything to go by. Either way, it would be put beyond doubt when he found Susan Hillfield. He would hunt her down to the ends of the earth, sparing no sacrifice and giving no quarter. Pausing only to retrieve the bag of weed he had hidden in the toilet, he stepped out into the street a man reborn.

Fran too left the room on something of a cloud. She was not about to march through the prison gates, but the depression that had been creeping up on her was gone. Reflecting on the sudden reversal in her fortunes, it occurred to her that she still had one gift left to open, in the form of the visit from Mr Briggs.

* * *

The row of lock-up garages was in a small private car park between a church and a block of flats. Overlooked at the rear by a trio of elm trees, it had an air of tranquillity and orderliness that made it a good place for storing stolen goods.

Bullock sat in a car across the road, lighting a cigarette from the glowing stump of its predecessor. His consumption had soared of late, ever since he had seen the CCTV picture of Knight with Merv in A&E, and another with Barbara Dawson. Further enquiries revealed approaches by Knight to Carol O'Brien and the Baldwins. Antonia Baldwin had called at the station to insist that Knight be arrested, provoking ribald comments from Bullock's colleagues about his chances with her. Picturing again the magnificent arse he made a mental note to look her up once Knight had been dealt with. At the Norfolk Terrace the foreign cow had been reluctant to help at first, but when he threatened to arrest her for obstruction she grudgingly identified Merv from the hospital photo.

The discovery that Knight had not only stitched him up with the hookers but was also interfering with his case called for a response. Yet for several days he had been caught between two fears. If he did nothing, Knight would encroach further into his territory, inventing red herrings for some smartarse barrister to dangle in front of a gullible jury. But if he moved against him he faced the humiliation of the photos going viral. The possibility that Fran might be innocent did not enter his mind.

In the end, it was the dread of losing the case that prevailed. There was no worse sin, in his eyes and those of his colleagues whose opinion mattered, than to let a slam-dunk conviction slip through your fingers. If it came to it, the photos could be put down to the wild demands of an ill-chosen girlfriend he had since dumped. He would claim he had been carried away in the heat of the moment and express his deep disappointment at her treachery. On the bright side he had a shrewd idea that many of his male colleagues would secretly admire him.

However, he had as yet no means of retaliation that were severe enough. The injury to the policeman at the hospital was not deliberate and a conviction for criminal damage would result merely in a fine. He wanted a lot more than that. There were people who would happily supply a beating in return for favours past and future, but there was a risk that the trail would lead back to him, especially if Knight died. Having said that, the thought of investigating his death appealed to him.

At last he received the call to say that the target was on his way. He alerted the uniforms in the next street and settled back to watch.

Hanrahan had been offered a quantity of games consoles from a warehouse on the retail estate. Having accepted enough of them to gain the thief's confidence he had tipped off his master over another session at Kalibanz.

A builder's van drove into the car park and discharged its burly occupant, a conman who had served time for charging fortunes to his elderly victims in exchange for spurious house repairs. For this Bullock bore him no ill will, though it would be a different matter if the contents of the garage were not worth his while.

When the man went into one of the garages Bullock called in the uniforms. Bev would not be among them. He was staying well away from her, biding his time until he was ready, and had pulled strings to keep her off the operation. When the plods arrived a few moments later he let them go in first in case it got physical; far better to wade in after they had taken the edge off, which was what they were for.

His spirits fell as he entered the garage. Far from the Aladdin's Cave he had hoped for, there were no more than a dozen console boxes stacked against the side wall. The warehouse had reported that a hundred were missing; either the rest had been shifted already or they were lying to up the insurance. He didn't care, all he knew was that he'd be tied up in paperwork for many hours in exchange for a result that would barely be noticed, just like the dead junkie still waiting to be identified.

The builder meanwhile was claiming that the consoles belonged to a friend who had asked him to store them and then gone abroad. Doubly irritated, because the ploy often worked, Bullock told the uniforms to take him away.

The consoles were the latest version of a system he already owned. In more favourable conditions he might have been tempted to go for an upgrade, but he could hardly walk out with a box under his jacket. Instead he worked his way along the shelves at the back, which contained tools and building paraphernalia. He had no interest in DIY, but there might be something small of high value, or even cash if he was lucky. You never knew, and criminals didn't complain when incriminating evidence went missing.

On the top shelf was a box with a paint roller sticking out. He took it down and went through the contents: a couple of tins of gloss, a few trays and several new brushes. He picked one up. The head was four inches wide, so it would fit into his pocket easily. He was considering taking it just on principle when he noticed that the handle was loose. Exasperated to be denied even this modest trophy, he pulled the handle from the bristle casing. With it came a small plastic bag, stuffed full of white powder. Checking first that he was unobserved, he opened the bag and dipped a finger in. The tang of cocaine on his tongue was unmistakeable.

He opened the other brushes and found four bags in all, getting on for a couple of hundred grammes he guessed. Either the building trade was going exceptionally well, or his prisoner was diversifying into new markets. Much more to the point, there was now a result worth having.

Feeling better disposed towards the man, he was about to have him brought back in when an even more pleasing thought struck him. Two hundred grammes had to be worth a three-year stretch, and he could think of someone far more suitable to serve it.

* * *

175

Chapter Twenty-Three

The Old Admiral Tavern stood at the end of a silent grey terrace not far from where Ryan had lived. Surveying the scene from his tattered sign, the ancient mariner would have been correct in concluding he had come down in the world, confronted as he was by a closed-down builder's merchant and a chicken shop that would soon be going the same way. At the back of the pub, had he been able to see it, was a slab of concrete that claimed to be a beer garden, and beyond it was a small adventure playground. The latter boasted a pirate ship of which he would have disapproved.

Regarding the pub's clientele, the Admiral would have felt marginally more positive, in that some of them might once have been useable fodder for a press gang. Previously the haunt of fishermen, the building that bore his name now provided a habitat for predators of a different kind, one of whom had been Ryan. According to Jen, this was the place where he had first met his mystery client.

He was as certain as he could be that the client was the woman in sunglasses, but it was hard to square her with the image of Susan Hillfield on the memory stick. Although the shape of the face was right, it was impossible to judge her build under the heavy coat. The hair was different too, though she could have been wearing a wig.

He had judged it better that they go in separately, so Merv waited in the car while he crossed the road. He held Knight's acting abilities in high regard, though on this occasion felt he was pushing his luck.

As Knight entered, the eyes of half a dozen afternoon drinkers turned to him as one. A trio of feral youths were playing pool while a small group of older men sat at the bar, listlessly drip-feeding their beer bellies. The landlady was a skeletal woman of an indeterminate age, who according to Bev, had run the place more or less singlehanded since her husband died. She had a son doing time – for fighting, she claimed, though everyone knew it was for the images on his computer.

She took a sip of her brandy and focused through rheumy eyes on the grizzled creature in the faded CND T-shirt.

'Large vodka, love,' he asked, in a faltering voice that he hoped was not overdone. He had needed a good few hours of YouTube to achieve a passable pastiche of Keith Richards, as good a model as any. She seemed to be buying it.

'Here you go, darlin',' she rasped. There was a sadness about her, a sense of defeat and tiredness in her eyes that no amount of mascara could disguise. Her face was hidden behind a wall of make-up that gave her the appearance of a painted doll, in contrast to the wizened skin on the backs of her hands.

'Nice place you've got here,' said Knight before she could turn away. 'Friend of mine told me about it.'

He had hoped she would ask who the friend was, enabling him to introduce the topic of Ryan's mystery client, but instead she replied dispiritedly, 'It's not what it used to be.'

'It looks alright to me.' He glanced around at the faded prints of sailing ships and the beer-stained carpet. 'What was it like before, then?'

She remained silent, contemplating better times. Shaking her head sorrowfully, she looked in the direction of the pool table.

'We didn't have that sort in here. Scum. Never done a day's work in their lives.'

Merv was by now at a table by a window in the far corner of the room, apparently engrossed in *Racing Post* but ready for action if needed. He was also keeping an eye on the car. Someone had broken a window in the night, although as far as they could tell nothing had been stolen. If anything, it made the damage more annoying.

A skinhead in a vest emerged from the staircase at the back of the bar.

'Barrel's back on, gran,' he mumbled as he rejoined the pool players. Knight had wondered who did the heavy lifting for her.

'Nice boy,' he said approvingly.

She pursed her lips as she watched him with his friends. It was obvious she didn't like the company he kept. Knight's instinct told him that she was not attempting to hide anything. She gave an impression of going through the motions, pickled against whatever further misfortune might come her way. When she emptied her glass and weaved her way to the optics for another dip into the profits, he moved to the table next to the pool players and waited until the game was finished.

'Anyone want to play for a pint?' He slurred his words enough to suggest incompetence but not outright drunkenness. Although the invitation was offered as if to one and all, he was looking at the grandson, who had a habit of clasping his arms about himself as if it were cold.

The skinhead inspected Knight, detecting easy meat. Only a real git would wear a stetson, especially one that was falling to bits.

'Yeah, alright,' he said. 'You got a quid for the table?'

Knight obliged and they started to play. His opponent made no attempt at conversation and swiftly racked up an unassailable lead. The others watched with amusement for a while, then got bored and went outside to smoke.

'Been a while since I played,' Knight ventured at length.

The skinhead paid no attention and sank another two balls in quick succession before narrowly missing the third.

Knight had not sunk a single ball yet, and even though he had not planned to win he was irked by his inability to get into the game. He felt unstable as he leaned into the table, straining to bend his back and get his eyes behind the ball. It was an easy shot into the middle pocket, which he missed by a fraction but in so doing sent the cue ball into the black. They both dropped into the corner pocket, bringing the game to a humiliating close.

'Bollocks,' he cursed, with no need for pretence. 'Fancy another one? Double or quits?'

Having earned the price of a pint in little over five minutes, the victor assented readily.

'Nice boozer this,' Knight began his opening gambit anew. 'Mate of mine told me about it.'

The youth muttered something unintelligible and went on playing.

'Yeah, old friend from the music business.'

This produced a flicker of interest. He stopped in mid-shot and considered Knight anew.

'You in the music business?'

'Was. Session musician, no one you've ever heard of.' He trailed off quietly, not wishing to provoke detailed enquiries about his career.

'What did you play?'

'Bass guitar.' Knight raised his glass in a toast. 'Happy days.'

The skinhead smiled for the first time.

'Bass, that's cool.'

It did feel cool. The spirit of complacent hedonism appealed to him, a welcome respite from the disquiet that had crept up since his return from London. For all the optimism he had experienced in Fran's presence, he knew that the case hung by a thread. Somewhere in the pub he had to find the link to Ryan's mystery client or for all practical purposes he would have reached another dead end.

'You still play?'

'Not any more, not since me fingers went.'

The skinhead looked at him with a discernible shred of sympathy. Knight pressed on.

'You here a lot then, helping your gran?'

'Yeah, most days.'

It was a crumb of hope. Glancing around as if to check that no one was in earshot, he said quietly,

'My mate said you could get good gear in here. I've got money if you know anyone.'

For a moment he feared he had made his move too soon. The skinhead missed his shot and scrutinised Knight closely.

'What makes you think I know anyone?' he asked, also glancing around.

'Never said you did son. Only...' he paused, and dropped his voice. 'The filth's cracking down in Brighton where I come from. My guy got put away.'

The skinhead was still staring at him, weighing risk against opportunity.

'You'd have to come back later,' he said, 'but it depends if you can make it worth my while.'

There was a discussion about paying a sizeable amount in advance which was eventually resolved when Knight produced a twenty as down payment on a finder's fee, with a promise of more to come. Then he played and missed again but didn't care. He was in.

* * *

As darkness fell, Bullock waited in his car in the side road next to Knight's building. His eyes were still sore.

The day had started badly. Well before sunrise he had entered the residents' parking bays behind the flats with a brick in a bag. The plan was simple enough. He would break into Knight's car and hide the cocaine under the driver's seat; in and out in thirty seconds. All would have been well had an insomniac dog walker not seen him as he prepared to strike. An ill-tempered woman at the best of times, she had been seething all day at the third cancellation of her operation for diverticulitis. The sight of a thug in a balaclava smashing a car window tipped her over, or rather was just what she needed. She accosted him furiously, careless of the risk to her octogenarian frame. When he swore at her she dosed him liberally with the pepper spray she had kept unopened in her bag for years and had been longing to use. She also managed to kick him in the groin, despite the discomfort this caused to her lower intestine, and watched with satisfaction when her equally bad-tempered Jack Russell bit his calf as he fled.

Bullock had driven home through a mist of rage and pain. He lay with a wet towel on his face until it was time to go to work, where he found some small satisfaction in intimidating a Pakistani landlord who claimed to know the dead junkie. The pleasure was short-lived when it became clear that the man could provide no details other than a name and the existence of a grandfather, which meant more work for him. In his fragile state, it did not occur to him to ask for the grandfather's description. As soon as he could, he had driven back to Knight's flat and waited.

A van was parking a few spaces ahead. Bullock's mood lifted a notch as Merv dismounted and made for the front entrance. A few minutes later he returned with Knight and they went together to the residents' parking bays. He noted with approval that Knight seemed frail and doddery compared to the last time he had seen him. For some reason he was wearing a cowboy hat.

* * *

'One thing I can't get my head around,' said Merv as they left the seafront, 'is whether she knew Ryan before they met in the pub, or if she just went there looking for smack and he was the first person she ran into.'

They had discussed every other permutation of what might have transpired between Ryan and his killer, but this was an angle Knight had not considered.

'I don't know,' he replied at length. 'Does it make a difference?'

'I'm not saying it does. But isn't it a bit odd that they go to all the trouble with the fake address and everything but they end up buying from someone who's connected to the home? Was that deliberate, or were they unlucky?'

Knight pondered the conundrum. It made little sense to pick a dealer who regularly visited the very place the crime was to be committed, unless he was already part of the conspiracy. But if he was, it made equally little sense to buy from him in a public place. It seemed more likely that the meeting had been unplanned.

'You're right, it doesn't add up. Maybe they didn't know he worked at the home because they were never in the garden. Susan Hillfield spent most of her time in her room and her son, if that's who he was, only came a couple of times a week to take her out.'

'So, if that's true, ending up with Ryan was their one little bit of bad luck, and our one bit of good luck, because if it wasn't for him we wouldn't have jack shit.'

Not that they did have much more than jack shit, Knight reflected. He stifled the doubting voice as they entered the warren of terraces. Visible life had been thin on the ground in daytime, but now it was entirely absent. They drove past the Old Admiral Tavern and parked opposite the playground, where the ghostly outline of the pirate ship loomed out of the darkness.

'Remember,' said Merv, 'you've got to get them into the garden.'

* * *

The bar was busier than before. The pool table was now occupied by a girl in her teens and a sunburnt man with a tattoo of a spider on his neck. A small child slumbered nearby in a pushchair, a soggy crisp clasped in its fingers.

Knight's erstwhile opponent sat in a corner beside a small man he guessed to be Filipino or Vietnamese. There was an empty chair to which the skinhead directed him with a discreet nod. Not wishing to appear over-keen, he went to the bar first, where the ancient landlady was less than welcoming but asked no questions. He felt her eyes following him as he went to her grandson's table and sat down.

'Cheers boys, appreciate you coming.'

'No worries,' said the skinhead without emotion. 'This is Ramil.'

Ramil was doing well for himself by the look of it, with a Rolex on his wrist and a wafer-thin leather jacket on his back. He was in his thirties, or perhaps a little older given the flecks of grey in his hair.

'Nice to meet you, son,' Knight greeted him.

He held out his hand and Ramil took it as briefly as possible. He stared intimidatingly, doubtless making an early claim to dominance in the negotiation that was to follow.

'Ramil's got some questions,' the go-between said.

'You go right ahead, son, can't be too careful these days.'

He could see that Ramil didn't like being called 'son'.

'Why you come here, to this pub?' he asked ill-humouredly.

'It's like I explained to the lad here,' Knight replied calmly, 'a good mate of mine come in here about a month ago. Kathy, nice-looking woman – maybe you saw her.'

Ramil turned to the skinhead. 'You know her?'

The boy shook his head, which was not surprising. The timing was a guess, and it didn't matter what Knight called her, nobody used their real name when they bought from strangers. Reassured by the nicotine stains on Ramil's fingers, he suggested a move outside.

Asserting the prerogative of age, Knight pointed with his stick to a table from which there was a clear line of sight to the top platform of the pirate ship, not twenty yards distant.

Merv was relieved to see them. Not wishing to draw attention to himself by appearing twice at the pub in one day, he had identified the ship as a vantage point from which to observe proceedings and intervene quickly if there was trouble. He adjusted the reception from Knight's fake hearing aid, which was stronger now they were outside.

'Yeah so, my mate,' Knight was saying as they lit up, 'nice-looking bird in her forties. You might have seen her, she told me she scored off this young bloke. Now what was his name?' He paused, apparently deep in thought. 'That's right, it was Ryan.'

To his satisfaction, the pair looked at each other sharply. The boy was about to say something when Ramil cut in.

'Ryan not around, he gone,' he said dismissively.

They clearly knew. Knight wondered if Jen had talked, and to whom. If this was Ryan's regular haunt there was every chance the skinhead knew her too. He was well aware of the risk that she might show up, but there was nothing he could do about it.

'That's a shame. What happened, he didn't get nicked did he?'

Ramil maintained a perfect poker face.

'No, he move away, not in Eastbourne any more.' Plainly not given to small talk, he added, 'You want buy, you buy from me.'

Knight nodded sagely, wondering where Ramil fitted into the picture. Was he a bystander or a player?

'How much you charging?'

'How much you buy?'

'Half a gramme to start with, see what it's like first.'

The skinhead looked disappointed. If he was hoping for a commission it wouldn't be much.

'Eighty,' said the Filipino.

Knight saw a way to bring the conversation back to the woman without arousing their suspicion. He winced for Ramil's benefit and said, 'I'm not a rich man, son. Kath said she only paid fifty.'

The Filipino frowned irritably. 'She tell you wrong, Ryan charge her more.'

Knight sensed his pulse rising. 'Hang on,' he said, 'how do you know that?'

Ramil was losing patience. 'Because he always buy from me. He get money up front then he charge his own price, maybe rip her off – you lucky you come to me!'

Still playing the canny consumer, Knight turned to the skinhead.

'How much did he charge her then?'

The boy turned to Ramil, as if asking permission to reply. Ramil shrugged indifferently.

'Hundred.'

Knight affected disbelief.

'A hundred!? Did you actually see this?'

'Course I fucking did, I was on the door for him in case the filth come!'

Knight rejoiced inwardly but maintained his air of incredulity.

'Well, fuck me,' he exclaimed. 'And you saw them too?' he asked Ramil.

'No!' snapped the dealer. 'You buy now or I go. Eighty pound!'

'It'll have to be a quarter then, that's all I've got enough for.'

Irked by the paucity of the deal, Ramil produced a small bag and took the money.

'You call me on this number.' He handed Knight a scrap of paper. As an afterthought he gave the skinhead a ten and left before he had a chance to object.

'I thought you was going to buy more,' he complained resentfully. 'You said you had money!'

If only. Knight took out yet another twenty.

'Maybe I will if it's any good. Here's what I owe you.'

The skinhead took the note without speaking and got up to go.

'Hang on son, I might have a bit more for you.'

On tenterhooks, Merv watched as the boy sat down again.

'It's like this,' he heard Knight say. 'I've got a bit of a problem with Kath.'

Merv didn't catch the rest. There had not been an opportunity to replace the shattered window or fit an alarm, so he was keeping a weather eye on the car. The man who had walked slowly past it a minute ago was now returning, his face obscured by a hood. After looking up and down the street he started unpicking the tape covering the broken glass. Although loath to leave his station, Merv decided that the situation in the garden posed no imminent threat. He climbed down to the bottom deck and sprinted to the road.

The skinhead meanwhile was digesting the surprising news that Kath, not that he recalled the name being used, was romantically linked to the old fart sitting opposite him. She was a fit-looking woman for her age as he recalled, too old for him, of course, but way too young for an ancient git in a stupid hat. He had never met anyone from the music business before and was beginning to think it wasn't what it was cracked up to be, if this was how they turned out.

'The thing is this,' Knight was saying, 'last week she pissed off somewhere, and now she's not answering my calls. I reckon she's got another bloke.' He paused and lowered his head as if ashamed. 'I didn't want to mention it before, it's not an easy thing when you're my age. But if you can take me to her, I'll make it well worth your while.'

Everything depended on the answer. They could be within a hair's breadth of finding Ryan's killer, but if the skinhead hesitated or prevaricated it would mean he was lying.

Merv by now was catching up on the lumbering figure ahead of him. A shout had been enough to send him off before he could open the door, which meant there was no compelling reason to pursue him. But Merv's limited forbearance towards the scum of the earth had been sorely tested of late. Another minute's absence from his post felt justified if it led to proper retribution. He might not have thought the same had he known it was Bullock and the bag in his gloved hand contained a brick.

Bullock was in meltdown, knowing he risked instant identification if the balaclava were removed in a fight. He had lost badly in his previous encounter with Merv and didn't fancy his chances any better in a rematch. Only twenty yards separated them as he turned a corner beside a high hedge. He stopped and turned, ready to swing the bag.

Merv was lucky, in the sense that the blow would have cracked his skull had it been the sharp edge of the brick that struck his temple rather than the flat surface. He barely glimpsed his assailant before collapsing.

Dropping the bag, Bullock ran.

* * *

Knight was alone in the pub garden. In his heart he knew it was over. He had known it the moment the skinhead paused uncertainly before claiming, hesitantly at first but then with mounting insistence, that he knew people who were sure to be in contact with Kathy, and to whom he would take Knight in return for a hefty advance payment. He became evasive and defensive when asked who these people were and how they knew her. As his claims became less credible, so his demands for payment grew more aggressive, until there was no doubt left in Knight's mind that he was lying. Finally he stormed off, shouting angry insults about Knight's age and sexual proclivities.

It didn't seem especially odd to him that Merv had not responded when he called. He would have heard the conversation and was doubtless licking his wounds too, not wishing to talk yet. Nor for that matter was Knight.

He went to the rear door and opened it a fraction. The landlady had her back to him, serving a customer. In the far corner her grandson was with some of his companions from earlier in the day. Sitting beside them was Jen.

With a sense of foreboding he opened the door a little wider and looked quickly into the other half of the room. Along with the chance of Jen showing up they had assessed the threat posed by Boyle if he was with her. Unhinged though he was, they had decided he would not resort to violence in a public place, and that Merv would make short work of him if he tried. To his relief there was no sign of him, though Merv was not there either.

The door to the street was no more than ten feet away. If Jen didn't turn in his direction he would be out in seconds without incident.

He realised his mistake as soon as he broke cover. The landlady moved aside from the customer she was serving. It was Boyle. He stared blankly at Knight as he passed by, then gaped in astonishment.

Knight pounded down the empty pavement. Even if Merv was not at the car he could lock himself in and let Boyle do his worst. If he tried to attack him through the broken window he would simply drive away, dragging him along the street if need be.

It was a race he was never going to win. Boyle was upon him with the ease of a leopard taking down an antelope. He slammed Knight against the side of a parked car and kicked his legs out from under him. Then he drew a thin blade from a sheath on his ankle.

'Remember me?' he leered.

He sniffed noisily and wiped his nose with his sleeve before unleashing a boot into Knight's chest.

'You know how much grief you given me, you fucking toerag?'

He started to gabble, his words swept along in a flood of bile.

'You know how angry I get when people do that?' he shouted. 'You wanna see what I do when I get angry? You wanna know what I do?'

Struggling for breath, Knight remembered. He did ears.

Boyle grabbed at Knight's left ear and thrust the blade towards it. Knight caught his wrist an instant before the point reached its target.

'Fucking let go of me!' Boyle screamed. 'Fucking let go or I'll do you properly!'

Unleashing a torrent of threats, Boyle used his other hand to try to break Knight's grip. The blade bobbed about erratically, nicking the rim of his ear more than once.

Knight's stick had fallen well out of his reach. He scrabbled for his car keys, but they were deep in his trouser pocket. He tried his jacket pockets, hoping vainly for a biro, anything with a point.

His fingers alighted on a ball of something that seemed to change shape beneath their touch. It was a bunched chain that led to a jagged object in the corner, where it had lain forgotten for nearly a week.

He withdrew the leaf-shaped pendant and clasped it tightly so that the end protruded like a miniature dagger. His grip on Boyle's wrist was weakening, the blade tearing against his skin as the arm-wrestle began to go against him.

He would only get one shot. The eyes were the obvious target, but Boyle's arms were in the way. It would have to be a sideways blow, but into what? The ear. An ear for an ear. He swung.

He would have missed had Boyle not shifted forward at that moment to bring his full weight to bear. Two inches of jewel-studded metal, tapering to a fine point, entered his left ear and pierced through to the drum.

Boyle sprang back as if electrocuted and staggered about like a drunk, his hand pressed tight to his ear. Knight hauled himself up on the door mirror as Boyle rounded on him, waving the knife wildly. He lunged clumsily, scraping Knight's cheek.

Grasping the chain in both hands, Knight forced it down over his head and around his neck, then turned his wrists until they would go no further. He was convinced that the links would snap, but they held long enough for Boyle to abandon the knife and claw frantically at Knight's fingers. Still the chain held. Boyle's eyes began to bulge. Knight maintained his grip for what seemed an eternity until, with a prolonged gurgle, Boyle sank to his knees. Another minute would kill him; he counted to twenty and let him slump to the ground. As an afterthought he wiped the wrap of heroin clean of his fingerprints and put it in Boyle's pocket.

Ten minutes later Merv became aware of someone slapping his face and repeating his name. He opened his eyes to find Knight kneeling over him, his face streaked with blood. Then he was slumped in the car while Knight felt his skull and shone a torch in his eyes. He was asked to recite the alphabet quickly, then backwards, then test his motor skills by calling Knight's phone. Bit by bit, the memory of a hooded man flickered to life, a chase and a blow from something heavy in a bag. Eventually Knight seemed satisfied and they drove away.

It wasn't until they reached the seafront that he thought to ask about the blood on Knight's face. He expected to hear there had been a fight with the skinhead and that their long quest had ended in failure, so he was surprised by Knight's reply.

'Wait until we get inside. I've got something to show you.'

* * *

Chapter Twenty-Four

Knight held the magnifying glass under the desk lamp. A moth fluttered insistently around the bulb, ignoring or forgetting his attempts to make it withdraw.

'There, do you see?'

Merv's mind had cleared, more or less. There was a large bruise above his cheekbone but the throbbing had stopped. He had suffered worse in drunken brawls at Aldershot.

The images on the back of the pendant resolved into some symbols and an inscription. He didn't know what the symbols meant, but he could read the inscription.

'With all my love, Kitty.' He stared at Knight blankly. 'So who the fuck's Kitty?'

'That depends on where it came from, but she could be a wealthy lady. Look at those marks.'

Merv squinted at the hallmarks.

'The one on the left tells you it's high purity platinum. The chain's platinum too, which is why it didn't break. The one beside it tells you that the markings were done twenty years ago, but the really interesting one comes next.'

Merv could make out the letters F.E. entwined in an intricate embrace.

'So what does that stand for, "fucking expensive"?'

'Not unless it's the name of a jeweller. It's the maker's mark, it tells you who made it.'

Merv frowned. 'OK, so we have a rich bird who gave an expensive bit of jewellery to one of the old biddies. Where does that get us?'

It was the question Knight had been mulling ever since he had dragged Boyle behind some bushes in the park then sat in the car peering at the pendant. As he drove off in search of Merv he reflected grimly on the lapse of memory that had allowed it to lie unexamined in his pocket for the best part of a week.

'The curious thing about an expensive piece like this is why Ryan didn't sell it? We know he needed money, so why did he give it to Jen?'

'Because it was the price of getting his leg over? He'd have had to be desperate, though.'

Knight had thought of this too and discounted it.

'There's no way he'd have put sex before paying for heroin. But suppose he stole it on the night of the murders? He might not have been that bright, but perhaps he wasn't stupid enough to leave a trail that would make him the prime suspect.'

Merv saw the ray of light that had given Knight fresh hope.

'So, who did he nick it from?'

'He told me he went into an empty room on the ground floor. I'm betting it was Susan Hillfield's.'

Merv studied the maker's mark with renewed interest.

'So F.E., whoever he is, made this thing for Kitty, whoever she is. And if Kitty gave it to Susan Hillfield, then she must know who she is.'

Merv sat back and closed his eyes. The effort of thinking had made his head throb again.

'How do we find F.E.?'

'I'll go to a few jewellers,' Knight said casually. 'Sooner or later I'll find one who recognises the mark.'

Merv looked at him suspiciously.

'What's with the "I"? You thinking of going alone?'

Knight hesitated. He had been putting the moment off and had reached the point where it could be delayed no further.

'I'm not sure it's right for you to continue with this.'

'You what?'

'You're lucky you weren't brain-damaged back there. It's not right for you to be taking that kind of risk.'

Merv was looking at him in disbelief.

'And how exactly do you think you're gonna do this without me?'

He caught the tremble in Merv's voice.

'With great difficulty, I admit. But this isn't your fight, you know it isn't.'

Merv exploded.

'Do you think I could be the fucking judge of what's my fight and what isn't!? What do you take me for if you think I'd pull out now?!'

He stormed off, leaving Knight wondering what raw nerve he had touched. It occurred to him that he might still be embarrassed about the panic attack in the van at the hospital, but then he saw it went deeper than that. In Merv's own eyes he was no longer Knight's occasional accomplice but a brother soldier. He had tried to take that away from him, and it had stung.

He was standing at the terrace door, smoking.

'I'm sorry,' said Knight. 'I didn't mean to insult you.'

Merv nodded, but didn't look at him.

'I'm not a mug, Tom.' His voice still trembled. 'I can tell something's up when there's two attempts at breaking into the car in one day. I'm not sleepwalking into anything here.'

'I didn't think you were, I…'

Merv held up his hand for silence. He turned and stared at Knight with an intensity that was alarming.

'Whatever goes down from here on, I am going to be there with you. Do you understand that?'

There was no denying him, nor did Knight wish to.

'I do. And I'm grateful, please believe me when I say that.'

Merv appeared to relent.

'Alright. You go there again, I'll hide your stick somewhere the sun don't shine, you daft bugger.'

Knight permitted himself a wry smile.

'I would expect no less of you.'

And with that it was over.

'Good. Now go and roll us a nightcap.'

As he sat down at the coffee table, Knight realised he still had the pendant in his hand. He ran a finger down the diamonds and emeralds, pressing it against the sharp point that had saved his life. He shared Merv's conviction that the two attempts on the car were not a coincidence. They were heading into treacherous terrain and he was glad that he would not be facing it alone.

As to the pendant, it might prove to be no more than a temporary reprieve. But there was something in the way the tiny stones sparkled in the lamplight that tempted him to believe otherwise.

* * *

F.E. proved easier to find than Knight expected. With the aid of a shave and a linen suit, the crumbling rocker gave way to a slow-witted member of Eastbourne's upper crust bent on the purchase of an expensive anniversary gift. Recognising a good thing when he saw one, the manager of the first shop was more than happy to oblige the additional request to value a family heirloom inherited from a recently deceased cousin. A trade database identified the mark of Felix Edelman within seconds, after which the highly promising customer seemed to lose interest in the bracelets he had been inspecting.

Not only was Felix Edelman alive and well, he was in Eastbourne.

Tucked away behind a parade of shops in the town centre was an enclave of narrow streets and terraced cottages known as Little Chelsea, though unlike the full-size version in London it counted no footballers or hedge fund managers among its occupants. Here, accessible by appointment only, were the studio and showroom of a Master Craftsman in Timeless Treasure, or so his website claimed.

As they waited to be buzzed in, Merv ran a finger over the white surface of the front door. It was cold to the touch.

'Solid steel,' he murmured, conscious that the camera in the portico was probably recording their voices as well. 'No one gets in and out of here in a hurry if our Felix doesn't want them to.'

Merv was wearing a chauffeur's uniform. Beside him, Knight adjusted his MCC tie and removed the Panama. He enjoyed posing as a member of the filthy rich. It seemed to come naturally, allowing him to toy with the fantasy that this might yet be his destiny.

Behind a second steel door a young woman in a severe black dress introduced herself as Chloe. Merv's part in the charade now over, Knight dismissed him with a lordly air and followed her down a short corridor. The showroom was in the style of a salon, with antique furniture tastefully arranged around glass display cases. She thoughtfully selected a high-backed Chippendale chair that would be easy on his legs and went to fetch tea. She seemed to have no qualms about leaving him alone and it was not hard to see why. Each display case was fitted with an alarm, while a quartet of cameras nestled in the ornately carved cornices.

Chloe returned with fine bone china on a silver tray. She offered him milk and sugar, but he decided that his discriminating alter ego would prefer lemon. He watched as she deftly placed a slice in his cup with a pair of delicate silver tongs.

'Mr Edelman will be joining us shortly, but perhaps you'd like me to show you some of his work first. I believe you said you might be interested in a necklace?'

She had a deep, confident voice that suggested a familiarity with horses and trust funds.

They went to a display cabinet containing examples of the master's oeuvre. There were gold chains embedded with diamonds and sapphires, loops of platinum encrusted with rubies and emeralds, strings of pearls the size of garden peas. Little of it was to his taste but the reek of money was pungent. There was one piece he liked, a platinum halter with four rows of square-cut diamonds. He imagined the expression on Fran's face were she to see it lying on her pillow one Christmas morning, and how she would look at him when he laid it on her neck and did up the clasp.

'This is rather good,' he mused, as if to himself. He held it up to the window and let the light play through the stones.

'You know, one shouldn't rush into these things, but I think this could be the one. Before I get carried away I suppose I ought to ask you how much it is.'

Learning that the price was more than the value of his flat, he made a show of being pleasantly surprised.

'Really?' he said, nodding appreciatively. 'I wish I'd known about Mr Edelman earlier.'

He caught the glint in Chloe's eye. It was time to roll the dice.

'Which reminds me, there's something else I must ask you about before I forget.'

Replacing the halter in the cabinet, he produced the leaf pendant and handed it to her.

'I picked this up at a jewellery fair in London. It's a magnificent piece; in fact, it's the reason I thought of you for my wife's necklace. But can you confirm it's definitely one of yours?'

Chloe took the unexpected turn of events smoothly in her stride.

'I'm sure it is,' she said brightly, inspecting the hallmarks. 'Before my time though, I'm afraid. Would you like me to check?'

'I'd be immensely grateful. You see…' he frowned, as if contemplating something disagreeable. 'When my wife and I are both gone I imagine my children will want to sell the collection, so I feel obliged to keep it well documented. What I really need is the provenance of the piece, who commissioned it, who owned it and so on. Would you be able to do that while I'm making my mind up about the necklace?'

'I'm sure I could find out for you. Would it be possible to leave it here for a day?'

Knight emitted a small grunt of irritation. He thought he saw Chloe flinch.

'Well, normally that would be fine, but we're off to the south of France tomorrow for a few months and I was hoping to get the provenance sorted out at the same time as my wife's necklace. Two birds with one stone sort of thing.'

It was her turn to hesitate. It was strictly against the rules to reveal a client's identity without their permission. On the other hand, she was within touching distance of a six figure sale. Eventually her public school education rode to the fore and she went for the money. Producing the thinnest of laptops from a bureau, she opened up the firm's archive while he wandered among the cabinets.

Given the price of the necklace, the stock had to be worth millions. From the very beginning he had believed that the murders were motivated by money. Here in the presence of boundless wealth he felt more sure of it than ever.

'I think I've found it.'

Knight crossed the room briskly, his pulse rising, but before he could reach the bureau Felix Edelman appeared in the doorway. He was a short, thin man in his sixties with delicate features and taut skin that could only be the work of a cosmetic surgeon. He also had dark, inquisitorial eyes that made Knight feel his mind was being read.

'Good morning,' he said in a silky voice. 'It's Mr Douglas isn't it? I do hope Chloe is looking after you.'

He came forward and shook Knight's hand with a surprisingly firm grip. As he did so he noticed the pendant beside the laptop.

'Ah, one of mine if I'm not mistaken.'

He picked it up and inspected it fondly. 'Have you brought it for a valuation?'

'Mr Douglas is actually interested in the diamond halter,' Chloe said pointedly. 'But he's also a collector, and he's asked me to look up the provenance of the pendant.'

Edelman's hitherto fixed smile wavered for an instant.

'I see. I take it you've asked the client for permission?'

Chloe confessed that she hadn't, explaining the urgent nature of the request and mentioning the necklace once more.

'Ah.'

Edelman was torn between a lifetime's habit of obsequiousness to the rich and his equally rigid rule never to divulge the merest snippet of information about them. Outwardly he betrayed not so much as a flicker of concern.

'I quite understand,' he reassured Knight in a tone designed to indicate compliance when none was forthcoming. 'But I'm sure you'd appreciate that we always ask for permission first in these cases. I'd be more than happy to call the client and make the request myself.'

Knight's mind raced. The call might indeed get him what he wanted, but if the request were refused the chances of getting Edelman to change his mind would be low. Beneath the obliging exterior he sensed a steeliness about the man; he would stick to his guns.

'You're absolutely right,' he replied approvingly. 'In fact, I should have thought of that myself. Call them whenever it's convenient.'

He felt sorry for Chloe, visibly squirming at the implied rebuke.

'Back to the important business. I'd like to take a look at those earrings as well.'

He pointed his stick at a cabinet behind the bureau. As far as he could see, Chloe had not closed the page. If he could get between the cabinet and the bureau he would have a direct line of sight to the screen.

While she unlocked the cabinet, he extolled the beauty of its contents to the creator, intending to drive the question of the pendant as far from his mind as possible. The tactic seemed to work, for Edelman lit up with pleasure at the praise heaped upon him. When he seemed sufficiently distracted Knight chanced a quick look at the screen, but although he could see the pendant the client details were too small for him to read.

'Now is there anything that perhaps catches your eye more than the rest?' Edelman purred.

Knight chose a pair of roses encrusted with tiny rubies that roughly matched the colour of the carpet. Chloe placed them in his hands, which had acquired a tremble not present before.

'Magnificent,' he declared, holding them up to the light. The trembling intensified, as if the excitement was too much for him, and the earrings fell to the floor beside the bureau.

'Oh my god!' he cried.

Before they had a chance to react he sank to his knees, sliding his hand down the stick to steady himself, and scrabbled on the floor. With his body masking the earrings from view, he flicked one of them under the bureau. As Chloe and Edelman knelt beside him, he pointed out where he thought it might be and left them to retrieve it, apologising profusely for his clumsiness.

Knight heaved himself up again, his knee protesting angrily despite the double dose of morphine he had injected. He considered it a small price to pay when his face reached the level of the screen and he was able to read the address of Catherine Elizabeth Cavanagh, though he had mixed feelings when he saw he would have to visit another care home.

***

196

Chapter Twenty-Five

Carol was down to her last bag of crisps. They were salt and vinegar, which she disliked, but they had come in a multipack on special offer. She thought about saving them for later but then discovered that she had opened the bag. It soon lay empty on the floor of the car among a dense carpeting of cake boxes and empty cans.

At first the cards had merely continued to confirm what they had revealed after Knight's visit, that destiny had at long last brought her its most precious gift. It was cause for celebration, and in the succeeding days she drifted happily on a current of Tesco Sauvignon Blanc, reliving the moment he had put his arms around her. Soon their first meeting was followed by others in which they made love on the roofs of Greek villas and chose furniture at Debenhams. Then had come the fateful encounter in the woods, throwing her into confusion. There had been nothing in the cards to indicate this, nor did they give any hint as to when he might appear again.

For situations such as these she had the dousing ring. She had last used it when Max disappeared, although not without difficulty. Several times it had directed her to points on the map where he was meant to be found, but he was never there when she arrived. For this she blamed herself; either her technique was at fault or she had not been quick enough. But the power of the ring was vindicated when he reappeared through the cat flap three days later.

The challenge was to keep her hand steady as she held the silver chain with the ring attached, slowly moving it over the city with her eyes closed. Sometimes the energy came in the guise of a pull, sometimes she could feel the chain swaying as the ring swirled around something that interested it. More than once she found herself being invited to pursue her quest in the sea but put this down to the way she'd folded the map.

She couldn't say the same when the ring directed her to the Arndale Shopping Centre. Here she was convinced she had found him in Smith's, and barged through the queue only to startle an elderly gentleman out shopping with his grandson. It happened again in Marks and Spencer, only this time the object of her attention had just entered a changing cubicle. He objected robustly when she pulled back the curtain, and she was ejected by security.

It was at the sewage works that she experienced serious doubt. She was disappointed enough that there was no sign of him, but what bothered her more was why he might be there at all. Surely the only people to be found at a sewage works were the people who worked there? There had to be more to him than that. And so she reverted to the cards.

They did not let her down. The appearance of The Star could only mean that truth and love were about to descend upon her, and the very next day she received the call from Bullock. The revelation that she had been deceived by a private investigator did not offend her in the least, indeed it added to his stature. It also explained his elusive nature, for wherever he went – including, quite legitimately, the sewage works – he would be slipping through the shadows, invisible to those who did not possess his skills. She pressed Bullock for the man's name and whereabouts, and subjected him to a torrent of abuse when he refused to tell her.

She rummaged among the remnants of her dwindling supplies and found a pack of economy sausage rolls. The third of these was about to meet its doom when Bullock came down from his flat again. She left it a few seconds before following, pleased with the thought that she was getting the hang of working in the shadows.

Adding urgency to her quest was his promise that the impostor would be made to pay for his actions, which meant it fell to her to stand between him and his prey. And if Bullock would not tell her who and where her lover was, he would lead her to him instead.

She nearly lost him when he turned onto the seafront. He was several cars ahead of her and the Friday evening traffic had not yet eased off. Several times in the past week she had been forced to give up and go home, unable to keep pace. It meant starting all over again, either at his flat or at the police station, where her quest had begun. Sustained by copious provisions, she clung to him like a limpet, fell off and returned to cling again.

She reached the front of the queue and gave the finger to a taxi driver who objected to her cutting in. To her relief she could see Bullock less than a hundred yards ahead, moving slowly towards the pier. He had come this way before but on both occasions she had lost him. This evening, however, she saw him turn into a side street beside a smart apartment block. Fearing she was about to lose him again, she turned the corner in a state of agitation only to find him parked and sitting in his car. Further down there was a space on the opposite side.

After the sausage rolls she would be down to the doughnuts and the mini Scotch eggs. The prospect of hunger disturbed her, so much so that she found herself eating the last sausage roll without intending to. She dealt out the cards onto the passenger seat, confident they would confirm that her quarry was nearby, and was rewarded for her faith when The Star appeared, followed immediately by The Lovers.

* * *

Chapter Twenty-Six

Montague Hall catered for the opposite end of the market from New Horizons. For close on ten thousand pounds a month its residents had the run of a Jacobean mansion in a quiet valley to the north of the Downs. An abundance of highly qualified staff catered for every conceivable need, while in the nursing wing the medical team rendered hospital visits redundant for all but the most complicated surgery. It would not be a bad place to live, it seemed to Knight, and not a bad place to die. But one had to be stinking rich, like Kitty Cavanagh.

It had taken hours of trawling before he found her, or at least a wealthy woman who seemed to fit the bill. Ten years ago the Cavanagh Centre had opened its doors in Brighton, with the declared aim of supporting LGBT teenagers through the tribulations of coming out. There was a picture of the eponymous benefactor, a frail woman who looked to be in her seventies then. She had provided two million pounds. How many Kitty Cavanaghs could there be with that kind of money? As to the source of her riches, the same article made mention of her grandfather, the founder of a private bank that still bore his name. With the aid of a genealogy site he was able to construct a family tree of sorts and conduct searches on her nearest relatives.

For all their riches, the Cavanaghs had not been blessed with much happiness. Kitty was the youngest of four children. Both her brothers had died on the beaches of Normandy, and her sister had perished in a light aircraft on the second day of her honeymoon in Kenya. The continuation of the line thus came to depend on Kitty, who remained resolutely single.

Knight wondered why there hadn't been a husband. Was it a fear of gold-diggers, or had she waited too long, believing perhaps that someone in her position should settle for nothing less than perfection? Either way, it followed that a large proportion of the family fortune would have found its way into her hands.

An alternative explanation for her spinsterhood presented itself in an oblique reference to an incident at Hampstead Ponds in London when she was in her twenties. It seemed that she and an unnamed woman had been arrested for an alleged affront to public morality. Although the charges were dropped, she left London and retreated to the family villa in Italy for several years. Taken together with her sponsorship of the Cavanagh Centre, the story suggested that Kitty Cavanagh might be gay, which in turn raised new questions about the recipient of the pendant.

'So now we've got a killer dyke on our hands. That makes a change.'

They were approaching Montague Hall along a gravel drive that meandered through an arboretum of redwoods and Scots pines. As they rounded the final bend the house came into view, its symmetrical facade of grey stone and mullioned windows proclaiming order and plenty. In front of it lay an immaculate lawn the size of several tennis courts.

It was Saturday morning. The visitors' car park was already filling up and the Skoda looked out of place wedged between a Jaguar and a Bentley. Not that it mattered, for the spendthrift Mr Douglas and his chauffeur had been replaced by plain Mr Evans and his long-suffering carer. To complete their anonymity they had switched plates before entering the estate. On private land there was no risk of a random check by a patrol car.

The story would be that they had found the pendant on the beach and wished to restore it to its rightful owner, Mr Evans having little confidence in the police to take the necessary trouble. It might, of course, seem odd for a man of his age and apparent respectability to hold the police in such low esteem, so he would be an eccentric, a borderline obsessive with too much time on his hands.

The entrance hall had the aplomb of a superior country house hotel, with settees arranged before a vast fireplace and oak panels hung with reassuring landscapes in weighty frames. At the reception desk a young blonde woman in a blazer sat beside a large Chinese vase full of lilies. A shiny enamel badge identified her as Vilma.

'Good morning, how may I help you?' She had a faint Scandinavian lilt.

Knight hadn't made an appointment. If Kitty Cavanagh was somehow mixed up in the conspiracy he didn't want to give notice of his arrival.

'Good morning to you too,' he declared, somewhat pompously. 'My name is Giles Evans and I have a piece of jewellery that I would like to return to one of your residents. This is my carer, by the way.' He motioned offhandedly to Merv, who was meant to be looking bored but was staring dreamily at Vilma's breasts.

He produced the pendant and showed her the inscription.

'There, Kitty Cavanagh. Would it be possible to speak to her, please?'

What was possibly a shadow of disquiet passed over her face, but the default smile returned so quickly he thought nothing of it.

'Please wait here, Mr Evans, I will be one minute.'

She came out from the counter and made her way between a pair of marble columns into a corridor linking the hall to the east wing. Knight was about to propose a move to the settees when a resident appeared through a matching pair of columns on the opposite side of the hall, shifting himself at a fair rate on a frame. He was smartly dressed in a tweed jacket and sharply creased slacks.

On seeing Knight he stopped and looked him up and down as if assessing his worth.

'Thinking of joining up, or just visiting?' he enquired in a reedy voice, though not without a measure of authority. Save for a few liver spots his face was chalky white, dotted with small scraps of tissue covering the morning's shaving wounds.

Knight confirmed that he was a mere visitor.

'Pity, we need more men here. Only two others apart from me and they're as mad as hatters.'

'You're outnumbered by the fair sex then. That's not always ideal, is it?' The exchanges across the tea table at New Horizons were fresh in Knight's memory.

'Outnumbered and surrounded. Still, what can you do? I bid you good day, gentlemen.'

Knight noticed that he was wearing a regimental tie. He was wondering how he paid the fees on an army pension when a wrathful cry pierced the silence.

'Mr Knight!'

Bearing down on them was a squat middle-aged woman in twin-set and pearls, whose general demeanour marked her as a wielder of power in the home's hierarchy.

'I beg your pardon?' he said, not finding it hard to look astonished.

'You are Tom Knight, a private investigator. We've been warned about you, and thanks to the alertness of my staff you've been stopped in time!'

Knight bristled credibly enough, though he knew the battle was lost before it had begun.

'Stopped in time for what? This is absolute nonsense, I've never heard of the man! Who on earth has told you this rubbish?'

She pursed her lips and scowled, jutting her chin out aggressively like an angry Pekinese.

'I am not at liberty to say, Mr Knight. But what I will say is that you fit the description exactly and if you don't leave immediately I shall call the police!'

* * *

She watched them from the entrance as they drove back down the drive. Knight had blustered and fumed, more out of stubbornness than any hope of turning the tables. It was a cardinal rule never to back down when a false identity failed, but the repeated threat of the police made retreat unavoidable.

'Who the fuck told them we were coming?'

Merv was unnerved by the encounter. Of the many deceptions they had contrived, none had been exposed so suddenly and unexpectedly. He was steering with his knees, fumbling agitatedly for a cigarette. Knight took the pack and lit up for them both, wishing they had brought something stronger.

'I haven't the faintest idea. The only people who know what we're doing are Bev and Fran, and even they don't know we're here. Bullock couldn't know unless he got an exact description of the pendant and went to see Edelman, and I don't buy that. Even if it was him, why make a tip-off anonymously? If she'd been warned by the police she'd have said so.'

He thought he glimpsed something moving between the trees, but it vanished from view as they rounded a bend.

'What about Edelman?'

Knight thought back to the end of his visit. Edelman and his assistant had not seen him look at the computer, though they could have worked out what he was doing. But he had departed on good terms, leaving them convinced that he would return the following morning to complete the purchase. Besides which, how could Edelman have found out his real name?

He saw the movement again.

'Stop the car!'

Some twenty yards from the drive the man they had seen in the hall was making his way towards a bench under a tree.

He looked up in alarm as he heard Knight approach, but then relaxed. 'Ah, it's you. I thought it was the Gestapo.'

Noting the puzzled reaction, he nodded to the cigarette in Knight's hand and produced a pack of his own.

'That bloody woman has her spies on my trail from dawn to dusk. I wouldn't be surprised if they're looking for me now.'

Knight reached for his lighter but the old man already had one in his hand, sucking greedily as the flames engulfed the tip of the cigarette.

'I keep telling them, if it hasn't got me by now it never will, and I don't care if it does. They won't listen, of course.'

He inhaled deeply and sat back, gazing up into the tree as he blew out a perfect ring of smoke. Knight watched appreciatively as it drifted up, like a halo taking leave of its owner.

'I haven't seen one as good as that for a while,' he said, 'but then one expects nothing less of the Sappers.'

The fugitive smoker smiled peacefully, savouring the bracing effect of the tar on his lungs.

'Not bad for eighty-nine. I suppose one should be grateful.' He took another puff. 'So you've done a bit of soldiering yourself by the sound of it?'

'Intelligence Corps mostly. Malaya, Germany, usual places. How about yourself?'

He ignored the question and peered at Knight curiously.

'One of them, eh? So what kind of intel are you after from me? I don't imagine you stopped just to pass the time of day.'

He was clearly nobody's fool. Knight decided there was no point in prevaricating; in any case, his cover was already broken.

'You're quite right, I'm a private investigator now. I was rather hoping to see Kitty Cavanagh, but I got the bum's rush from your delightful manager. Any idea how I might get hold of her?'

He had hoped that the reference to the manager would kindle a spark of complicity between them. Instead the old man let out a short sigh.

'I'm afraid I can't help you there. Kitty passed away a bit over a week ago.'

Knight felt the familiar thud of the brick wall. First Ryan, now her. To be the last lead in this investigation was apparently lethal.

'I'm so sorry, I had no idea. Was she a friend of yours?'

'Not really. She was a perfectly nice woman, of course, but when people lose their minds it's not possible to have a proper conversation with them. So you can't make friends.'

He shrugged with an air of resignation.

'Why did you want to see her?'

'I was hoping she could identify the owner of a piece of jewellery she once gave as a gift.'

He took out the pendant and passed it over. The old man held it in his palm, rubbing a finger lightly over the stones.

'Looks like the sort of thing she might have given. She was a very generous woman in her time from what I've heard. And very wealthy too, though you probably know that.'

He gave the pendant back.

'And why do you want to find this person, or is that none of my business? The name's Harding by the way,' he added, holding out his hand.

There had been a General Harding from the Royal Engineers who had made it to chief of staff while Knight was still serving, though they had never met. Idle gossip had it that his aristocratic wife had pulled strings to get him the job. It may or may not have been true, but it would explain where the money for the fees came from.

Knight had a sense that he wanted to trade information, not with a view to using it but to be part of the action in some small way.

'It's possible that whoever she gave it to could help me find a murderer. It's a long shot, but it's all I have at the moment.'

Harding's eyes widened.

'Kitty? Involved in a murder?' He shook his head. 'I don't think so old chap, not in her condition.'

205

'Well, that's the thing, I know very little about her. Would you mind if I asked what she died of?'

Enlivened by the prospect of a puzzle to be solved, the general opened up. Kitty Cavanagh had lived at Montague Hall for seven years. Her dementia was already apparent when she arrived, and as time passed it stripped away her ability to perform all but the most basic tasks. She had died of kidney failure after an illness lasting several months, mercifully unaware of the reason for her transfer to the hospital wing.

'Did you go to the funeral?'

'Half a dozen of us went, all from here. She had no family, you see.'

'Did anyone ever come to see her?'

Harding looked sombre.

'Not that I can remember. Even if they had it wouldn't have meant much to her.'

Knight thought of Brenda and wondered if Kitty had lived in a vibrant fantasy world or whether she sat staring into space like Sheila.

'So, who are your suspects?'

'The people I'm most interested in are Tim and Susan Hillfield. Probably not their real names, but do they mean anything to you?'

Harding thought long and hard.

'Can't say they do. Sorry.'

Knight was nearing the bottom of the barrel again, and the general seemed to sense it.

'It sounds to me you're a bit stymied,' he went on. 'If Kitty was your last hope, and you don't know the real name of your suspects, what else can you do?'

Knight felt like a junior officer being put on the spot by the top brass.

'I don't know yet. Is there anything else you can tell me about her? Anything at all?'

The general thought hard again. It crossed Knight's mind that he may have heard some rumour about her sexuality that he was too discreet to mention, not that it would help unless he could come up with a name.

'It's as I said,' he said eventually. 'You couldn't really have a conversation with her. To be honest, the only thing we had in common was that we used the same solicitor. I saw mail lying out for her once or twice and recognised the name on the envelope.'

Before Knight could say anything, a shrill voice rang out.

206

'General Harding! Are you there?'

Even at a distance, the imperious tone of the manager was unmistakeable.

'Bugger it, she's onto me!'

Instantly flustered, he stamped the cigarette out and rose to his feet, intending to escape deeper into the arboretum. But he was too slow, for now she advanced through the trees, her face turning to thunder when she saw Knight.

'I'm calling the police,' she shouted. 'General Harding, I must ask you to come inside at once! This man is a trespasser and you are not to speak to him!'

For all the authority he must once have exercised, the woman appeared to trigger some deep-rooted fear. He seemed set to obey meekly and started shuffling towards her. In a desperate last roll of the dice, Knight laid a restraining hand on his arm.

'How much are they paying you?' he bellowed at the manager. 'Why don't you tell the general how much you've been bribed to cover up a murder?'

It was a wild accusation with nothing to back it up. Nevertheless, it stopped her in her tracks, allowing him to press home the attack.

'I'd be very happy to speak to the police and ask them to investigate whoever it is you're covering up for. So please go ahead. And in the meantime may I remind you that this gentleman did not give a lifetime of service to our country so that people like you could tell him who he's allowed to talk to!'

She looked to be on the brink of a seizure, but managed to disengage from Knight's piercing glare and address herself to Harding.

'You will come with me,' she said slowly, unable to prevent her voice from shaking.

It was out of Knight's hands now. If he tried to force the general to stay he would only be offering him a choice between bullies; he would probably stick with the devil he knew.

Harding had hitherto displayed a pronounced stoop but now he straightened his back as if he were on parade.

'No,' he said. 'Bugger off and leave me in peace.'

She gaped at him in disbelief.

'What did you just say to me?'

The general swallowed hard.

'Are you bloody deaf, woman? I told you to bugger off. Now do it!'

Without another word she turned and walked away. He stood still for a moment, breathing heavily as if he had run a race, then turned to Knight.

'I should have done that years ago. Places like this are no good, they soften you up.'

He took the cigarette that Knight offered and held it in the flame with a trembling hand. Knight's hand was shaking too. It was one thing to tear a strip off a squaddie, but it came less easily with a woman.

The general took a couple of puffs and fixed Knight with a twinkle in his eye.

'Now then young man, I expect you'd like the name of that solicitor.'

* * *

208

Chapter Twenty-Seven

Bullock awoke from a torrid encounter with Antonia Baldwin to find a seagull eyeing him through the windscreen. For a moment he was seized with panic but it was only a little after five in the morning; he had been out for just over ten minutes. Having repelled the bird with the windscreen wipers he took another Dexedrine.

The drive back from the Old Admiral had been the stuff of nightmares, the empty roads flitting by in an otherworldly hallucination as he calculated the chances that he had killed a man. Back in the safety of his flat it took half a bottle of Scotch to persuade him that no one had witnessed the blow or seen him run to his car.

The next day at work started badly with the news that a man had been found unconscious near the pub. His joy knew no bounds when he learned that the victim was Colin Doyle, who by all accounts was refusing to say what had happened or why there was a wrap of heroin in his pocket. Of Mervyn Watson there was no mention, which emboldened him to return to Knight's flat that evening. Fuelled by amphetamines, he kept watch all of Friday night.

He had decided that there was no point in using a brick again as it must be obvious to Knight that he was being targeted. The car had to be left unlocked for a moment, and he had to be nearby when it happened. Sooner or later his moment would come, it was a question of nerve and faith.

Knight and Watson did not appear until after ten on Saturday morning. He followed them out of town towards the Downs only to lose them when a learner stalled in front of him at the lights. There was no option but to return to the flat and wait. Knight returned at noon and didn't come out again for the rest of the day. With the singlemindedness of a bomber pilot he fought off sleep, keeping his eyes on the Skoda as he chain-smoked his way through Saturday night.

A van sped past bearing the Sunday newspapers, and a pair of sleepy teenagers wrapped in sleeping bags came up from the beach. Wishing that he'd done so while it was dark, he relieved himself again in the telephone box, one of the few left in the town. He did not consider this antisocial. Normal people had mobiles, only scum used public phones now.

Returning to his car he thought he saw a movement in a battered Fiesta parked further up the road. It occurred to him vaguely that he had seen it before, but as he settled back to resume his vigil a van drew up. It was marked 'South East Painters and Decorators', and out of it stepped Mervyn Watson.

* * *

Knight was already up. In contrast to Bullock he had slept soundly, although he felt queasy from the two injections he had taken. He returned to the kitchen table and nodded in the direction of the coffee pot.

'Milk's in the fridge.'

Merv said nothing; it was not a time of day that required conversation. He noticed there were only five phials of morphine left in the fridge. By his reckoning there should have been at least a dozen.

'How many of these have you had? You been doubling up?'

'It's not a problem, I can get more tomorrow.'

Merv sensed that further comment would be unwelcome. The coffee was tepid and he poured it down his throat in one go.

'When you're ready then. Let's go and see our learned friends.'

* * *

Crocker and Sharkey was a small firm of family solicitors whose partners had grown fat on clients who valued gentility over vigour. Their website boasted testimonials from grateful widows and divorcees, which were necessarily anonymous and almost certainly fabricated. They occupied a Victorian town house in a leafy avenue between the station and the sea.

210

Merv found a space by the entrance and looked in the mirror. There had been a black BMW behind them earlier, but now it was gone. He failed to notice that Knight had already opened the passenger door and was swivelling his legs out.

'Oi, where you going?'

'You're going to need help with the ladder.'

'No I'm not!'

'Well I'm out now.'

Knight slid the last few inches and landed lightly enough on his good leg, its injured comrade following close behind. Merv was about to point out that he would now have to hoist him back into the van if they needed to leave in a hurry, but thought better of it.

The house was set back from the pavement, opposite a nursing home. What had once been the front garden was now under tarmac, with space for a handful of cars. The view to the street was partially obscured by iron railings and a newish hedge that had yet to fill out.

Merv positioned the top of the ladder between a first floor window and the alarm box. The higher he ascended, the better he felt about Knight holding on below.

Knight noted that his overalls had not been washed since the stake-out of Barbara Dawson's house. Merv's were no better, but it made no difference to the credibility of their charade, two tradesmen completing a window repair job before the staff returned on Monday. He was feeling awake now, almost wanting a cigarette.

He wondered if the general had revealed their interest in the firm. His gut told him that the man would hold fast, but there was no telling how long his defiance would last under pressure from the dragon woman. If she had passed that information on to the killer they were potentially sitting ducks. It was a chilling prospect, but it came with an upside. In order to get to them, the killer would have to break cover.

A car was approaching. Through the hedge he glimpsed an indistinct shape, followed by a smaller one a few seconds later. He could not identify the makes, but they weren't police cars and they didn't stop. He breathed a little easier and decided he was ready for the cigarette.

Bullock drove slowly round the block, at a loss to understand what he had seen. He naturally assumed they were up to no good, but whatever they were doing it would almost certainly not send them down for long enough. There was also the remote possibility that Watson was simply earning himself some money, though he had to be scraping the barrel if Knight was all he could get for a helper.

Passing the building again he assessed his chances of planting the coke in the van. Even though Knight's view was obscured by the hedge, Watson would have a clear line of sight from the top of the ladder to the pavement. He drove round to the top of the avenue and waited for his luck to change.

Carol was equally dumbfounded. When Knight had appeared with the other man outside the flats her intention had been to run and warn him, but the cards had not prepared her for the sight of him in overalls, filthy ones at that. Besides which, he looked ten years older than when she had last seen him. They drove off while she was still dithering, with Bullock following shortly after.

When she saw Knight holding the ladder she thought again about warning him and was almost resolved to act when she saw her own haggard face in the mirror. Her nerve failed and for want of a better idea she continued to follow the BMW.

At the top of the ladder, Merv had heard the cars but stayed facing the window, not daring to show his face. The blinds on the inside were dilapidated and did not close fully, affording him a view of an open plan office that had likewise seen better days. Downstairs, where the blinds were open, he had seen an imposing reception desk and an equally grand private office, presumably belonging to one of the partners. But little money had been spent up here where clients never came. The computers were ancient and a wall of shabby filing cabinets lined one side of the room.

A quick recce had indicated that the alarm was a cheap DIY job, and so it proved to be; the partners' penny-pinching ways evidently extended to the matter of security. The alarm was even more ancient than the computers, and as far as he could see there were no motion detectors inside the office. The only obstacle to entry was a vibration detector attached to the inside of the window pane, from which a much-painted wire disappeared into the woodwork. He had seen them on the lower windows too. Assuming they worked, they would set off the alarm if the glass was shattered.

Knight watched apprehensively as Merv took a cordless drill from his toolbelt. Two more cars had driven past a few moments earlier, possibly the same ones as before, but he was too intent on what was happening above him to pay them much attention. If the drill set the alarm off they would have to run, and he didn't have a Plan B yet. Yet the risk was worth it. If Ryan had stolen the pendant from Susan Hillfield, and if she had once received it from Kitty Cavanagh, there was a chance that Susan Hillfield was also a beneficiary of her will. He tried not to think about the number of ifs.

The drill whined like a choir of mosquitoes. It felt like an eternity until the early morning stillness returned, broken only by a gang of seagulls tussling over some chips. The alarm box remained silent.

Merv swapped the drill for a foam gun and inserted the nozzle in the hole. The foam would expand and fill the box, encasing the ringer in a tomb of polyurethane as it hardened.

'Coming down!'

Ignoring Knight's offer of help, Merv collapsed the ladder quickly and carried it to the van. He was sweating, though the air was still cool.

'Get back in, you're done.'

Knight raised no objection as he was hoisted into the van. Without further comment, Merv took a large carpet tile from the back and went to a garden door between the side of the building and the boundary wall. Now it was an electric saw that sang out as he cut away a small panel to expose the bolt on the other side. According to Google Earth the rear of the building looked onto a scrap of concrete and a high wall, beyond which was a hotel.

Shielded by the wall, Merv inspected a pair of sash windows. One looked into a private office like the room at the front, the other into a small kitchen. They were both fitted with the same ancient vibration detectors and thickly painted wiring. Choosing the office window, he engraved a circle the size of an orange and covered it with duct tape. He placed the carpet tile over the circle and struck it with a hammer.

The muffled thump was followed by a barely audible tinkle as the glass fell onto thick carpet. He prepared to run, the alarm bell shrieking in his imagination, but silence reigned. When night fell, they would be back.

* * *

Chapter Twenty-Eight

Fran had not expected flowers. It was a mixed bouquet of gerberas and carnations, a burst of bright colour in the drabness of the visiting room. She thought they looked expensive.

'I hope these are what you like. I'm not much good at flowers.'

'They're lovely. Thank you, Mr Briggs.'

'No, please, call me Matt.' He seemed suddenly flustered. 'I didn't think to bring a vase, I'll make sure you get one.'

He was a big man, a northerner, with close-cropped hair and a nose that looked as if it had been broken more than once. In partnership with the cauliflower ear it suggested he had once been a rugby player.

'You saved my life, Fran. I can call you Fran, can't I?'

She nodded assent.

'I don't know how I'll ever be able to thank you. If it wasn't for you I'd be in the ground now.'

She had witnessed him in action against disruptive inmates, unyielding to their fury though never disrespectful, but there was an earnestness about him now that she hadn't seen before.

'I'm just glad I was able to help. How are you?'

'Not bad, doctors say I have to take it easy for another few weeks, so that's what I'm doing.'

That would explain the chinos and the lambswool sweater. His shoes were highly polished; she wondered if he always dressed smartly or if he had made a special effort.

'There's something else I wanted to tell you.'

He held back, as if some inappropriate confession were about to surface.

'I'm not really supposed to say things like this, but I wanted you to know that I've never thought you did what you're accused of. I've done this job for twenty years and I'm seldom wrong.'

She found herself buoyed in a way she hadn't experienced since Knight's last visit. He hadn't been in contact for nearly a week, and while she still believed in his promises the dreary routine of prison had sapped her optimism.

'Thanks. I need to hear that from time to time.'

'I'm not supposed to do this either, and I've no wish to pry, but you can tell me what really happened if you like.'

He listened carefully as she told him the story of the deaths and her arrest, not disguising his shock when she revealed that her fingerprints were all over the syringes. She didn't mention Knight.

'And you've no idea how they got there?'

'Yes. It happened while I was asleep. I was probably drugged, but the bottle I was drinking from wasn't there in the morning and I didn't think about having a test until it was too late.'

Unsurprisingly, he looked dumbfounded. She had seen that expression of incredulity more times than she cared to remember.

'I wouldn't blame you if you changed your mind.'

'No! I just... I mean who'd want to fit you up like that?'

Knight had asked her not to tell anyone about Susan Hillfield. Trustworthy though Briggs seemed, she wouldn't betray the confidence.

'We think we know who, but we don't know why.'

'We – that's you and your lawyer?'

'No, it's someone else.'

She couldn't leave it at that, he was hanging on her every word. She would have liked to unburden herself of the hopes and fears that swirled around her mind during most of her waking hours, but she reined herself in.

'He's a private investigator.'

He was wide-eyed now.

'You've hired a private investigator?'

'I haven't hired him exactly, he's doing it for free. I'm sorry, that's all I can really say.'

He was clearly bursting to ask her more, but kept to his assurance not to pry.

'Well I hope he gets you out. And good on him.'

Not for the first time it worried her how indebted she was to Knight, and how much more she would be if she walked free.

'Anyway,' he was saying, 'I want to do everything I can to make it alright for you while you're in here. I've had a word with the other officers to make sure you're looked after, so if there's anything you want you just ask. Anything legal, that is.'

They both laughed. She wondered what he would have done if he'd caught her with a lump of hash in her pocket.

'So, when will you be back?'

A flicker of regret crossed his face.

'Well that's it you see, I won't. They've offered me early retirement off the back of this, and it's a good package so I'm taking it. But if you have any problems my mates can't sort out, I want you to feel free to call me.'

He produced a slip of paper with a number on it.

'This is definitely against the rules, but it's what rules are for, right?'

They laughed again, which helped disguise the disappointment she now felt.

'I hope you enjoy your retirement. I'm sure you deserve it.'

He stared at her oddly for a second, his colour rising.

'I wouldn't be able to if it wasn't for you. I'll not forget that, Fran, not ever.'

He was blushing. The cauliflower ear, however, remained resolutely pale and thereby all the more conspicuous. It was an unattractive feature, of that there could be no doubt. On the other hand, he did have perfect teeth.

* * *

Chapter Twenty-Nine

Knight's dream of a jungle tryst with Fran fell dismayingly short of consummation. His first thought on awaking was that an intruder had broken in from the terrace, but it was only a glass falling from the coffee table, dislodged by a billowing curtain in the breeze that had sprung up.

He had only meant to lie down for an hour but it was already dark and there was much to be done before Merv returned. He had injected twice today, yet already his knee twinged as he made his way to the front door. Outside, he crossed to his neighbour's flat at the other end of the shared landing and listened for sounds of life. They were wealthy weekenders from London who usually left in the late afternoon, and so it proved on this occasion.

In the middle of the landing was the lift, and beside it, at floor level, the fire extinguisher cupboard. The cupboard was built into the wall and was wider than the door suggested. He dragged the fire extinguisher aside and reached in along the inner wall. Eventually his fingers found the ledge. On it lay a steel cashbox, which he carefully withdrew before hobbling back to the kitchen.

The key was at the bottom of a jar of coffee. He wiped it clean and opened the box, revealing the leather pouch that contained the Browning. It was not his service pistol, which he had been obliged to return when he left the army. This one was from a cache beneath a slurry pit on a farm in County Armagh, revealed by an IRA informant in what turned out to be his final betrayal. The Browning, by contrast, had lived on in good health, meticulously maintained though never fired in anger. Always kept at a deniable distance, it was an insurance policy that no one else knew existed.

As he disassembled and oiled the gun he rehearsed the operation again. They would take two vehicles; Knight would keep watch at the front of the building while Merv went in at the back. This time he would have a lightweight Kevlar ladder fitted with grappling hooks. At any sign of trouble he would go over the wall and make his way out through the hotel, posing as a lost guest if necessary, while Knight drove round to collect him. It was not the most elegant of escape plans, but it was serviceable. When he got up to fetch a cloth for some spilt oil his knee sang out again, forcing him to steady himself on the kitchen table.

There was no point in delaying the inevitable, besides which he didn't want to be injecting when Merv arrived. Leaving the gun he took the last of the morphine from the fridge. By now the skin around his knee was as pitted with needle marks as Ryan's arm, but eventually he managed two phials. The question he now asked himself was whether they would be enough. He had to drive the car without mishap and possibly help Merv make a speedy exit if things went wrong in the hotel. Were that to happen, Merv couldn't afford a deadweight on his hands. His eyes still watering from the last injection, he loaded the remaining phial.

As he reassembled the Browning his fingers felt cold and clammy. The spring fell and rolled across the floor. Cursing, he raised himself from the chair and bent down to retrieve it. The knee raised no objection, but when he sat down again his ears were ringing, as was the doorbell. Merv was early.

'Coming!' The effort of shouting made his head spin. He hurriedly put the gun back together with a full magazine and slipped it into his coat pocket. Merv was banging on the door now.

Walking made him feel dizzy, the ringing in his ears was getting worse.

'Jesus Christ, what's happened to you?'

Merv was appalled. The colour had drained from Knight's face; he looked paler than when he'd been wearing make-up.

Without replying, Knight turned and fled to the bathroom. With a mounting sense of dread Merv followed him and watched him being violently sick.

'I think I need to lie down for a moment,' he managed to say before retching again.

'Have you got a pain in your chest?'

'No.'

'Are you sure?'

'Yes! Just get me to the bed if you would.'

It was scant reassurance to Merv that his voice retained a note of command. He helped him to the bedroom and onto the bed.

'I'm calling an ambulance.'

The bedroom was spinning.

'No ambulance, I'm not having a heart attack.'

'Then what the fuck are you having?'

Merv was fumbling with his wrist, trying to find his pulse.

'I think I OD'd on the painkillers.'

'You what?! Jesus wept!'

'I'm sorry.'

'Never mind sorry, you still need an ambulance!'

'No!'

This time he managed something approaching a bark. A fresh wave of nausea rolled in, though not as strong as before.

'I'm fine, I just need to rest for a few minutes before we go.'

Merv found the pulse. It was weak, but regular.

'We're not going anywhere, mate. If you're not going to hospital we're staying here!'

* * *

The trailing edge of a cloud rolled away from the full moon, so that for a moment the sea glowed with a silver sheen. A few drops of rain fell on the van's windscreen as Merv drove along the seafront.

An uneasy compromise had been reached. The raid could not be postponed, on this they had finally agreed. The broken glass would be seen the next day and the building would be put on a watch list. So on the solemn promise to call if his condition deteriorated, Knight agreed to stay in the flat while Merv went alone, with a remote camera to cover the front of the building.

On balance, he was not unhappy with the arrangement. Even without the overdose, Knight's lack of mobility presented a complication that he would now not need to worry about. He was in any case no stranger to breaking and entering. The last outing had involved a quantity of DVDs which his cousin had persuaded him to remove from a warehouse after the client failed to pay. The cousin was a flash bastard who fancied himself as a player in the porn business, but the money had been excellent, even allowing for the incident with the dog. He feared dogs almost as much as the police.

At Knight's suggestion he left the van in the same street as the hotel behind Crocker and Sharkey. If he was going out the back way he wanted it as close as possible; the calculation was that he wouldn't be in a hurry if he was going out the front.

The vantage point he'd chosen for the remote camera was a gateway opposite the solicitors. The size of a matchbox, it perched discreetly on the brick gatepost, covering the street for thirty yards in either direction.

He switched on the feed to his phone and went to the side door. The leaf he had left in the bottom of the frame remained undisturbed. Things were going better than he'd dared hope.

Having unrolled the ladder he hooked it over the rear wall at the first attempt. He could see the top two floors of the hotel beyond, where all the lights were out. To either side, the neighbouring houses were likewise dark and the camera showed no change at the front. For the moment at least, he was invisible.

He worked steadily, cutting vertical and horizontal lines across the entire windowpane, then applied the carpet tile and began tapping with the hammer. The tinkling was louder than before, but no light came on or curtain twitched to suggest he had been heard. He removed the shards and climbed in.

First, he stowed the computer screen beneath the desk to prevent its light escaping outside. Kneeling on the floor, he switched the machine on and loaded the programme from the disc Knight had given him. As predicted, the ancient contraption yielded its password in minutes, revealing that this computer was Sharkey's. If Kitty Cavanagh was his client it would contain a file for her.

He told himself he was doing well. But then the warehouse job had started well too. A bribed guard, a key and the precise location of the boxes, in and out in ninety seconds while the alarm rang uselessly. That was the plan until the guard forgot to lock the dog up. It was fortunate, though not for the dog, that Merv had been accompanied that night by Jabril.

God bless Jabril. He was one of the regulars in the van when Merv occasionally provided transport for a local gangmaster. A trained butcher reduced to casual labouring since quitting the sun-kissed shores of Somalia, he was good with dogs if you needed to get rid of them. He had saved Merv after he ignored his warning not to run, and then he had gone back for the boxes.

He found the client directory and rejoiced when he saw the folder with her name on it. In another five minutes he would be done.

Considering how long she'd been a client, there wasn't much to read. He found a letter from Sharkey accepting her instruction to take Power of Attorney and another confirming the firm's role as her executor, with a reference to the will held at the office. It could only be a matter of seconds now.

But the will wasn't there.

A second trawl proved equally fruitless, except in one respect. He saw now that there was not a single item of correspondence from her to Sharkey. Everything went one way, nothing came back except for an email from an accountant about her tax status.

A sickening possibility began to gnaw at him as he quickly inspected several other client files. Here too, the only incoming correspondence was by email. It seemed that nothing that had arrived on paper had been scanned, which meant that the will had to be upstairs in one of the filing cabinets. Having felt well-disposed towards Sharkey for the ease of access he had afforded, Merv now cursed him and all lawyers for their sloth.

Apart from a pair of armchairs and a small side table, the only other furniture was a bookcase that ran the length of one wall. The moon briefly reappeared, illuminating shelves full of dusty legal volumes but no client files.

He was about to abandon the office when he noticed a small door behind the desk. It was about two feet square with an ornately carved frame, set at knee height in the wall. His hope that it might be a safe was quickly dashed; the door had been thickly painted over and its handle removed. At a guess it was some ancient but unused feature of the house that had been kept for show.

Merv's spirits sank. There seemed little point in searching Crocker's office at the front given that she was not his client. It could be that the document was stored on one of the computers on the first floor, but he fancied his chances better with the filing cabinets. After replacing the screen and keyboard exactly as he had found them, he texted an update to Knight and went upstairs.

In a rare nod to security, the cabinets were locked. Rather than hunt for the keys, he took a crowbar from his rucksack and worked it into the top drawer. It sprang open with a loud crack that rattled him. He wished Jabril was there.

* * *

Merv's news brought Knight's mood to a new low, if such a thing were possible. The better he felt physically, the more frustrating it was to be separated from the action. Having acknowledged the message he stepped out onto the terrace to think in the cool air.

Despite his conviction that the woman calling herself Susan Hillfield was behind their unmasking, he could not shake off the notion that Bullock was onto them too. Bev was keeping as close a watch on him as she could, but was not privy to his every movement. He looked down at the cars parked along the deserted seafront, but they were too far away to see if any of them were occupied. This was paranoia, he told himself, it was the weed talking, he should smoke less, but he went to the office anyway to fetch a pair of binoculars. He was opening the drawer when the phone on his desk rang.

It was his public phone, the one whose number appeared on the website, so it could not be Merv or Bev. He hoped it was not a new client calling in the middle of the night with a desperate plea for his attention.

'Mr Knight?'

It was a young man's voice, on a withheld number.

'I'm sorry to call you so late but I have some information you need. Please don't hang up.'

There was nothing distinctive about the voice. It was anodyne and classless, yet he knew immediately he had heard it before. He switched on the call recorder.

'Who is this?'

'I can't tell you my name. All I can tell you is I'm a friend of Ryan's, and we want the same thing.'

Knight felt a cold shiver pass down his back.

'And what might that be?'

The dizziness was returning; he had to sit down.

'I can tell you where Susan Hillfield will be in thirty minutes. Get a pen.'

* * *

Chapter Thirty

It took him a moment to realise he'd put the pen down somewhere. His mind racing chaotically, he scrabbled in the desk drawers until he found a stub of pencil. It infuriated him that he couldn't put a face to the voice.

'Go to the McDonald's on the Uckfield bypass and park near the exit. Go inside and sit at the far end so you can't be seen from the car park. You got that?'

'Yes. How do you know about me?'

He didn't expect an answer, it was a question of keeping the man talking until he remembered the face.

'It's not safe here any more, I gotta go.'

The line went dead. Slowly gathering his wits, Knight played back the recording.

The caller had been brisk and organised, dominating the conversation as if reading from a script like a salesman. Only it wasn't a sales script. 'All I can tell you is I'm a friend of Ryan's and we want the same thing.' There was something oddly clichéd that put him in mind of the soaps at New Horizons. 'It's not safe here any more, I gotta go.'

That still didn't tell him who it was.

He was on the point of calling Merv but stopped with his finger on the key. Merv would not want him to go alone, which would mean argument and delay. They would also forfeit their chance to find the will if he abandoned the search to come with him, which he surely would.

That left Bev. The situation clearly called for backup, but this wasn't something she could do off the books, and he didn't want the police arriving mob-handed. If need be, he could call her later. Reassured by the presence of the Browning in his jacket pocket, he left the flat.

Having extracted a high price, the extra dose of painkiller was paying him back handsomely. He fairly glided to the car, only to realise he had left his cigarettes behind. The craving was a distraction he didn't need. Deciding there was still time, he drove to the all-night shop in the road behind the flats.

* * *

Merv was sweating again. The sharp crack as each drawer opened was an assault on his nerves, no matter how much he told himself it would scarcely be audible outside. The blinds worried him too. The winding mechanism was old and partly jammed, preventing the slats from closing properly. He was at risk of letting the light from the finger torch seep through, even though he only switched it on when his hand was inside the cabinets.

The first five had yielded nothing except personnel files followed by records of dealings with the firm's suppliers and the council. There was no apparent system, and no way of telling where the client files might begin.

He checked the front of the building on his phone and opened the sixth cabinet.

* * *

Bullock ignored the red light. There was no camera, and the road out of town was empty save for Knight two hundred yards ahead and a pair of headlights some way back. It wasn't a patrol car; he was listening to the police radio and the nearest one was approaching from the west.

His mental state when Knight appeared from the flats had reached the point where he wondered for a moment if he was dreaming. If it was a dream, it wasn't a bad one. He had followed Knight to a shop where he went inside without locking the car. There was no time to think. Stopping at the next corner, he sprinted to the passenger door of the Skoda and shoved the package under the front seat.

He was already on the phone to Hanrahan when Knight came out. The Irishman had not been pleased to be roused from a drunken slumber, but didn't hesitate to keep the highly profitable promise he had made. Minutes later, in response to an anonymous tip-off, the late shift was alerted to the presence of the Skoda and its cargo. Among them was an ambitious constable who thought Bullock was helping him to escape into C.I.D. He had just received a text telling him Knight's present position.

Blue lights appeared up ahead. Bullock slowed down as the car pulled out from a warren of bungalows and followed Knight, its siren starting up. A sense of awe stole over him. He had hung tough, pushed himself far beyond his limits and won. His exhaustion a thing of the past, he stopped to watch.

* * *

When Knight saw the lights behind him his thoughts flew to the gun, but there was no time to dump it. The car was on his tail, the siren deafening, then it was pulling in across him as he stopped by a bus shelter. He wound the window down as two constables approached, and heard himself address them with unlikely assurance.

'Good evening officer, is something the matter?'

'Will you get out of the car, please?'

The request was cold and curt, compliance taken for granted. Knight pleaded his leg, to no avail. Ignoring his protests, one of them lifted him out while the other went to the passenger door. He was about to open it when the loud blast of an air horn made him look up. A truck was bearing down on them, flashing its lights at an oncoming car.

Carol had no idea she was over the white line. She had intended to pull in beyond the police car, and in truth there was enough space between the approaching headlamps and the flashing blue lights for her to pass through unscathed. But she had entered a delirium that went far beyond any state she had reached before. Starved, drunk and stricken by double vision, she swerved away from the truck as it sped past and clipped the back corner of the police car.

She was already braking when she hit it, but the impact was enough to send her into an uncontrollable spin. Shops, trees and bus stop flashed past the windscreen until she came to a halt on the far pavement, astonished to be alive.

Badly shaken, Knight steadied himself against his car. The two policemen were running to the stricken Fiesta, one of them already calling for an ambulance. Looking round for somewhere to ditch the gun, he saw that the vehicle blocking his path was now mostly in the bus shelter.

They looked up when he started the engine. He heard shouts and beating on the roof as he drove away, though what struck him most was a glimpse of the woman staring at him through the windscreen of the crashed car. Bizarrely, she reminded him of Carol.

* * *

For Bullock, the dream was fast disintegrating into the foulest of nightmares. He had thought nothing of it when the car behind him stopped for a moment, then pulled out and drove past. Now, approaching the scene of the accident, he was greeted by the sight of his brother officers struggling under the weight of a vast and hysterical woman, who was pointing at him and shouting that she had seen him 'put it in the car'.

'Put what in the car?' Bullock's protégé asked her. The other one was staring at Bullock oddly.

'A package!' she howled. 'You've got to stop him! I've done everything I can, it's up to you now!'

Bullock's mouth was dry.

'What did you find?' he rasped at the protégé, while the woman continued to rave and hurl accusations. He'd placed her now, the nutter with the weird cards.

'We didn't find anything, he got away before we could search the car.'

Bullock could taste bile in his throat. He understood what needed to be done. Whatever it took, he had to get the cocaine back.

* * *

The eighth cabinet cracked open. Merv flicked through insurance policies and bank statements, but almost at the back was a file marked Aaron, and behind it Abbey.

Two cabinets later he found the Cs. Cable, Cadwallader, Carey; he sensed the finishing tape awaiting him. The next one was Cazenove.

He went back to the beginning of the Cs, then forward into the Ds, but he hadn't missed it. There was no file for Kitty Cavanagh.

* * *

The McDonald's shared a car park with an all-night filling station. Knight drove round slowly once, but the Peugeot wasn't there, just a handful of cars and a pair of breakdown vans. It was worrying that the place was overlooked by two main roads, making him easily visible to an observer or a police car. Ignoring the instruction to park near the exit, he left the Skoda between the breakdown vans where it couldn't be seen from the road.

Just inside the door was an alcove with a payphone. Beyond it were empty tables and a handful of late-night travellers. None of them remotely resembled the Hillfields, and none looked up as he went to the counter and ordered a coffee.

He knew that things were spiralling out of control. The police had known exactly where to look for him and could find him again at any moment. Meanwhile he was dancing to someone else's tune with no idea what the next few minutes might bring. It was time to call Merv.

The phone had other ideas. 'Network unavailable' was its stony response to his repeated attempts. Apprehension turned to fury. What kind of company failed to provide a signal next to a main road on the outskirts of a large town? A few tables away a young couple were complaining to each other about the same thing. Somewhere deep inside, a wilful demon put it to him that he was getting too old for this.

'Excuse me, is your name Knight?'

He hadn't noticed the young man who had come out from behind the counter.

'Someone left this for you.'

Knight took the envelope, inspecting the messenger closely. The stars on his badge made him the manager, though he didn't look more than a boy. It wasn't the voice he had heard on the phone.

'When was this?'

'About twenty minutes ago.'

'What did he look like?'

He stared at Knight blankly. Customer service training hadn't covered this.

'Sort of forties maybe? Brown hair. He said to look out for an old man... I mean a gentleman with a stick.'

Knight dismissed him and opened the envelope. Inside was a slip of paper with a printed message followed by a number. 'Too dangerous for me to come. Call from the payphone immediately.'

He knew for certain now that he hadn't been gifted an unexpected ally. Whoever had left the message knew that he couldn't use his phone, which meant they wanted him in the alcove for a reason.

With his hand on the gun he walked back through the restaurant. From the alcove he could see the petrol station and the car park; nothing was moving.

The number answered after one ring. It was the young man again.

'Stay where you are, she's coming now,' was all he said before hanging up.

At long last, Knight remembered where he'd heard the voice.

A pair of headlamps had entered the car park. A blue Peugeot was approaching the restaurant. Knight had no doubt he had just been talking to one of the occupants, but also that the young man didn't exist. What he'd heard was a voice-change app, a download that he'd used himself more than once. It was cheap and cheerful, a standard voice you couldn't customise, but better than nothing if you were in a hurry.

The Peugeot stopped a few yards from the entrance. It was a public place, not one he'd choose for an assassination, but he put his hand back in his pocket and flicked off the safety. The passenger door opened and Susan Hillfield got out.

She came straight towards the glass door, her hands empty. He could make his move now, or wait for her to enter, but as she saw him her mouth contorted into a wide grimace. She cupped her hand in front of it in an expression of pantomime horror and fled nimbly back to the car while Knight struggled with the door.

As the Peugeot drove away he caught sight of the man he remembered as Tim Hillfield at the wheel. It puzzled him that they should perform the clumsy charade only to retreat. The charade continued at the exit, where they appeared to stall while Knight hurried to the Skoda. Just as he reached it the Peugeot conveniently started again. In no particular hurry it turned onto the road and headed north. It was a blatant invitation to follow and there was no way he could refuse.

* * *

Merv sat on the floor beneath the window, longing to be gone but unwilling to break the news to Knight. With the missing file had come a sense of menace. The enemy had been here and might be watching him even now.

As he wavered, his eye fell on the computer beneath the nearest desk. It was, he supposed, just possible that he was wrong about the scanned records. Perhaps they were stored away up here where the work was done.

The disc was in the rucksack, which he had left by the filing cabinets. He switched the finger torch back on and crawled along the floor until he found it.

In the nursing home across the way, one of the town's nocturnal army of carers and nurses was checking on the peacefully departing occupant of a first floor room. Opening the window to let in some air, he saw a flicker of light through the blinds on the other side of the road.

* * *

Knight's eyes were locked on the tail lights a hundred yards ahead of him. They were speeding along a twisting country road past farms and dense woods.

There was nothing subtle about the attempt to lure him. Unlike the slickly executed murders of Ryan and the three women, it smacked of desperation. They must know that one call to the police could see them caught and their identities exposed. But they also seemed to know it was a call he wasn't able to make. There was still no signal, even though he had just passed a radio mast.

Headlights were approaching, fast. As the car sped by he glimpsed blue and yellow stripes. He watched in the mirror as the brake lights glowed and it slowed to turn. Thus distracted, he nearly missed the bend, the back of the Skoda hitting the banked earth on the far side as he wrenched the wheel. The police car had yet to reappear, but when it caught up there would be no escape. He would be arrested, and the Hillfields would vanish again.

Unless he had them as evidence. They were passing through a twisting tunnel of closely spaced trees on either side. Knowing it was madness, he accelerated, intending to run them off the road.

But then the Peugeot slowed and turned off the road. As he drew level, he saw its tail lights disappear down a dirt track.

* * *

Bullock swore when he heard where Knight was. After abandoning his colleagues to Carol's ravings he had continued as far as the McDonald's and quickly driven round the car park. But the route forked at this point, one way going through the hills towards Kent and one heading west. He was on the wrong road.

He pulled into a layby and swung around. He hadn't gone a mile when slightly better news crackled through the radio. They had lost him.

* * *

The Peugeot stopped at the bottom of a hill. Knight had killed his lights as soon as he turned onto the track, seconds before a flash of blue flew past behind him. He switched them on again now, in time to see two figures get out and hurry away.

As he drew nearer, the trees gave way to the small field into which the figures had vanished. He could make out a dark shape, no more than a shadow until a break in the clouds brought it to life. In the middle of the field, surrounded on three sides by trees, stood a derelict oast house.

The Peugeot was parked beside the track, fifty yards or so from the ruin. Knight drove slowly past, ignoring for now the crude invitation to follow them. At this distance, in his car, he was a poor target for anything less than a machine gun or an RPG, which he doubted they possessed.

Or a bomb.

He stamped hard on the brake pedal. Peering through the drizzle for signs of disturbance in the track ahead, he found himself questioning his sanity for the second time in as many minutes. What were the chances of an IED in East Sussex? But why not? A few clicks were all you needed to find the instructions.

He reached a passing place and turned the car around. He had a better view of the oast house as he drove back. The roof had caved in, so that the building resembled the stump of a round tower. There was no sign of an entrance, which he assumed must be on the far side, facing the trees at the top of the field.

When he was out of sight he stopped and turned the car sideways across the track to block their exit. He tried Merv again; still there was no signal. Then he doubled back to where the woods gave way to the field.

At the corner he went into the trees and took a long look at the oast house. He cursed himself for forgetting the infra-red binoculars, but now that his eyes were accustomed to the darkness he could see the creepers that had taken root around the top, providing a screen for anyone able to climb up there. If they had a gun, the open space around the building was a perfect killing field.

From where he stood he was still about fifty yards away, but behind the oast house the distance to the trees was more like twenty. That was where he wanted to be.

* * *

Bullock opened the window to let the cigarette smoke out. According to the satnav he was on the stretch of road where Knight had last been seen. To his north the patrol car was scouring the lanes on either side, without success.

It didn't make sense. The next turning was over two miles ahead, more than enough for them to have caught up with him. They had obviously missed something. He slowed down almost to walking pace and saw the track.

* * *

Knight tapped his stick like a blind man. A torch would betray his presence, so to keep his bearings in the dark he had to stay close to the edge of the wood.

His energy was on the slide. More ominously, there were rumblings from his knee. Yet again he had fallen into the trap of thinking like a young man, the price of which might be that he would have to crawl on all fours.

Pausing to rest for a moment, he tuned his ears to the life around him. Far away an owl hooted, from closer by came the rustle of a fox or a badger brushing through saplings. From the oast house there was nothing. He might have misread their intentions entirely, even now they could be just yards away, waiting to take him. Fear was slipping its cold tentacles around his mind, disrupting his judgement in a way he couldn't account for, until he realised he hadn't eaten since midday.

Burrowing in his pockets he found the remnants of a long forgotten packet of peanuts and shook some of them into his mouth. The tentacles withdrew a little. His instinct was to eat the rest, but he stopped himself; the night might have a long way to run.

He crept on, tapping cautiously through the ferns and nettles. It was not far now, he told himself. He was still in the game and the odds were about even, it was nothing he hadn't dealt with before.

His stick came up against a tangled tree root. As he picked his way across it, slowing almost to a halt, he heard the faint but unmistakeable hum of a car engine.

* * *

Bullock was face to face with the Holy Grail. He didn't ask himself for one moment why the Skoda was parked across the track, all that mattered was that he had found it before his colleagues.

He took a minute to find a suitable rock, after which came a moment of savage abandon as he plunged it through the window. He retrieved the bags of cocaine and held them in his hands with the reverence of a cardinal contemplating a holy relic.

* * *

Merv was on the fourth computer when he heard the voices outside. Engrossed in his work and preoccupied with Knight's lack of response to his latest update, he had neglected to check the front of the house for some time. He stared in disbelief at the shadowy image of the police van and the dark blobs at the hedge. Confirming their presence, a ray of torchlight played on the window.

He threw the disc into the rucksack and ran for the stairs. At the broken window he gashed his shoulder on one of the remaining shards, barely sensing it as he sprinted to the ladder. He had reached the third rung when the top of the wall disintegrated.

Merv fell onto the concrete amidst a hail of ancient bricks. The voices were at the side door, and now it was opening. With no way out on the other side of the building the only option was to haul himself back in through the window.

The voices reached the courtyard, debating whether the intruder had crossed the wall, then they were at the window.

'I'll go in,' one of them said. 'You get the dog.'

Cowering under the desk, Merv's only thought was to surrender to the man climbing in through the window before his colleague returned with the animal. As he rose his eyes came level with the in-tray on the small table beside the desk. It contained a folder bearing a printed label.

The name on the label was Kitty Cavanagh.

He ducked down as the policeman entered. The torch shone round the room and the light went on. The floorboards creaked as he moved, in what direction Merv could not tell, then came the sound of boots on the kitchen lino.

Merv stuffed the folder into the rucksack. The front door had a mortice lock and thick glass, impossible. The back was out of the question. The seconds ticking down, his eyes fell on the small carved door in the corner of the room.

The Stanley knife sliced through the paint and levered it open. Behind it was a shaft of some kind. He had seen one before on a decorating job, a laundry chute.

He climbed in backwards, squeezing his hips down into empty space. His feet dangled in thin air but his shoulders were tight against the sides, which encased him as snugly as a coffin. He dragged the rucksack in and pulled the door shut as far as it would go. From the courtyard came monosyllabic commands accompanied by the scrabble of claws on concrete.

There was just enough space for him to press his hands against the walls and push himself downwards out of reach. He could hear the dog in the room now, followed by the handler's curses as he cut himself. A moment later the door would open and the stinking breath would be in his face. He heard a shout from upstairs. They left the room, and he breathed again.

Merv tried to pull himself back up to the door but his hands slipped uselessly on the old plaster, sending fragments tumbling below where they hit something hard. Seized by a fit of claustrophobia he scrabbled like a trapped rodent, trying to push himself down again, the rucksack hard against his ribs.

His shoulders budged a centimetre, then another. The pressure on them seemed to be decreasing slightly. It had barely occurred to him that the chute was widening when he dropped like a stone.

For a moment he was in free fall, about as long as a hanging he reflected afterwards, until his feet broke through something brittle and he tumbled onto a hard stone floor. In total darkness he lay gasping, waiting for them to come for him. There was silence.

He switched on the torch. Around him were the scattered remains of the rotting plywood that had covered the bottom of the chute, and along the walls were racks of bottles. At the end of one rack he made out a staircase leading up to the ground floor. He crept over to it.

At the top of the stairs was a door with a faint thread of light across the sill. He was in the rear corner of the house, opposite where the laundry chute came out, which meant that he was looking up at the kitchen. If the door was not locked he was seconds away from the open window and freedom.

He mounted the stairs and listened, then turned the knob. The door swung open, blinding him with light. A few moments of stealth and patience were all it would take, but the promise of release overwhelmed him. He bolted blindly across the kitchen and crashed into a waste bin.

It barely delayed him but now there were shouts from upstairs. Even as he dropped from the window he could hear the dog in the kitchen, and as he ran for the side door it landed in the courtyard. He wasn't going to make it.

He felt for the Stanley knife but it had gone in the cellar. Instead, his fingers fastened on something smooth and slippery. It was a spare pair of latex gloves, and with them came the memory of something Jabril had told him.

Flattening himself against the wall, Merv offered his clenched fist to the Alsatian's open jaws as it leapt. He felt the stab of its teeth on his wrist, but his fingers were at the back of the dog's mouth, squeezing the balled-up gloves into its throat. It relinquished its grip and fell back, retching.

He was already at the corner of the street when he heard one of the policemen shouting. The van was a hundred yards away, uphill. His chest was clamped in a vice but the rest of his body was on fire, ignorant of its limits.

The key stabbed wildly at the lock, then somehow he was in the cab and pulling out into the road, the policeman a distant figure in the door mirror.

* * *

Chapter Thirty-One

Knight peered between the trees at a new ally. Previously invisible, a hay bale wrapped in black PVC stood halfway between him and the oast house.

The engine must have been someone turning round. He had wanted it to be the police, but there were no shouts or flashing lights, no cavalry. It was down once more to the poor bloody infantry.

He could make out an empty space where there had once been a door. If he fired the gun to distract them, he might make the ten yards from the bale and take control of the entrance. From there he could shoot again, upwards into the roof, and with luck terrify them into submission. Assuming, of course, that they were in there and he was still alive.

It dawned on him that he had blundered. The better plan would have been to stake their car out and hold them at gunpoint when they returned, whenever that was. He looked despondently across the field, contemplating the long trek back. The Peugeot's outline was just visible but something about it wasn't right. An object appeared to be sticking up above the roof on the far side. The object moved. Indistinct though it was, when it reached the front of the car it took on human form.

Bullock didn't recognise the vehicle, and the bare interior shed no light on the identity or intentions of its owner. He had stashed the cocaine in some nettles beside the track and made his way down the hill, surprised to find the Peugeot and the oast house. It seemed obvious that whoever had left it there must be inside the ruin, and very likely Knight too.

There was no sign of a window or doorway. Confident he could not be seen, he stepped into the field and walked quickly to the building, where he flattened his back to the wall and crept round in search of an entrance. When his fingers detected a break in the brickwork he ran them lightly up and down, making out the side of the empty doorway. From inside came the faintest rattle of a stone on a hard surface.

He craned his head to peer in. The last thing he remembered was an excruciating jolt of pain that seared his scalp.

To Knight it seemed that a small object had glanced off the interloper, causing him to collapse to the ground. He didn't see where the object landed because at that moment two figures emerged from the doorway. One of them shone a torch over the body.

He could hear her voice, remonstrating angrily. The words weren't clear, but he had little doubt as to the gist; they had got the wrong man, and Tim Hillfield was to blame. He passed something to her, something large it seemed, and curved. Then he took the body by the legs and started dragging it across the field straight towards Knight.

This was his best chance. Same plan as before, shock and awe, but out in the open. Still hidden in the trees, he aimed over their heads and pulled the trigger.

The Browning clicked uselessly.

* * *

Merv had almost forgotten about the will.

Racing across the empty town, he was tormented by imaginary sirens, convinced at every corner that the police would appear. He had made things worse by heading instinctively towards Knight's flat only to realise that he couldn't leave the van on the street. Now, in a quiet alleyway behind a row of shops, he skipped through the preamble and searched for the beneficiaries.

At first, it seemed she had left everything to charity, until he saw that there was also a legacy. It was for ten million pounds. The amount was not especially surprising given her wealth. What shocked him to his core was the name of the intended recipient, and the fact that if she died before Kitty Cavanagh, the money would go to her next of kin.

* * *

Knight pressed his back against an ancient oak, sickened at himself for botching the assembly of the gun. A torch beam danced around him as the sound of the body bumping over the earth drew nearer. He caught fragments of a fiercely whispered quarrel, no choice, should have waited, find Knight, then they were feet away and passing by. He couldn't see the face of the body but got a glimpse of the object Susan Hillfield was carrying. It was a hunting crossbow, with a rifle butt and a telescopic sight. It was unloaded and had one bolt in the quiver.

When the light receded he shuffled after them. The land began to slope downwards, reducing him to a snail's pace for fear of falling, but they were moving no faster. Still mourning the Browning, he reassessed the odds. Two against one, crossbow against stick.

The light stopped. He inched closer, fully expecting to be betrayed by the snap of a twig. The torchlight played across a mound of earth and beside it a large hole. It was a grave, no doubt intended for him but now about to acquire the additional occupant that Tim Hillfield was dragging towards it. The light passed over the body, and Knight saw Bullock's bloodied face.

They were facing away from him towards the grave. If he could take out one of them quickly the odds were nearly even. As he prepared to move, Bullock moaned.

Tim Hillfield dropped the legs and sprang back.

'Christ, he's alive!'

'Then do something about it!'

'No! Enough is enough!'

With a sharp hiss of contempt, she put the crossbow down and took something from her pocket.

'Then I will! Get out of my way!'

As she knelt at Bullock's head Knight saw the syringe in her hand.

'No!' he roared.

He was nearly halfway to them before the light shone at him.

'Get him!' she screamed.

Tim Hillfield suddenly had a shovel in his hand. He held it out in front of him, as if he were keeping a wild animal at bay. Knight tightened his grip around the end of the stick, willing him to come closer.

'Do it you moron! He can't hurt you with that!'

He lifted the shovel above his head and took a step forward. They both swung at the same time, as if conducting some arcane duel. Knight's blow landed first, the metal handle catching his opponent on the ribcage, level with his heart. The shovel glanced painfully off Knight's shoulder. Tim Hillfield stood swaying with a look of bemusement on his face while an unnerving rasp erupted from his lungs. When the second blow landed on his head he fell beside Bullock.

Susan Hillfield had vanished, but from behind the pile of earth came a series of clicks as she ratcheted the crossbow. Knight turned and fled, hobbling recklessly into the trees, which lit up as she gave pursuit. Nearly losing his balance, he lurched to one side even as the bolt whistled past his ear. The odds were even again, or would have been had he not tripped on a fallen branch.

He was tumbling down a steep bank, the stick no longer in his hand. Tree roots and rocks flew by, then near-total blackout as he crashed through a dense patch of ferns, the fronds ripping at his face. He burst through the other side and landed hard on damp earth.

He was lying in the bed of a narrow rivulet that summer had reduced to a few meandering ribbons. Downstream was a small stone bridge, above him the curtain of ferns that covered the steep bank. The torch beam shone out, probing the trees on the opposite bank. He could hear her moving down the slope.

It had only been seconds since the bolt had missed him, not long enough for her to have found it in the dense undergrowth. Her game plan must be to finish him off with the syringe before he had time to get away.

He had no chance if he remained where he was. Staying close to the bank, he set out on a commando crawl to the bridge while the torchlight played above him. When he reached the opening he attempted to stand up and steady his back against the wall, so that he could at least face her on his feet. But the fall down the bank had forced the final surrender of his knee, and his good leg no longer had the strength to lift him on its own. He felt for a gap in the brickwork with which he might claw himself up by his fingers, but there was none. For want of a better plan he crawled further in and slumped against the wall.

Outside, he could hear her brushing slowly through the ferns. He hoped she hadn't seen the lost stick, which would tell her how far the odds had swung back in her favour. It was a syringe versus his bare hands now.

He felt around for a sharp stone, again without success. His armoury amounted to his keys and his phone. More out of habit than hope he looked to see if the signal had been restored.

The message light was flashing.

As he read Merv's text he felt a bizarre mixture of emotions. Disbelief came into it, as did shame and self-reproach at the way they had comprehensively outwitted and outmanoeuvred him. Most of all, even though he faced the prospect of death, he could not help but marvel at how exquisitely they had played their hand. They had kept their cards hidden until the very end as surely as if they had buried them in the grave they had dug for him.

He heard a clump as she landed on the river bed. She shone the torch both ways and saw him immediately.

'You're a meddling old fool, Knight. You nearly cost me ten million pounds!'

At the sound of her voice he pictured her the first time they met, scarcely believing it possible that she could have transformed herself into the grisly spectre now approaching him, syringe in hand. He held the car key ready.

'My partner knows who you are!' he shouted hoarsely. 'He's already told the police about the will!'

He heard a sharp inhalation of breath. She was standing over him now, shining the torch in his eyes.

'So pay for it, you bastard!'

She dropped to her knees and grabbed him by the neck. He lashed out with the key but it glanced off her arm and then the needle was in his skin.

He pushed her wrist back, but she was strong. It would not be long before the initial spurt of heroin began to pacify him. The image of Colin Boyle flashed through his mind, the knife pricking the same spot. Roz was suddenly there, greeting him it seemed. It was not unpleasant, the sense of acceptance that was seeping in, the comforting notion that none of it mattered any more. Fran was there too. She was on his sofa, pulling him towards her. Was she saying goodbye, or was she urging him to stay?

The tip of the needle was on his skin again when he remembered what he had read about her those few weeks ago, in another life. He scooped out a handful of peanuts and thrust them at her mouth, grinding them with his flattened palm onto her lips and teeth. He felt her judder as she identified the taste and began to panic. Her wrist slackened, enough for him to pull it aside and smash the syringe into the wall behind him. With his last drop of strength he jabbed the key into her neck and she pulled away.

He needn't have bothered. Already her throat was tightening, her blood pressure falling, unconsciousness beckoning.

'You shit,' she murmured, and toppled over.

Knight didn't care if she lived or died. He was serene, free of pain and fear. Her head lay not far from a ribbon of water that branched out from the main channel. As if claiming his prize, he washed away the make-up and revealed the face of Antonia Baldwin.

* * *

Chapter Thirty-Two

It was time to turn the cutlets in the marinade.

Knight pulled himself up from the kitchen table and slipped the crutch under his arm for the short journey to the fridge. He didn't want her to see him in this state, but an operation beckoned, followed by weeks of convalescence before he could walk again. There could be no question of waiting that long.

The painkillers were tightly rationed now. At the hospital there had been shock at the extent of his self-medication, which the track marks around his knee made impossible to disguise. Not that he had paid much attention, drowsy as he was from the heroin and distracted by the knowledge that Antonia and Harry Baldwin were under police guard not three cubicles away while Bullock lay in a scanner.

He pounded the garlic into the salt. The squish of the bulbs breaking under the pestle was pleasing. It was a simple, wholesome task, the ideal therapy for the minutes until she arrived.

Bullock had been lucky. The bolt had grazed his scalp and fractured the top of his skull. Had it struck a fraction lower he would have died instantly. Merv had found him after carrying Knight up from the bridge, beneath which Antonia Baldwin lay trussed with a belt. Harry Baldwin was still unconscious.

Before the police and ambulances arrived, Bullock awoke sufficiently to grasp the main events that had led to his present state. Kitty Cavanagh had left ten million pounds to her one-time lover and lifelong friend Joan Baldwin. But were Joan to die before her, the money went to her next of kin, which was Harry Baldwin. The latter had been entirely truthful in telling Knight that his aunt's estate went to a cats' home. What he neglected to add was the potential size of the estate had his aunt lived long enough to inherit it.

Antonia Baldwin had no intention of letting ten million pounds slip through her fingers. When she realised that her husband lacked the spine to do the job alone, the Hillfields were born. The deception was built on solid ground. Neither of them had ever been to New Horizons, so by applying her working knowledge of make-up it was not difficult to create the pretence of mother and son, and to pass herself off to Ryan as a heroin addict. It said something for her skill that he didn't recognise her when he went to her house intent on blackmail. It said more for his desperation and naivety that he believed in the instantly fabricated junkie sister who would meet him in the woods with a wad of cash.

Her one misfortune was not knowing that Ryan worked at New Horizons. Never having been there she had never seen him, and during her brief stay she had never ventured into the garden. Nor would it have mattered had she not at some point removed the pendant from Joan's room, doubtless to extinguish any trace of a link between her victim and Kitty Cavanagh. But in the end the pendant had led Knight straight there. Antonia had in any case taken the precaution of warning the manager of Montague Hall that Knight might come snooping and asked to be informed if he did. If he got that close he would have to be silenced.

He opened the olive oil. There was nothing flashy about aioli. It couldn't be construed as seduction food, the effect on one's breath saw to that. It was a display, a gift to lay before her, a fiery sensation they would share. That was as far as his intentions ran, at least for now. There was certainly no Viagra. That is to say, there was none readily to hand. He knew where the packet was and could not prevent it springing to mind occasionally. He had thought about throwing it away, but it seemed wasteful.

He added the oil drop by drop, knowing that a moment of impatience could turn the paste into a muddy liquid, the magic destroyed. It seemed an appropriate analogy. It would not serve his cause to presume her won already, despite the heroic status he doubtless commanded in her eyes. He would go slowly, patiently, and she would come to him.

When the aioli was done he went out onto the terrace and smoked a cigarette.

More pieces of the jigsaw had come to light as the Baldwins confessed, or rather as Harry Baldwin crumbled once removed from his wife. Three electronic signal blockers were found, one in the oast house, one in the restaurant and one on the underside of Knight's car. Desperate to shift the blame, Baldwin swore that his wife had intended to kill Fran as well, and had not done so only because he had put his foot down. The framing was the resultant compromise, from which he took credit for saving Fran's life.

It was a disgraceful claim, but Knight could well believe it. If Antonia Baldwin was prepared to kill three women, why not a fourth?

His deepest regret was Carol. The deal he had struck, even as the first police car was arriving, gave Bullock full credit for solving the case in exchange for ensuring that no charges would be brought against him or Merv. Despite the fact that he had saved Bullock's life, no more than an uneasy truce now existed between them, neither side inclined to acknowledge the full extent of their plotting against the other. But when it came to Carol, Bullock's writ did not run far enough to conceal the drunken destruction of a police car. According to Bev, she was being held in a secure psychiatric unit where she continued to proclaim the truth of the cards. She was also insisting she had seen Bullock put something in Knight's car. In the absence of any evidence, no one believed her, though Knight did.

There was little he could do. He would appear as a witness for her defence, not that it would help much, and he would visit her to apologise, a prospect he did not relish. She was a casualty of a war that he had started, and not the only one. He did not blame himself for Ryan, but there was every chance that in thwarting the boy's attempted burglary, he had driven him to his inept attempt at blackmail.

Merv at least had signed up of his own free will. He had been embarrassed when Knight tried to thank him and amused when he solemnly vowed never to involve him in the like again. Never say never, he could remember him saying with a strange smile on his face. Yet he was haunted by the thought that Merv could easily have been a casualty too. He would hold to his vow.

Sensing his mood grow sombre, Knight reminded himself that today was not a day for gloomy introspection. Besides, there was one debt he had managed to pay, or so he hoped, for he had invited Penelope and General Harding to tea together the following week at the Grand Hotel. Merv had accused him of playing Cupid, which he could not entirely deny. Was it ever too late? He hoped not, for even now Fran was walking from the corner of the street towards the entrance.

* * *

It seemed an age until the bell sounded. He had been waiting at the door until he realised how odd it would seem if he opened it the moment her finger was off the button. Retreating to the kitchen, he remembered that the peppers were still in the oven and was getting them out when she rang. He burned his finger and hurried back to the door as fast as caution would permit.

She had a bouquet of lilies and a bright red gift bag.

'Hello, Tom,' she said, a little nervously, her eyes flying to the crutch. When she put her arm round his neck and kissed him on the cheek he was possessed by the desire to pull her to him and hold her tight, but the flowers were in the way.

'For you.'

She stepped back, holding the offering out in front of her.

'They're beautiful, thank you,' he heard himself reply. They were indeed beautiful but their unexpected arrival had thrown him. She was looking at the crutch again.

'Come in, I'll put them in water.'

Clutching the bouquet he completed the journey to the sink without incident, but here a fresh dilemma arose in the form of the gerberas he had bought for her. Had he overdone it? Might they diminish her pleasure in giving him the lilies? She had been here less than a minute and he was on tenterhooks; he had to relax.

'It seems we both had the same idea. These are for you.'

There was another moment of awkwardness as the gerberas were presented then replaced in the sink beside the lilies. At last they could go out.

The champagne was on the lunch table, which he had placed in the corner of the terrace so that he could lean against the wall while he opened the bottle. There were olives and almonds, and a plate of asparagus wrapped in prosciutto.

'I thought we might celebrate. Would you like a glass?'

'Yes, please.'

She seemed tense, too. They both needed a drink.

'You're looking well.'

In truth she looked tired. Her skin was paler and the bags under her eyes were darker than when he had last seen her. But he would change all that, given the chance.

'Thank you. What happened to your leg?'

'It's fine, just needs a bit of straightening out.'

'What sort of straightening out?'

'A minor knee op, no big deal apparently.'

It wasn't quite what he had been told. He was lying to her again, but now the cork was out and he was pouring the champagne.

Fran watched, impressed that the froth bubbled up to the rim and no further. It was not an accident; he repeated the feat with his own glass. Yet despite the smooth shave and the uncrumpled linen jacket she was distressed by his appearance. It wasn't just the crutch. His face was, if anything, even more bruised and misshapen than the last time she had seen him, and his eyes were deep pits of exhaustion. They clinked glasses and drank.

Knight had prepared a high-minded speech of sorts about her not owing him anything, but she seemed to have prepared a speech of her own and was quicker to the draw.

'I want you to know I'll never be able to thank you enough,' she began.

There was perhaps a stiffness to her words but they blew over him like a warm, scented breeze. She was wearing a denim skirt that went well below the knee and a loose blouse with a cardigan over it. To a more discriminating eye the ensemble may have seemed shapeless, but Knight felt his body awakening. He saw the Viagra box again and swatted the image away.

So fulsome was her praise that when she finished he was convinced she would reach out and kiss him again, but instead she picked up the gift bag.

'This is also for you. It's a very small token.'

At the bottom of the bag was a parcel wrapped in tissue. He stripped it away to reveal a portentous cardboard box embossed with the logo of Felix Edelman. It contained a silver-plated half pint tankard which must have cost a fortune. Running around the inside of the rim, the engraving said 'Thank you for everything, I will never forget you. All my love, Fran.'

Even though he seldom drank beer, he marvelled at his trophy. There was something about the inscription that faintly jarred, but he wasn't going to let it bother him.

'It's beautiful, you shouldn't have, I really wasn't expecting this.'

Now was the moment. He was still leaning against the wall with the crutch next to him, about three feet away from her. With faultless execution he gathered in the crutch and stepped towards her, reaching out to put an arm around her shoulders. Obligingly, she leaned forward, turning her head so that he kissed her on the cheek. Strictly speaking he had intended no more but couldn't help noting how quickly she turned to avoid their mouths meeting. Recalling his vow to proceed slowly, he released her and stood back.

'How about a top-up?'

'I'm fine for now, but don't let me stop you.'

She had only taken a sip of her champagne in the time it had taken him to drain his glass. He refilled it and proposed lunch.

The barbeque was set up beside the table, the coals timed to perfection. She helped him bring out the food and watched while he cooked the cutlets, complimenting him on the feast and declaring that he should not have gone to so much trouble. Until now they had only spoken once, he in a hospital bed and she in the governor's office, scarcely able to believe in her freedom. It was a disjointed conversation, but he'd managed to tell her the bare bones of the story and, more importantly, she had accepted his invitation to lunch. Now, as they ate, he told her the rest.

Eighteen months ago, when Joan Baldwin was moved to New Horizons, Harry Baldwin was prevailed upon by the council to clear out her rented bedsit. It was the only service he would ever perform for her, but it proved to be a fateful one. While going through her papers he found a copy of her will, naming a bank as the executor and leaving her meagre savings to a cats' home. He would have thrown it away had he not also found a letter from Kitty Cavanagh that made reference to the presence of her own will at Crocker and Sharkey, and to the fact that Joan was a beneficiary.

He knew the story of the lovers, and that his aunt supposedly had a rich friend with whom she occasionally went on holiday. His father, not a broad-minded man, had broken off all contact with her. Reading through the correspondence between the two women, which petered out as they were taken in turn by dementia, Harry Baldwin learned two things. Despite living in near poverty, his aunt had refused many offers of financial assistance from her friend, which to his mind was profoundly stupid. Far more to the point, Kitty Cavanagh clearly had money. It did not take long to find out that her wealth could be counted in tens if not hundreds of millions.

Antonia was determined to discover how much Joan had been left. It took a few months, but eventually she managed to get temping work at Crocker and Sharkey, no doubt subjecting the partners to the full force of her charms. She left as soon as she found the document, and with it the chance of gaining or losing a fortune. Her husband would only inherit as next of kin if Joan died before Kitty.

Forgery was not an option. There were bound to be other copies of the Cavanagh will, and Joan's will was held at the bank. Nor was there a realistic prospect of getting her to change it. In the absence of any family support, her affairs had been taken over by the Court of Protection, which would not look kindly on such a request from those who had abandoned her. Thus it all came down to who died first.

For over a year Harry Baldwin hoped that his aunt would oblige them, but although her mind continued to decay, her body remained depressingly robust. When it seemed likely that Kitty had begun her final illness, Antonia declared they could wait no longer.

Fran's mood had been lightening as she listened to the story, forgetting for a moment what must soon be done. A shadow passed over her as she learned of Baldwin's grisly assertion about saving her life. She also found herself reflecting yet again how she might have spent most of her remaining life in prison had it not been for Knight.

She could not stay silent for much longer. She had considered not telling him at all, but her daughter counselled otherwise. Nothing less than complete honesty would suffice, she owed him that at the very least. There was a second, equally compelling reason. If she didn't tell him now he would never give up, that much was obvious from the tenacity with which he had pursued the case. Timing was all – too soon would be brutal, but too late would be no better. Cruel to be kind, her daughter's phrase kept coming back to her, though she felt anything but kind. At least she had heeded the advice to go easy on the alcohol, much though she craved more.

Knight was relaxing at last. He was on his second glass of the Brouilly, soothed by the way she hung on his every word. True, she had only taken a few sips and barely touched the aioli, but he had a comforting sense of being on track.

'Tom, there's something I need to tell you.'

Knight set his glass down slowly, alarm bells ringing. The sadness in her voice was palpable, the type that usually precedes news of a death.

'I've met someone.'

There. She'd said it.

A breeze of a different order blew over him now, icy and toxic. It contained phrases such as wasn't meant to be, always be friends, nothing's happened, only early days.

'I see,' was all he could say when she had finished. He continued to stare at her blankly, numbness giving way to the paralysing fear that this wasn't a dream or a vision, that it was actually happening. He had, of course, been dumped before, though not frequently enough to acquire immunity to the immediate ravages. There was a convulsion of some sort in his guts and he wanted to cry out that she must be mad.

'That's a... surprise,' he added eventually. A sudden instinct to preserve his dignity saved him from asking who it was.

Fran was watching him apprehensively. Despite everything her daughter had said, she felt unclean. But it was done now. So far he was taking it better than she had expected.

Knight clung to his stiff upper lip like a drowning man to a lifebelt.

'I can't say I'm not disappointed, but... well, it's not as if we're a couple, so...'

So, what exactly? So it didn't matter that he had rescued her from a long prison sentence? That he had risked life and limb for her?

'So, I'm pleased for you. That's wonderful news.'

She must know he didn't mean it. He willed her to say as much, but she didn't.

'Thank you,' she said instead. 'You're an amazing man, Tom, you really are. I hope you can forgive me, I don't deserve it.' Her eyes were filling with tears.

'There's nothing to forgive,' he lied again, wanting to scream that, if he was so amazing, why on earth would she want to leave him?

'As you say, it probably wasn't meant to be, especially considering my behaviour.'

She couldn't tell him that it wasn't the lie, but rather that something had snapped when she learned his true age and saw him minus his tooth. It was an animal instinct, one that told her there simply wasn't enough of him left. It was doubly cruel that he had awakened that instinct in the first place, and with it the willingness to take a chance. She wasn't in love with Briggs, but there was an ease of being with him that made her want more, and on top of that she knew she fancied him, despite the cauliflower ear. She couldn't tell Knight that either.

'I really am sorry, Tom.'

'Honestly, it's fine.'

He sensed that she wanted to go. She was like a fish released from the hook, desperate to swim away; it would be cruel to detain her. At the door she kissed him again when they said goodbye. This time he held her tightly and she responded. A ray of false hope flickered but then she was in the lift.

At once, he wished he had pleaded with her, insisted that she was wrong, implored her to stay. Panic-stricken, he resolved to pursue her. The lift would take too long so he hurried to the terrace and looked down just as she came out into the street. He shouted her name several times but she didn't hear him over the traffic, or perhaps she did. She turned at the corner and was gone.

Knight was halfway back to the lift before he saw the hopeless idiocy of it. His chest felt tight, he had to sit down.

Slumped in business class, he wondered again who his rival was. He was still glad he hadn't demeaned himself by asking, but his murderous thoughts needed a target. Next he raged at the sheer ingratitude of her behaviour. What had he not done for her, what risk to life and limb had he not taken? Did the state of his body not call for something more than a fucking tankard?

It was an ugly thought. He allowed it to roll around in his mind for a moment and then dismissed it. But an unavoidable question was left – would he have done it all had he known it would end like this? He had told Merv more than once that he was driven by the search for justice;

he clung to that thought now. Justice was the reward, though as rewards went it felt little better than the tankard.

He picked up the newspaper he had meant to show her. On the front page was a picture of Bullock outside the oast house. It should have been him, and the TV interviews too, he reflected bitterly. Why had he not insisted on taking the glory? Because he hadn't been thinking about glory, he had been thinking of her and her alone.

He tossed the newspaper aside and wondered whether to call Merv, but he knew what Merv would say and didn't want to hear it. What he really wanted was a spliff.

It was his first cheering thought for some time, yet it withered swiftly on the vine. The cupboard was bare, they had smoked the last of what they had on the afternoon of his release from hospital. Another kick in the teeth, why not? After a moment of crushing disappointment, he had a vague recollection of Merv losing a half-smoked joint. The search had not lasted long, it being deemed quicker to roll a new one. So where was it? He climbed unsteadily to his feet and embarked on the quest.

The kitchen yielded nothing, even after he emptied the bin. Nor was it in his sitting room, bedroom or bathroom. His hopes took longer to wither on this occasion, but eventually reality could no longer be ignored. The joint was gone.

For want of a better idea he returned to the terrace and lay with the seat reclined. The afternoon had cooled and grey clouds were rolling in, flecked with an early troupe of starlings. After grieving for the lost joint he grieved for Fran again while the flock dissolved and reappeared above him.

There was a clatter. He raised the seat enough to see that a seagull had landed on the lunch table. It was the same one as before, he was sure of it. Its beak was in the aioli. He waved his crutch and shouted, but the bird took no notice. Knight looked around for a projectile. There was a champagne cork on the floor, but it would mean getting up.

The bird was company of a sort, he supposed, and there was a scrap of comfort to be had that the wreckage of the afternoon contained something of value to a fellow creature. Yet even this small consolation had its own bitter taste – how sad was it to find solace in the company of a seagull, having started the afternoon with the woman of one's dreams? Perhaps this was indeed all she was, a dream, an illusion he had conjured up and allowed to grow into an article of faith. He thought again about phoning Merv.

His new companion meanwhile had transferred its attention to the floor, mopping up a pair of stray olives. It stopped a few feet away, eyeing him cautiously. Knight remained stock still, wondering whether to feel flattered by its trust or affronted by its lack of respect. It seemed to be weighing up an important decision. Without warning it lunged under his seat and scrambled awkwardly out again, flapping its wings as it hopped to a safe distance.

However, the prize it had found was evidently not to its liking. Lacking the capacity of the large creature sitting opposite to appreciate such a treat, the seagull dropped the half-smoked joint on the terrace floor and flew away.

Thanks and Acknowledgements

I would like to thank the following for their invaluable advice and encouragement, without which the book might not have seen the light of day. Andrea Collins, Harry and Chris Duffin, Jo Evershed, Lucy Fawcett, Michael Fishlock, Andrew Gordon, Carolyn Grindle, James Greenwood, Ben Hodges, Nick Hodges, Soraya Khan, Felicity Maidens, Kate Malone, Richard Phillips, Dr Julie Trew, Chrissie Warren, Roland Wilmer and Marie Wright. In addition, very special thanks to my agent Gaia Banks for her warmth and wisdom, and above all to my wife Kate for her patience, faith and unstinting support.

Preview

Live Bait
(A Tom Knight Mystery 2)

Knight's surveillance work has dried up and he's reduced to accepting a gig as a life model for a reclusive painter. When she's found dead in the same location as a suspicious death thirty years earlier, instinctively he knows they're connected – but cannot find the proof.

Enter a femme fatale in her sixties who puts Knight on the trail of priceless stolen Chinese art, shady dealings in a country house – and a dangerous con man. Even with decades' experience, he finds himself unexpectedly in the grip of events, and at the business end of a shotgun.

Proving that you're just as young as you feel, the Tom Knight mysteries combine delicious comedy with a precision engineered plot.

About the Author

In a glittering career since leaving university, **Charlie Hodges** has worked as a TEFL teacher, a marketing quack and Father Christmas in a department store. He has also written extensively for television, with credits ranging from *Emmerdale* to *Shaun the Sheep*.

Charlie was born in Durban, South Africa. He lived there until the age of fifteen before moving to England where he was educated at Tiffin Boys' School in Kingston upon Thames and Jesus College, Cambridge. He lives in Tunbridge Wells with his wife, two teenage sons and a bad-tempered Jack Russell. *Vanishing* Act is his first novel, introducing 73-year-old private detective Tom Knight, ex-SAS, as he squares up to the challenges of sex, death and old age in Eastbourne.

Note from the Publisher

To receive updates on special offers and news of other humorous fiction titles to make you smile – sign up now to the Farrago mailing list at farragobooks.com/sign-up.